*An investigation into the comparability of two tests of English as a foreign language*

**STUDIES IN LANGUAGE TESTING...1**
Series editor: Michael Milanovic


Also in this series:

**Test taker characteristics and test performance: A structural modeling approach**
Antony J. Kunnan

**Performance testing, cognition and assessment: Selected papers from the 15th Language Testing Research Colloquium (LTRC) Cambridge and Arnhem, 1993**

# An investigation into the comparability of two tests of English as a foreign language

**Lyle F. Bachman**
**Fred Davidson**
**Katherine Ryan**
**Inn-Chull Choi**

**With an introduction by Bernard Spolsky**

CAMBRIDGE
UNIVERSITY PRESS

Designed and desktop published by Helen Goring

Published by the Press Syndicate of the University of Cambridge
The Pitt Building, Trumpington Street, Cambridge CB2 1RP
40 West 20th Street, New York, NY 10011, USA
10 Stamford Road, Oakleigh, Melbourne 3166, Australia

First published 1995

Printed in Great Britain
at the University Press, Cambridge


*British Library cataloguing in publication data*

University of Cambridge, Local Examinations Syndicate
An investigation into the Comparability of two tests of English as a foreign language

Lyle F. Bachman
Fred Davidson
Katherine Ryan
Inn-Chull Choi

1. Education. Assessment 2. Education. Tests. Setting

ISBN  0 521 48167 8 hard cover
      0 521 48467 7 paperback

# Contents

# Series Editor's note

This volume is the first in a series of EFL research-related publications from the University of Cambridge Local Examinations Syndicate. It documents a major study, carried out between 1987 and 1989, which was intended not only to compare statistically two Cambridge EFL examinations with the Test of English as a Foreign Language (TOEFL) but also to investigate similarities in test content, candidature and use. It reflects a view of Cambridge EFL before 1988, and this short note tries to describe some of the developments that have taken place since that time, in part prompted by the study documented here. The first and perhaps most significant development was the establishment of an EFL Division in 1988 which was set up to enhance the management and development of EFL examinations around the world.

The University of Cambridge Local Examinations Syndicate (Cambridge) is a major provider of educational assessment services throughout the world. It is involved in school examinations in the UK and many other countries, examining over 700,000 candidates annually, and is also heavily involved in the examining of English as a Foreign Language (EFL), examining over 400,000 people in 1993. In providing these services, it is important that Cambridge EFL examinations should be useful. Usefulness in this context is defined as a combination of reliability, validity, impact and practicality. The precise quantity of any of these qualities is a function of the purpose to which examinations and tests are being put. An up-to-date and detailed discussion of these issues can be found in Bachman and Palmer (forthcoming).

Test development and subsequent validation require a great deal of information about candidates. One of the first innovations made to procedures after 1988 was to increase the amount of information routinely gathered on candidates. The Candidate Information Sheet (CIS), introduced in 1990 and now routinely administered to most EFL candidates, has improved the systematic capture of relevant information. This has helped to inform the many examination revision projects that are being continuously undertaken by the EFL Division. The information is also being linked to score information which allows for the investigation of differential test and item functioning on the basis of candidate background.

In addition to the routine information captured by the CIS, work with UCLA to produce a bank of questionnaire items to be used on a sampling basis is nearing completion. This bank will allow for the study of a range of candidate characteristics, such as motivation, anxiety, cognitive and metacognitive strategies and communication and learning strategies in relation to performance and demographic characteristics. Information gathered from instruments based on this bank will allow for feedback to teachers, textbook writers and students. This type of feedback contributes positively to the impact of Cambridge EFL examinations.

Since 1989 there has been a great deal of rationalisation in the capture of information about candidates, and a similar process has also taken place with regard to information about test questions. The pedagogically useful nature of Cambridge EFL examinations has always been a prime consideration in the development of item types. This has sometimes meant that the lowest levels of statistical information about items have been difficult to capture routinely. Since 1988, techniques have been developed to ensure that item level data on all questions in Cambridge EFL examinations can be routinely captured without affecting the nature and quality of the items themselves. Where possible, changes have been made to existing papers, and where not, changes have been scheduled to coincide with revised versions of examinations.

The rationalisation of data capture outlined above has a number of advantages. First, it allows for more systematic validation of test materials and facilitates the on-going process of their change and development. Second, it allows for valuable research on the eventual triangulation of characteristics of test content, candidate background and test performance. Indeed, the second volume in this series, authored by Antony Kunnan, investigates just this area. Third, it frequently means that systems are made more efficient, which helps to improve the level of service offered to test takers.

Cambridge is committed to the direct assessment of language skills through tests of speaking and writing. It is well known that these areas of assessment are particularly difficult to deal with on a large scale. The EFL Division has devoted substantial time and effort to the rationalisation of a support system for oral examiners throughout the world and the development of training and standardisation materials. Research projects that have looked at marking approaches, candidate and examiner language and the development of rating scales have been carried out to support the direct assessment of spoken and written skills.

A number of major revision and development projects have taken place in the EFL Division since 1989. Perhaps the most important development has been the introduction of a five-level system covering the main EFL examinations. At Level 1, a new examination has been developed, the Key English Test (KET). The test content is based on the Council of Europe Waystage Level 1990 (Van Ek and Trim 1991b) specifications. At Level 2, the Preliminary English Test (PET) has been reviewed and revised in line with the Council of Europe Threshold Level 1990 (Van Ek and Trim 1991a) specifications. Cambridge, along with the British Council and BBC English, was a major sponsor of the 1990 revision of the Council of Europe's Waystage and Threshold specifications. At

Level 3, the First Certificate in English (FCE) has been extensively reviewed and revised. It appears in its new form in December 1996. At Level 4, the Certificate of Advanced English (CAE) was introduced in 1990. At Level 5, the Certificate of Proficiency in English (CPE) is currently being reviewed and a revised version will be available from 1998.

Apart from the main suite five-level framework, a number of other examinations of a more specific nature have also been developed or revised. The Certificates in Communicative Skills in English (CCSE) were introduced in 1990. The Cambridge Examinations in English for Language Teachers (CEELT) were introduced in 1988 and revised in 1993. The Certificate in English for International Business and Trade (CEIBT) was introduced in 1990. The International English Language Testing System (IELTS) was introduced in 1989 and is currently being revised for 1995. IELTS is particularly interesting in that it is a truly international test with materials being developed by teams of item writers in the UK and Australia. The administration of the test is also international in that it is conducted jointly by the British Council and the International Development Programme for Australian Universities (IDP). Another related development is the setting up of an Institutional Testing Service in 1992. This service is designed to develop materials for test users who have needs that cannot be readily satisfied by the main examinations offered on fixed dates throughout the year.

Extending the quality and quantity of personnel involved in the development of testing materials has also been a priority. Item writer training programmes have been prepared and are now delivered on a routine basis, not only in the UK but also in Australia where substantial amounts of IELTS materials have been developed.

Pretesting is fundamental to good practice. It involves the systematic trialling of test materials prior to their use. This is an important quality control measure and provides a clear indication of the statistical characteristics of materials. This in turn allows for the calibration of materials and the effective equating of test forms. The EFL pretesting service is now in place and it processes 30–40,000 pretests a year.

In the European context, perhaps one of the most significant developments that Cambridge has been involved with in recent years is the Association of Language Testers in Europe (ALTE). This association has eleven institutional members as of 1994. Each member is responsible for the testing of its own language as a foreign language. ALTE has three main objectives. These are:

1  to establish common levels of proficiency in order to promote the transnational recognition of certification in Europe;
2  to establish common standards for all stages of the testing process: that is for test development, question writing, test administration, marking and grading, reporting of results, test analysis and reporting of findings;
3  to collaborate on joint projects and in the exchange of ideas and know-how.

ALTE has now developed an initial framework that allows for the comparison of examinations in different languages. This will be of great benefit to employers and employees in the European context and further afield as the work force becomes more internationally mobile. ALTE has also produced and published an international code of language testing practice.

In the area of technological developments, a comprehensive computer-based item banking system has been developed by Cambridge EFL which allows for the storage and retrieval of test materials. It also allows for the efficient construction of EFL tests which are equivalent not only in statistical terms, but also in terms of content. A joint long-term research project with UCLA, to develop test content analysis instruments, has been supported by a considerable amount of work at Cambridge to refine the descriptive systems that lie at the centre of the item banking approach to test development and construction.

In addition to item banking, work has proceeded on computerising the administrative systems available to Cambridge Local Secretaries around the world. For example, it will soon be possible to carry out the range of administrative functions related to Cambridge EFL examinations using a computer alone, and transferring information either on diskette or by modem. Such developments will improve the quality of service available to the users of Cambridge EFL examinations.

Another example of the impact of technology has been the development of EFL computer adaptive testing systems. These have taken two forms. The first was developed in Singapore in partnership with Singapore Telecom. This is a diagnostic system which allows Telecom users in Singapore to log on and take a test on their own computers in their own homes. The second development is a computer adaptive testing system. It is anticipated that this system will soon make use of CD-ROM technology which could pave the way for the testing of listening and possibly even speaking in a computer environment.

A large number of research projects have taken place since 1989 either in the EFL Division or by researchers sponsored by Cambridge. The list below represents a few of the areas that have been focused on:
the systematic description of test content;
the nature of test takers' strategies and cognitive processes in relation to test
   performance;
the strategies markers use when evaluating EFL compositions;
the discourse of oral interview interaction;
the nature of oral examiner language;
the development of rating scales in listening and reading tests;
the development of rating scales in oral and written assessment;
the relationship between what candidates can actually do in the language and test
   performance.

Where appropriate, reports are being produced of these and other research projects, and will be published in this series.

Cambridge EFL Division now participates fully in international language testing seminars and conferences. For example, the first leg of the 15th International Language Testing Research Colloquium was held in Cambridge in August 1993. Several smaller seminars and conferences are also hosted every year.

The EFL Division produces two newsletters. The first, *Research Notes*, appears twice a year, and is intended to inform the Cambridge network as well as universities and colleges throughout the world of EFL research and development projects. The second, *ALTE News*, also appears twice a year and is widely distributed to parties interested in this European venture. The content describes and explains the activities the group are engaged in.

In conclusion, I would like to express Cambridge's thanks to Lyle Bachman and his team for all the hard work they put into the project reported here. They undertook to engage in a difficult comparative study which required a great deal of expertise and sensitivity. I would also like to thank the Advisory Committee for their comments and advice and in particular Bernard Spolsky for his introduction to this volume. Finally, I would like to thank Helen Goring, who organised the design and desktop publishing.

Michael Milanovic
Cambridge, January 1994

# Preface

In July 1987, during a trip to England, I was invited to visit the University of Cambridge Local Examinations Syndicate (Cambridge), and during that visit was asked if I would be interested in conducting a study to determine the equivalences between scores from Cambridge EFL examinations, specifically the Certificate of Proficiency in English (CPE), the First Certificate in English (FCE), and the Test of English as a Foreign Language (TOEFL). My initial reaction was that I didn't personally find the study of score equivalences very interesting as research, and that before such a study could be done, one would need, at the very least, to provide evidence that the test batteries measured the same abilities. When I was asked what that would involve, I indicated that I thought that comparability of both test content and test performance needed to be investigated, and sketched the outlines of a program of research that I had no idea would be taken seriously. But as the discussion intensified, it became clear to me that Cambridge was genuinely concerned with better understanding its EFL examinations and increasing its own research capability, and might actually be interested in funding such a program of research.

The research program that I had sketched out hastily in Cambridge was further refined in meetings with Peter Falvey and John Foulkes in Illinois and with Alistair Pollitt in Cambridge later that year, thus beginning the Cambridge-TOEFL Comparability Study and what was to become a very busy three years for a number of other individuals and myself.

During the conduct of the study, we were blessed by being able to attract and involve a number of very capable and dedicated people. In particular, the other co-authors of this report, Fred Davidson, Kathy Ryan and Inn-Chull Choi, were invaluable and indefatigable throughout the study. They suffered through the agony of data collection and management and shared in both the process of analysis and the reward of trying to make some sense of it all. They were also an integral part of what was a collective effort of writing the final report on the study.

A crucial ingredient in the successful conduct of the project was the resourcefulness and managerial dexterity of John Foulkes, of the Council for Examinations Development, Cambridge. It was John's efficiency and sense of humour that sustained us through many a crisis, as we constantly weighed the demands of the research design against the realities of dealing with an operational test administration at eight different sites around the world.

We also benefited from the wisdom of a number of distinguished scholars and researchers – our Advisory Committee – who took the time to comment on and discuss with us the results of the initial pilot study, the design and conduct of the main study, and the final report.

The final project report was prepared for use by Cambridge, and contained a number of specific recommendations, both for modifications in the exams themselves and for follow-up research on the exams. I am pleased to say that virtually all of these recommendations have been seriously considered and are being implemented by Cambridge. Because of its purpose, the final project report was not written for a general audience, nor was it intended to be published. However, because the Advisory Committee recommended strongly that the central findings should be made available, and because of the interest the study has generated in the field, it was decided to edit the original report so that it would be suitable for a more general audience. The task of editing the original report has been facilitated by the collaboration of Michael Milanovic of the EFL Division, Cambridge. The manuscript has been greatly improved for having been sifted through his editorial eye, and he has our sincere gratitude.

Looking back over the study and its findings, I feel that there is little I would have done differently. Had I known at the time what would be involved, I might not have accepted the responsibility so eagerly. At the same time, I believe the study demonstrates that language testers in different countries, with different traditions, both in measurement and applied linguistics, can find a way to collaborate productively in the investigation of questions of common interest. I thus feel that one of the most important outcomes of the study has been a greater sense of collegiality, cooperation and mutual respect between American and British language testers.

Lyle F. Bachman, Principal Investigator
Cambridge-TOEFL Comparability Study
Los Angeles, March 1992

# Acknowledgements

This study could not have been completed without the cooperation of many individuals, in many capacities. Our greatest thanks must go to the over 1,700 individuals who gave up their weekends to endure what to them must have seemed to be an endless succession of English tests. While we hope that they benefited from the experience, there can be no question that we did, and for this they have our sincerest gratitude.

We would also like to thank the following individuals and institutions in particular for the parts they played in the study:

Braj Kachru, Director of the Division of English as an International Language, University of Illinois at Urbana-Champaign, who graciously provided both an organizational home and a physical location for the study at Illinois;

Gillian Brown, Professor and Director of the Research Centre for English and Applied Linguistics, Cambridge University, who graciously made available facilities for the entry of the data from the FCE and CPE;

Brian Lynch, who organized the pilot study test administration at the University of California, Los Angeles, collaborated in every stage of the content analysis, and whose comments and suggestions on that section of the report were invaluable;

Kathleen Bailey and her staff at the Monterey Institute of International Studies, who rated the TEW scripts for the pilot study;

Marianne Tyacke and her staff at the University of Toronto, who rated the TEW scripts for the main study;

Barbara Plakans and her staff at Iowa State University, who helped organize and conduct the SPEAK ratings for the main study;

Angela Pitard, whose patience, cheerful disposition and common sense held the Illinois half of the study together on a day-to-day basis, and who mastered the mysteries of two word-processing programs, arcane statistical symbols and interlinear scribbles in the preparation of the original manuscript. Without her superhuman efforts, this task might have taken as long the study itself;

Members of the study's Advisory Committee and Respondents to the Pilot Study and Final Project Reports: John L. Reddaway, Gillian Brown, J. Charles Alderson, John L. D. Clark, Alan Davies, Braj Kachru, Robert Kaplan, Alan Maley, Alistair Pollitt, Bernard Spolsky, Charles Stansfield, Peter Strevens, John Upshur;

Cambridge Personnel: Data Processing Division: Dave Sanders, Mike Geach, and Mike O'Rourke;

EFL Division: Peter Hargreaves, Patricia Aspinall, Janet Bojan, John Walker and Colin Dean;

Examinations Division: Hillary Foster;

Susan Rolfe, University of Cambridge, Research Centre for English and Applied Linguistics;

University of Cambridge Computing Service;

University of Illinois at Urbana-Champaign Project Personnel: Kevin Curry, Jennifer Derksen, Pearl Goodman, Laura Hahn, Leanne Hohulin, Kimberly Houk, Jim Kapper, Lubitsa Katz, Marilyn Larink, John Levis, Bonnie Mills, Carolyn Quarterman, Margaret Qureshi, Rachel Shelton, Jan Smith, Susan Sullivan-Tuncan, Cathy Wesolek, Robin West;

University of California, Los Angeles Project Personnel: Patricia Card, Patsy Duff, Jan Eyring, Alice Fine, Juan Carlos Gallego, Antony Kunnan, Anne Lazaraton, Karl Lisovsky, Diana Savas, Swathi Vanniarajan;

Polytechnic of Central London Project Personnel: Peter Symonds, Enid Nolan-Woods;

Site Coordinators for the main study and their institutions, without whose cooperation and diligence the study could not have been conducted:

Noel Artist, Cambridge Local Secretary for EFL Exams, Madrid

James Hull, Cambridge Local Secretary for EFL Exams, Zürich

Robert Turner, Cambridge Local Secretary for EFL Exams, São Paulo

Alan Preston, Cambridge Local Secretary for EFL Exams, Toulouse

Carol Clark, CIT English Programs, American University in Cairo

Michael Thornton, Cambridge Local Secretary for EFL Exams, Cairo

Malinee Chandavimol, Director, Chulalongkorn University Language Institute, Bangkok

Ian Stewart, Cambridge Local Secretary for EFL Exams, Bangkok

Michael Milanovic, Department of Languages, City Polytechnic of Hong Kong

Steven Ross, Department of General Education, Kobe University of Commerce

John Hodge, Osaka Gakuin Senior College, Osaka

Richard Cowley, Cambridge Local Secretary for EFL Exams, Montevideo;

Content Analysis Raters: Terry Santos, California State University at Los Angeles, Mark Harrison, John Foulkes, Brian Lynch.

And last, but not least, we would like to thank our families, who patiently endured our crises, anxieties, deadlines, lost weekends and our long hours at computer terminals.

# Introduction
# A not-too-special relationship

This book reports the results of the three-year research project carried out by Bachman and his colleagues. My goal in this introductory essay is not to summarise or comment on their work, but rather to provide some of the historical and ideological context for it, in the hope that its significance may be even more apparent. The encounter reported in this monograph between the University of Cambridge Local Examinations Syndicate (Cambridge) and the Educational Testing Service, the proprietors of the two currently most widely used and most profitable English tests for foreign students, had long been a possibility. For about sixty years, the earlier versions of the transatlantic English tests had lived in relative mutual ignorance, with only occasional indirect contacts. In 1987, however, Cambridge invited a leading American language tester to make a detailed side-by-side study of the two tests, and this monograph reports the results. Each battery of tests had developed in its own way, for its own purposes, so that the differences found by the study are probably much better understood against the historical background that this introduction attempts to sketch.

The Local Examinations Syndicate, begetter of the present investigation, was created by the University of Cambridge in 1858, responding to pressures from several Exeter residents who persuaded both Oxford and Cambridge universities to take on the responsibility for examining students outside the university. From this initiative evolved the system of secondary school leaving examinations that still dominates English education. Cambridge had its first experience with overseas testing as early as 1863, when it sent papers out to the West Indies, but only fifty years later did it start to examine the English of foreign students.

## The Cambridge Examinations in English for foreign students up to 1939

In 1913, the examination for the Certificate of Proficiency in English was instituted, intended for "foreign students who sought proof of their practical knowledge of the language with a view to teaching it" in foreign schools (Roach 1945:34). The new examination reflected contemporary interest in direct method teaching, which required that teachers possess "reliable command of the language for active classroom use" rather than academic or descriptive knowledge of the language. In testing a candidate's ability to use the language, the examination was judged a revolutionary break from established academic approaches to testing content knowledge.

In its earliest form, the new examination assumed the traditional language syllabus for native speakers of English, employing the essay as the principal testing method. Roach (1983:4) surmised that the Cambridge initiative was a breakaway by Exeter University College from an existing London examination. Both examinations, he recalled, were based on a course for foreigners, and were "heavily academic", including a paper on phonetics set by Professor Daniel Jones. The demand for the examination was at first quite modest and it "teetered along" with about fifteen candidates a year. There was the paper in phonetics, another on a literary period studied in advanced classes in English secondary schools and a third that required translation into English, the two source languages regularly offered being French and German.

The First World War temporarily interrupted the activities of the certificate. After the war, in 1925, when John Roach was appointed Additional Assistant Secretary to the Syndicate, his tasks included final decisions on the award of grades for the English examination, "a hole-in-corner affair of fifteen minutes" (Roach 1983:5). "It was not then realised," Roach recalled, "that English was, for foreign candidates, a 'modern' language." Shortly afterwards, Roach was given full responsibility for the examination and he prophesied that he would spread it round the world in ten years. By 1939, he later triumphantly noted, it was in fact being offered in 30 countries.

Under his direction, the English examination slowly changed. From 1926, papers requiring translation from Italian and Spanish were offered regularly; translation from other languages was possible by special request. In 1930, a special literature paper for foreign students was included. In 1931, a major revision was published, to take effect in 1932: the phonetics paper was dropped, and the examination was to be offered at centres other than London. As a result, the numbers of candidates started to grow rapidly.

**Candidates for the Cambridge Certificate of Proficiency in English**

| 1931 | 1932 | 1933 | 1934 | 1935 | 1936 | 1937 | 1938 | 1939 |
|------|------|------|------|------|------|------|------|------|
| 15 | 33 | 66 | 140 | 202 | 278 | 412 | 678 | 752 |

(Roach 1945:34)

In 1935, there were centres at Cambridge, London, Edinburgh and Rome. In 1936, a paper in Economic and Commercial Knowledge was offered as an alternative to the English literature paper, and three levels of pass, Special Mention, Good, and Pass, were instituted. In 1936, the examination was also offered at Rome, Naples, Hamburg, Paris and Holland, Sweden and Switzerland.

The Certificate of Proficiency in English received a major boost in 1937 when the University of Cambridge recognised it as "the equivalent of the standard of English required of all students, British or foreign, before entrance to the University". Oxford took a similar step in 1938. In 1937, centres listed included Dublin, Paris, Berlin, Marburg, Hamburg, Florence, Rome, Naples, Milan, Hilversum, Lausanne, Basle, Malmo, Helsinki, Budapest, Belgrade, Zagreb, Ljubljana, Sarajevo, Vienna, Gdynia, Warsaw, Bucharest, Athens, Smyrna, Rabat, Beirut, Baghdad, Jerusalem, Shanghai, Oslo, Stockholm, Amiens, Bordeaux and Dakar. By 1938, translation papers were regularly set in Arabic, Chinese, Dutch, French, German, Greek, Hebrew, Italian, Serbo-Croat, Spanish and Swedish, and other languages were available on request. A new alternative to English literature in that year was English Life and Institutions.

In 1939, Roach proposed the introduction of a new Lower Certificate of English. Because of opposition from the British Council, Roach (1983:6) decided to restrict overseas centres, but in 1943 it was also offered at home centres for members of the Allied Forces who were stationed in Britain. The Lower Certificate examination in June 1939 consisted of a dictation, a two-hour English composition and language paper, and a two-hour literature paper. Candidates were required to write a letter of between 80 and 100 words on one of the three topics. There were also three topics offered for the required 250–300 word composition. In another question, candidates were asked to propose a title for a short narrative, demonstrate knowledge of the meaning of six out of twelve underlined words, write a four-sentence summary of the main points of the story, and rewrite in good English some sentences in Aboriginal pidgin in the story. The literature questions were based on the prescribed texts, which were *A Tale of Two Cities, The Oxford English Course: Reading Book Four, Gulliver in Lilliput*, and *Arms and the Man*. There was also an oral examination, described in some detail in Roach (1945) and discussed in Spolsky (1990a).

At the outbreak of World War II, when many foreign centres became inaccessible, the Cambridge examinations were well established as a respected method of testing the English language proficiency of a small but significant number of foreign learners of the language. The emphasis was clearly academic; the examination was seen as the embodiment and natural conclusion of a carefully considered and controlled educational programme. Its focus was on an élite group of foreigners who aimed at the high levels of English skills that would qualify them to teach the language.

## Early US testing of foreign English

In America, the testing of English for foreign students started later than in England, in 1930. The College Entrance Examination Board, which offered the first English Competence Examination (CECE), had itself been set up at the turn of the century in order to establish some degree of uniformity in admission standards for the élite Ivy League American universities (Butler 1926). The motivation for the American English test for foreigners was, in marked contrast to that behind the Cambridge examinations, political and eugenic rather than educational.

The US Immigration Act of 1924 had owed its passage in part to the evidence of psychometrists like Carl Brigham, concerning the deleterious effects of permitting non-Nordic immigrants to contaminate the American gene pool. The Act contained a substantial loophole in that it allowed the granting of special visas to any foreign alien whose purpose was to study in the United States. After its passage, the number of foreign applicants seeking admission to US educational institutions grew rapidly. In 1926, the US Commissioner General of Immigration wrote in a memorandum that:

> *The experience of the bureau in the past two and one-half years is to the effect that many non-quota immigrant students gain admission to the United States totally unfit, because of insufficient knowledge of the English language ... THEREFORE, IT IS REQUESTED THAT ALL SCHOOLS INDICATE IN THE CERTIFICATE OF ADMISSION THE EXACT KNOWLEDGE OF THE ENGLISH LANGUAGE A STUDENT MUST HAVE BEFORE HE CAN BE ACCEPTED.*
> (Excerpt included in the file of English Examination for Foreign Students, Educational Testing Service archives.)

In December 1927, the American Association of Collegiate Registrars adopted a resolution asking the Board to deal with this problem by preparing "a special examination designed to test the ability of a foreign student in such use of the English language as is required for attendance by an American collegiate institution, and to offer this examination to prospective foreign students in connection with their regular June examination".

In April 1928, the College Board set up a commission of English instructors and admission officers which reported six months later that an examination to test "ability to understand written English, to read English intelligibly, to understand spoken English, and to express his thoughts intelligibly in spoken English" would be desirable. The aural comprehension test should include "simple English prose read slowly" and "simple directions given conversationally". The test should include passages of varying difficulty and "with different subject matters"; the report should break down the result by section. Such an examination was "financially feasible" but the candidates should bear its full cost (College Entrance Examination Board 1929).

The Board accepted this report, and a commission of English instructors presented a detailed outline for the examination: four one-paragraph passages followed by plus or minus (true–false) answers; a longer passage with open-ended questions; a direct dictation, and the reproduction from memory of a dictated passage; an oral test, with ten topics prepared for the examiner; and a

250–300 word composition. The commission believed that the main value of the examination would be its diagnostic accuracy. "It is important to know the candidate's strength or weakness in knowledge of words, command of English construction, and grasp of the logic and continuity of English speech." The plan of the examination was approved, a grant of $5,000 was received from the Carnegie Endowment for International Peace to cover its cost, and the first examination was taken in April 1930 by third-year candidates. The following year, 139 candidates were examined at centres in seventeen countries. In 1932, the test was offered in 29 countries, but as a result of the world-wide depression, only 30 candidates offered themselves at twelve centres.

A new description was approved for the 1933 examination (College Entrance Examination Board 1932). Part 1 was changed to consist of several passages, ideally fifteen, with true–false and other questions testing understanding; altogether, about 30 questions were planned. The direct dictation continued, but for this, and for the second dictation, the candidate no longer needed to rely on memory, but would be allowed to take notes and then reproduce the substance of the passage. The composition was unchanged. The oral test was to be based on "ten or fifteen minutes of discussion or conversation".

Sufficient funds remained from the Carnegie Endowment for International Peace grant to finance the April 1933 examination. In 1933, seventeen candidates took the examination, and the following year, 20 (College Entrance Examination Board 1934). In 1935, the funds were exhausted (College Entrance Examination Board 1935) so that the College Board was unable to answer requests to administer the examination in 1938 for Jewish doctors and lawyers seeking to emigrate from Nazi Germany (Saretsky 1984).

In 1938, the New York State Board of Education made the first comparison of the American and the Cambridge examinations when they agreed to accept either of them as evidence of English knowledge by German refugees. The similarities between the two tests no doubt justified this decision to equate them. Each was intended for foreign students learning English at the end of secondary education; each was concerned with "testing the language" rather than "testing academic knowledge about the language"; each covered much the same kinds of skills (reading, writing, oral ability).

The most significant difference, one that was to continue to grow into the fundamental difference of approach highlighted in Bachman's investigation, was that the Cambridge examination maintained the traditional principle of using subjectively scored items, with fairness and standardisation maintained by a process of moderation and discussion, while the College Board examination already included objective or "new-type" items under the growing influence of the psychometrists like Brigham who were starting to control test production in the United States. The American initiative collapsed because there was not a market for it, but it demonstrated the paradigmatic differences that were to come to divide traditional and scientific language tests.

# The 1947 College Board Examination

This tendency was even more marked in the case of the 1947 College Board English Examination for Foreign Students. The 1930 test was never reused, but soon after the war was over in 1945, the US Department of State approached the Board and suggested that such a test would be helpful "in eliminating at the source foreign students desirous of federal or other support for study in this country, whose command of English is inadequate" (College Entrance Examination Board 1946). An advisory committee of people with experience in the field developed two forms of the test, one for use by member colleges, and one to be administered through the Department of State, at cultural centres overseas and other foreign centres (Saretsky 1984).

The experimental forms of the new examination included a number of paragraphs on historical and cultural topics recorded on gramophone records with multiple choice questions in a booklet. The final battery of tests provided seven separate scores: reading comprehension, correct and incorrect grammatical forms, pronunciation, vocabulary, auditory comprehension, English composition, and non-verbal reasoning. The test was used a few times, but there were serious administrative problems and claims of poor cooperation from the Department of State. In January 1948, the English for Foreign Students test was one of those that was handed over to the newly created Educational Testing Service.

From the reviews of the test in *The Fifth Mental Measurements Yearbook* (Buros 1959:256), the continued influence of the psychometrists and the firm establishment of multiple-choice items was evident, leading one reviewer to describe scornfully the unforgettable experience for foreign students – a week of studying the practice book, five hours of testing time in two sessions for the student, a long laborious scoring procedure for the adviser, with complex instructions on how to get the converted scores to be compared to the limited norms. In any case, the funds to support the test soon ran out, and copies of the old versions were sold only occasionally.

# The Cambridge examinations in English after Roach

The 1945 Cambridge examinations were the last for which Roach was directly responsible, as he left the Syndicate in that year. From the kind of questions being set, evidently the objective question had no place in the thinking of the Cambridge examiners. Examinations were invitations to the candidates to display their linguistic prowess in a variety of formally prescribed situations. The examiner would then apply educated and moderated judgment to arrive at a fair and equitable decision on the standard that had been achieved.

We have no detailed account of the concern taken within the system to assure that this moderation worked in written examinations, but we know from Roach (1936) that he and his colleagues were well aware of the evidence that Hartog and Rhodes (1935) had produced in support of Edgeworth's demonstration of the nature of marking error. We can see particularly in Roach's (1945) fascinating and sensitive discussions of the oral examination the kind of care that the Cambridge examiners considered must be taken to make these judgments as fair as humanly possible. But a belief in the need for fairness did not necessarily entail the use of objective testing.

The attitude of Cambridge to objective tests emerges from the minutes of the Joint Committee on the English Examinations, established in 1941 by Cambridge and the British Council. (I am grateful to the Syndicate for permitting me access to these archival materials.) Much of the work of the Committee appears to have been routine: the confirmation of examination centres, the approval of examiners and dates and changes in syllabus. On 21 November 1945, there was a report of a standardisation meeting of examiners in Egypt. In March 1947, it was decided to continue research into the standardisation of oral tests, and to begin research into methods of testing knowledge of English. In June 1951, a Use of English paper for all candidates was proposed, and the staff was authorised to begin experiments in the "objective" methods of testing reading. The word *objective*, it is noteworthy, remained in inverted commas in the Committee's minutes for some years.

At the May 1958 meeting the Executive Committee (set up to share the work of the Joint Committee) was told of modifications being tried in the first part of the English language paper, with comprehension questions being used in place of the précis. The June 1959 meeting gave the Joint Committee an opportunity to consider new developments in testing techniques, and I cite in full the item from the minutes:

> *The possibility of using "objective" tests was briefly discussed, and it was agreed that this should be borne in mind in future. The possibility might well be a limited one, however, since examining bodies using such tests in English language use a test in composition of the type set by the Syndicate, and some of the Syndicate's questions (e.g. on the meaning of words and phrases) resemble "objective" questions to some extent.*

The comment is an interesting one, revealing that the Committee members had very little appreciation of the problems that objective testing was intended to deal with. They clearly lacked the sophistication that had been developed in members of the College Entrance Examination Board by their professional staff since Carl Brigham had begun their education in the 1930s. In England, seventy years after Edgeworth had shown the pervasiveness of error and forty years after Cyril Burt (1921) had demonstrated the usefulness of objective testing, the Cambridge English examiners were still to be allowed to continue in their traditional ways.

The "objective" question issue came back to the Joint Committee at its June 1960 meeting, when they received and briefly discussed specimens of the examination of the English Language Institute of the University of Michigan, and the syllabus of the programme of the American Language Center of the University of Pennsylvania. This event appears to have followed a visit to the Syndicate in 1960 by Robert Lado, who met, Shephard (1989) later recalled, the people in charge of the English examinations. Shephard believed that the Cambridge staff (and perhaps the Committee members) expressed surprise at the use of American English in the tests. In any case, they did not change their methods of testing.

However, Wyatt did make a visit in 1960 to Educational Testing Service in Princeton, and two staff members were sent to Edinburgh the following year to meet some of the applied linguists there. One of them, John Sinclair, was appointed to the Executive Committee in 1963, and Peter Strevens, who had had experience with English testing in West Africa, joined the Committee later. After he moved from the staff of the School of Applied Linguistics at Edinburgh to the new Chair of Contemporary English Language at Leeds, Strevens was invited to serve on the Cambridge English as a Foreign Language Executive Committee. His account of what was a frustrating experience is worth citing:

> *I had acquired a reputation for saying publicly that the UCLES exams, FCE and CPE, were already old-fashioned and should be modernised ... After two years with no visible signs of change in the exams being accepted, I rebelled, at a stormy meeting where the Chairman, with the full approval of the committee, said to me that the reason why the Cambridge exams should not be changed was that "... they force the teacher to teach according to the best possible methods."*
> (Strevens 1989:5)

But slowly the objective item battered its way in. In June 1962, the Joint Committee decided to enquire about the level of demand for a "more purely linguistic type of exam". At its meeting a year later, the words "more purely linguistic" in the minutes of the 1963 meeting were replaced by "more flexible". However, a letter seems to have already been sent out using the unwanted term. In any case, at the October 1963 meeting, the Executive Committee was informed that 49 centres supported a purely linguistic examination, 26 had some hesitations, and fourteen opposed it. A new syllabus was proposed with a compulsory English language paper and a choice of any two out of literature, use of English, and translation. A sub-committee was set up to consider "synthetic and analytic items".

At the same meeting, a sub-committee reported on a proposed new form of the examination as a whole to be introduced in 1965. Major changes were proposed. In the English language paper, composition would be reduced from

60% to 50%, and the formal précis would be replaced by comprehension questions and an informal summary. The Use of English paper would include "a series of short analytic tests of basic linguistic skills" (50%) and longer questions including varieties of English (40%). The committee was even more daring and called for

> *Further research to be done into tests of "objective" type, as a matter of urgency, with a view (i) to finding out the linguistic skills which could be most satisfactorily tested objectively and (ii) to building up batteries of tests which could be used in the Use of English paper.*

The Committee finally let the modern barbarians inside the gates in 1967, when it approved a revised Lower Certificate examination syllabus for 1970, which included multiple-choice items in an optional language test. A Research Officer with psychometric training, appointed to the Syndicate staff in 1970, criticised the absence of "a substantial compulsory element of objective testing as a yardstick for the assessment of candidates" and "incompatibility, in terms of measures of attainment, of the present range of optional tests". The absence of inverted commas seems to support the notion that psychometrics had at last broken its way into the Syndicate, but as Bachman's study showed, it was still to have no easy way once it was inside.

# Testing of English as a Foreign Language (TOEFL)

In the meantime, a third American effort to start an English examination for foreign students had been more successful. A suggestion in 1961 that the Educational Testing Service revise the English Examination for Foreign Students was dropped in favour of a decision to support an initiative from the Centre for Applied Linguistics and other Ford Foundation sponsored bodies to set up an independent body to develop a new test (Spolsky 1990b). When the National Council on the Testing of English as a Foreign Language was established in 1962, it gave a contract to the Educational Testing Service to provide technical assistance in editing, printing, administering and scoring the new test.

The form of test established was purely psychometric. In spite of the emphasis on integrative tests in the keynote address at the 1961 conference (Carroll 1961) and of extensive experience with writing tests and oral testing, the test that emerged was largely discrete point and strictly objective, with all its questions in multiple-choice format. After two years of operation, funding uncertainties forced the Council to hand over the test to the joint control of the College Board and the Educational Testing Service. Subsequently, the College Board gave up its share in ownership and the Princeton agency became the sole owner of the test, which proceeded to grow by leaps and bounds, until it is now the second largest programme at the Educational Testing Service.

During the thirty years since it was first designed by David Harris and Leslie Palmer with advice from Fred Godshalk at Educational Testing Service, the Test of English as a Foreign Language has remained virtually unchanged in form, structure, and psychometric purity; its standards even remain anchored to the first pilot testing population of thirty years ago. But in the meantime, extra tests have been developed, in response to strong external demand by the ultimate users of the test results – the American universities and colleges – to measure written and oral proficiency.

# The second encounter

The two giants of the EFL testing world lived for a time in peaceful complementary distribution, operating in a world divided by English educational allegiance to one or other side of the Atlantic Ocean. Each test continued more or less unchanged, but both testing agencies found it advisable to develop new tests alongside them to meet new markets.

Educational Testing Service added a Test of Written English, and in response to concerns about the qualifications of foreign graduate students in science and engineering to work as teaching assistants, a Test of Spoken English. The original aim of including integrative skills was thus met, although the promised research in language aptitude has never been carried out. There are also forms of the test for high school and for non-academic use.

Cambridge in its turn added a Preliminary English Test; it also took over responsibility for the innovative Royal Society of Arts communicative tests, and for the psychometrically developed tests of the International English Language Testing Service.

Thus each had developed a wide range of various kinds of tests. But the FCE and TOEFL remained the star performers, as it were, and on them attention was naturally focused. The beginning of more obvious competition came when TOEFL moved into Europe, not just as a requirement for the comparatively limited number of students seeking admission to US colleges and universities, but offered as a certificate. *Eurocert,* a form of TOEFL administered in Europe by CITO (Centraal Instituut voor Toetsontwikkeling), entered not just new geographical territory but also a quite novel area for Educational Testing Service, so long committed to offering scaled scores for expert interpretation, in that it promised a certificate of proficiency.

Faced by this direct competition, Cambridge decided to seek an answer to a simple-seeming question: would it not be possible to show that the CPE and the FCE that it conducted produced results that were more or less equivalent to those produced by TOEFL? If this were so, candidates for one might be able to use their results in institutions that normally required the other; the equating that the New York Board of Education had made in 1937 might be renewed and widened. This was the question that was posed to Lyle Bachman on his visit to Cambridge in 1987.

With the hindsight afforded by the trailblazing work of Lyle Bachman and his colleagues, there are a number of different ways that one can now imagine trying to answer the question posed by Cambridge. The simplest might have been to choose the method that satisfied the developers of TOEFL. In 1964, the new test was specially administered at the institutions so that its results might be compared. Some 2,315 foreign students, ranked by their teachers on a five- or six-point proficiency scale, at Columbia University, New York University and the University of Michigan, took the test. The total TOEFL scores correlated 0.78 with the proficiency ratings at one university, 0.87 at a second, and 0.76 at the third, as was reported to the March 25 1964 meeting of the Executive Committee, held in the Program Office in Washington. Fred Godshalk of Educational Testing Service remarked that comparison testing had yielded "an extremely high validity figure" (National Council on TOEFL 1964). Looking at the half-dozen studies published between 1963 and 1982 (Hale *et al.* 1984) comparing TOEFL and other tests, one can easily imagine that the 0.71 correlation reported in the present study by Bachman (Appendix E) between the FCE grade and the TOEFL Standard Score total would have satisfied many researchers that both tests were doing a similar job.

An ultimately more adequate (but technically and theoretically much more complex) approach might have been to attempt to discover the degree to which each test served as a useful addition to other predictors in making university admission decisions. Predictive validity studies of this kind, which have been conducted for TOEFL (see Hale, Stansfield and Duran 1984) and for IELTS, a stablemate of CPE and FCE at Cambridge (Criper and Davies 1988), are, however, inordinately time-consuming and still leave considerable doubts. The questions that Bachman and his colleagues wisely chose to answer were different, and they have produced as a result data of indisputable interest and usefulness.

While there is not space in this essay to do justice to the many detailed comments made by the eight members of the Advisory Committee on the Final Report, a good number of which have led to modifications in it that appear in this monograph, it is worth noting that all drew attention to the thoroughness of the investigation and the valuable contribution that it has made to language testing research. John Clark (1989) noted the "wealth of comparative information" that helped lay "substantial groundwork for the increasingly refined examination of these and other language instruments with respect to their fundamental measure-ment characteristics and operational utility". He also remarked on the difficulty produced by the reluctance of Educational Testing Service and their TOEFL program to collaborate directly in the study.

In other comments, Alan Maley (1989) drew attention to differences in the purposes of the tests, with the CPE and FCE serving only a minority of those seeking university admission. He also provided a charming metaphor when he characterised the ETS tests as representing a factory system, as opposed to the

Cambridge cottage industry. The latter produced, he suggested in a somewhat mixed image, a "herbaceous border, characterised by the charm of the unexpected, gradual approximation, and rule of thumb or eye". Peter Strevens (1989) carried this further when he noted the contrast of two paradigms, the one concentrating on measurement independent of prior experience and the other seeing it as part of the educational process. Strevens would have liked to see more attention paid to developing tests of the latter kind, rather than just giving in to the demands of psychometric reliability. Gillian Brown (1989) pointed out that in spite of their "scrupulous attempt to preserve an impartial view", the investigators had concentrated on questioning the reliability of the CPE and the FCE while not examining the assumptions underlying TOEFL. I will echo this comment in my own remarks at the end of this essay.

Fundamental issues were broached by Robert Kaplan (1989) concerning the political and economic questions involved in EFL testing. He was particularly concerned that tests like TOEFL and (to the extent that it can be used comparably) CPE are misused in the admission process, and with the way that test preparation schools take advantage of some test users' blind confidence in the accuracy and clear meaning of EFL test scores.

An important finding, which led to quick remedial action, was the revelation of continued problems in the administration and scoring of the CPE and FCE examinations and in their psychometric reliability. Ever since Professor Edgeworth's now classic paper before the Royal Statistical Society in 1888, examiners have no good defence when they claim ignorance of the existence of possible and probable error, the former avoidable and the latter part of the "unavoidable uncertainty" in all attempts to measure human abilities. There have been regular public lessons on the difficulty of achieving fair and reliable examinations, such as the reports in Britain of Sir Philip Hartog's committee between 1935 and 1941 (Hartog *et al.* 1941; Hartog and Rhodes 1935; Hartog and Rhodes 1936).

The Cambridge Syndicate, I noted earlier, was persuaded to introduce its first semi-objective paper for English as a foreign language only in the 1960s. Later, in the 1970s, an internal report convinced it of the need for more major changes in these examinations in order to increase their objectivity. The persisting problems detected by the present investigation were none of them unreported in the testing literature on both sides of the Atlantic, but their persistence was a cause for concern and Cambridge has taken remedial steps to make these examinations much more fair. In his comments on the study, Charles Alderson (1989) judged this finding to be the "most striking" one, while at the same time he pointed out that there were many other British tests (including some others offered by Cambridge) to which the criticism would not apply.

# A personal view

Taking full advantage not just of the opportunity to read and share in the discussion of the results of the investigations of Bachman and his colleagues, but also of a sabbatical year devoted to studying the history of modern language testing and to pondering questions that first became clear to me as I sat in meetings in Cambridge talking about the study, I want to conclude this essay with some general comments on the whole enterprise.

The history of modern language testing, it seems to me from this perspective, reveals an almost obsessive concern to do away with the "unavoidable uncertainty" that Edgeworth recognised over a century ago, with a resultant deification of reliability in objective testing leading to an increasingly narrow focus of what is measured. That a psychometrically pure test is reliable is unquestionable. What remains to be shown convincingly is the nature and relevance of what it measures.

The quest for perfection in tests (like the parallel quest for a holy scale in the assessment of more integrative language skills) founders ultimately, I believe, on the multidimensional, interactive, dynamic, affective and contextualised nature of language proficiency. Following a suggestion from Code (1991), I do not think that there is ultimate profit in treating language knowledge as purely cognitive and autonomous. The very preciseness and sharpness of psychometrically reliable instruments purporting to measure language ability make them unsuitable for this purpose. Like Gillian Brown and Peter Strevens whom I have cited earlier, I would therefore like to see much more serious consideration given to the alternative paradigm that informed the best aspects of the more traditional Cambridge tests: the close relations of tests to teaching, the emphasis on content validity, the recognition of the need for differences in standards of judgment and taste. For this, we will need a study of objective examinations from the more traditional point of view that will show the same degree of professionalism, thoroughness, research skill and creativity that has been shown in this study of traditional examinations from an objective point of view by Bachman and his colleagues. It is important to note that the wide range of English as a Foreign Language tests that the Syndicate now offers includes a number that show sensitivity not just to psychometric reliability but also to these more difficult issues of validity.

We must all be grateful to Lyle Bachman and his colleagues for their work, and even more, for the willingness of Cambridge to have the somewhat unkindly revealing glare of an investigation like this turned on their examinations, and congratulate them on their continued dedication to the development of high quality tests.

Bernard Spolsky
Bar-Ilan, Isreal, November 1992

## Table of events

| Year | England | US |
|------|---------|-----|
| 1858 | University of Cambridge Local Examinations Syndicate (Cambridge) founded | |
| 1863 | Exam in the West Indies | |
| 1899 | | College Board founded |
| 1913 | CPE offered for first time | |
| 1925 | Roach joins Cambridge | |
| 1930 | | English Competence examination – 30 candidates |
| 1931 | CPE – 15 candidates | ECE – 139 candidates |
| 1932 | CPE – 33 candidates | ECE – 30 candidates |
| 1933 | CPE – 66 candidates | ECE – 17 candidates |
| 1934 | CPE – 140 candidates | ECE – 20 candidates |
| 1935 | CPE – 202 candidates | No more funds |
| 1936 | CPE – 278 candidates | |
| 1937 | CPE – 412 candidates | |
| 1938 | CPE – 678 candidates | NY Board of Regents accepts CPE or ECE |
| 1939 | CPE – 752 candidates | |
| 1940 | LCE overseas | |
| 1943 | LCE in England | |
| 1945 | Roach leaves Cambridge | US State Dept approaches College Board |
| 1947 | | English examination for foreign students |
| 1948 | | Educational Testing Service founded; sells EEFS off the shelf |
| 1961 | | Testing Conference |
| 1962 | | NC – TOEFL |
| 1963 | | Test specification |
| 1964 | | TOEFL starts |
| 1965 | Objective items to be investigated | TOEFL loses independence |
| 1967 | Objective items to be added in 1970 | |

# 1 Overview of the study

## Introduction

The First Certificate in English (FCE), administered by the University of Cambridge Local Examinations Syndicate (Cambridge), and the Test of English as a Foreign Language (TOEFL), administered by Educational Testing Service (ETS), are widely used as measures of proficiency in English as a foreign language (EFL) throughout the world. Hundreds of thousands of individuals take these tests each year, and it is likely that for most of these individuals some sort of personal career decision, such as seeking employment or advancement in a career, or applying for admission to an educational program, is determined to some extent by their scores on these tests. Furthermore, many will submit applications for jobs or admission to several places. Thus, it is probably safe to say that the number of individual career decisions that are affected in some degree by these tests is well over one million annually.

While the EFL proficiency test batteries developed by Cambridge and ETS are designed to measure many of the same abilities, they nevertheless represent radically different approaches to language test development. The TOEFL is perhaps the prototypical "psychometric/structuralist" language test (Spolsky 1978), and its complements, the Test of Spoken English (TSE) and Test of Written English (TWE), while still developed in the psychometric tradition, represent an expansion of the structuralist linguistic framework, and incorporate features associated with a broader range of language abilities and test methods. The FCE, on the other hand, was designed and developed largely in the tradition of the British examinations system, which places emphasis on expert judgment and institutional experience in the production, scoring and setting of criteria for interpreting test results.

At the planning and design stage, the project team was aware of these obvious differences between the Cambridge and ETS tests of EFL, and for this reason felt that the study would have implications not only for these specific tests, but also for the field as well, as an example of a cross-national comparison of two quite distinct approaches to language proficiency test development and use. In order to conduct this comparison, we utilized a research design and procedures that reflect an empirical approach to research that we believe is compatible with educational research traditions in both the US and the UK. The officers of Cambridge clearly felt that this approach was appropriate for the comparison and were eager to have the FCE scrutinized according to the procedures and standards of this approach.

During the course of the study, we came to realize that the differences between the FCE and the ETS tests of EFL that we had felt to be interesting from the beginning were reflections of deeper and broader differences between educational measurement traditions in the US and the UK, and that an understanding of these differences would be essential to the appropriate interpretation of the results of the study. These deeper differences thus became an ancillary subject of discussion and research, and over the course of the project we gained considerable insight, we believe, into the nature of these differences as they are reflected in the FCE and the ETS tests of EFL.[1] Thus, although educational measurement tradition in the US and the UK was not an area on which the study focused, we feel that an awareness of these traditions provides a context in which the results of the study can be better understood. For this reason, we will provide a brief overview of what we perceive to be the salient differences between these two traditions.

Public tests, or examinations, play a vital role in both the UK and the US, in that an individual's future educational path and career are very likely to be strongly affected at some point in his or her life by how he or she performs on the particular test that is used as part of the screening procedure for educational or career opportunities. Despite the similarities in the roles that educational measurement plays in both countries, there is a major difference between the British and American systems in the role and function of the agencies that are responsible for educational measurement. These agencies are traditionally called "examining boards" in the UK, while their American counterparts go by a variety of labels, such as "service", "program" and "bureau".

Since their establishment in the 1860s, English examining boards like Cambridge have had a major influence on the contents of educational programs. They work with members of government, school administrators, teachers and other concerned parties on a regular basis to examine curricula and educational policy. Since the exams produced are the result of interaction with many other persons and agencies in British education, the concept of an exam represents more than just a test. In UK education, an exam is thus characterized as both a given measurement event and the curriculum or course of study leading up to that event. In this scheme, exams are usually seen as certifications, with scores reported as certified levels of achievement. In the case of the FCE, for example, the majority of individuals who take this exam will have completed a course of study aimed at enabling them to achieve a certificated level of proficiency in EFL. This notion of certification carries with it the implication of grades and a "pass/fail" level. In the UK, the examining boards, in cooperation with the schools, thus reinforce standards of achievement by setting grade boundaries, or pass/fail scores, in public examinations.

Large educational measurement agencies in the US generally do not see their role as advisory in the development of national curricular reform, as there is really no "national" curriculum in the US.[2] Testing agencies in the US have thus evolved a rather different role from that of their UK counterparts. In the US the testing agency, of which ETS is an example, is an independent, objective provider of reliable information that is useful for making placement, advancement and other evaluation decisions in the educational system. The information provided is devised and produced by a psychometric epistemology which itself is clinical and detached. Thus, while certain types of standardized achievement tests may be based on published teaching materials that are widely used, the content of the tests themselves does not constitute a national curriculum. Indeed, in the absence of a national curriculum, the tests are developed so as to be sensitive to local diversity. Test results are typically reported as norms, and testing agencies generally avoid recommending standards for grades or pass/fail performance.

This difference in the roles and functions of testing agencies in the UK and US is reflected in differences in test development procedures, scoring and score interpretation, as has been observed by Alderson (1987). In both the US and the UK, the development of tests begins with a plan, in the form of either a set of objectives or a table of specifications, or "blueprint", which is developed either by, or in consultation with, subject matter specialists. Test questions or items are then written according to this blueprint, again generally by subject specialists. At this point the two traditions diverge. In the UK, items are most typically edited, selected for use and combined to form the test on the basis of the expert judgments of the subject specialists – the examiners. In the US, on the other hand, after test questions have been thoroughly edited, generally by both content and measurement specialists, they are then tried out, analyzed statistically, and subsequently rejected or combined with other items largely on the basis of their statistical characteristics. With respect to tests of EFL, the writing and scoring of the TOEFL is effectively under the control of measurement specialists, with advisory input from subject specialists, while Cambridge examinations are set and scored by subject specialists, with limited input from measurement specialists.

Differences can also be seen in scoring procedures, where the primary difference appears to be in efficiency. In both traditions, correct answers are determined by subject specialists, but there the similarity ends. While the scoring of large-scale tests in the US is generally objective, efficient, clinical and detached, marking procedures in the UK are generally subjective, complex, holistic and involved. In the US, standardized tests are routinely marked by scanners. In the UK, on the other hand, very few tests are scanned by machine, and marking schemes are frequently characterized by full, partial and multiple marks, which are awarded on the basis of the subjective evaluation of examiners.

Finally, there is a critical difference in score interpretation and use that derives directly from the difference in functions of the testing agencies described above.

In the US, large-scale tests are typically either norm-referenced, with no specification of grades or pass/fail points, or domain-referenced, in which case scores are interpreted with reference to levels of achievement in a specific content domain. In neither case do the testing agencies themselves set criteria for either pass/fail or grading decisions. In the UK, on the other hand, grade levels and pass/fail points are set by the examining boards, as determined by the expert judgments of examiners who are subject specialists. This difference can be seen in the way the ETS and Cambridge tests of EFL are equated. Each form of the TOEFL is theoretically standardized on the first norming group from 1964, while the equivalence of FCE scores from form to form is based on the collective judgment of the examiners, who take previous standards into account.

In summary, the observable differences between the FCE and the ETS tests of EFL are, we believe, reflections of important differences in the educational measurement traditions from which these two test batteries derive. This is not to imply, however, that they are representative of the full range of EFL tests currently available in their representative countries. There are, indeed, widely used EFL tests in both countries that diverge considerably from these two measurement traditions, so that the results of this study do not necessarily apply to other widely used tests of EFL, whether American or British. However, the purpose of this study was not to compare either US and UK educational measurement or EFL testing practice in general, but rather to focus on two test batteries that have developed and are used within this broader context. The purpose of discussing this context is simply to provide a broader background for understanding and interpreting the study and its results.

## Objectives

The first goal of this study was short-term: to examine the comparability of these two English language proficiency test batteries. The most important aspect of comparability is that of the abilities measured, and so the first step under this goal was to investigate the construct validity of the two tests. This involved two different but complementary approaches to gathering evidence related to construct validity:

1 the qualitative content analysis of the two tests, including the specific language abilities and the types of test tasks employed;
2 the quantitative investigation of patterns of relationships of examinee performance among the different tests, both at the level of total test scores, and, where appropriate, at the item level.

Once the patterns of comparability of abilities measured by the different tests were ascertained, we proceeded to the second step, the examination of the comparability or equivalence of test scores.

The second goal of the study is long-term: to initiate a program of research and development that will lead to a better understanding of the nature of communicative language ability and of different approaches to its measurement. This long-term research agenda will include continued research into:

1 the characteristics of test content and the subsequent refinement of both the models upon which this is based and the procedures for operationalizing these models in the design and specification of language tests;

2 the relationships between aspects of the content of test tasks and test performance;

3 the characteristics of test takers and the relationships among these characteristics and patterns of test taking and test performance.

The second area represents a particularly important concern for both test developers and test users, since recent work has indicated a poor relationship between what "experts" believe a given test item measures and test takers' performance (Alderson 1990a; Alderson 1990b; Alderson and Lukmani 1989).

A crucial aspect of this long-range goal is the collaboration of British and American language testers and other applied linguists in research projects that are of mutual interest, and to which each can bring the best of their respective measurement and research traditions. It is our hope that such collaborative research will result in a cross-fertilization of traditions and perspectives that can most productively be viewed as complementary, and lead ultimately to a broader, integrated set of approaches to empirical research in language testing and applied linguistics in general. It is encouraging, in this regard, that this study has already stimulated a program of research and development aimed at both improving and maintaining the quality of current Cambridge tests of EFL and providing a research basis for the development of new tests of EFL.

## Implementation plan

The study was administered under the direction of Lyle F. Bachman, then of the Division of English as an International Language, University of Illinois at Urbana-Champaign (UIUC), with the advice and assistance of an Executive Committee and an Advisory Committee. The Executive Committee consisted of Lyle F. Bachman; Alastair Pollitt, then of the Godfrey Thompson Unit for Educational Assessment, University of Edinburgh; John Foulkes of the Council for Examinations Development, Cambridge; Fred Davidson, then a Research Advisor to the Council for Examinations Development, Cambridge; and Peter Hargreaves, Director of the EFL Division, Cambridge. The Advisory Committee consisted of John L. Reddaway, Secretary of the University of Cambridge Local Examinations Syndicate; Braj Kachru, Director of the Division of English as an International Language, University of Illinois at Urbana-Champaign; Gillian Brown, Professor and Chair of English as an International Language, University of Cambridge; and several internationally distinguished scholars and researchers in the fields of applied linguistics and language testing.

The study was conducted in two phases:

1 a small-scale ("pilot") study, conducted in 1988, with approximately 250 subjects, at UIUC, the University of California, Los Angeles (UCLA) and in the UK, concurrent with the content analysis of the tests;

2 a large-scale ("main") study, with approximately 1,450 subjects at eight sites around the world.

# Pilot study

The objectives of the pilot study were as follows:

1 to complete a preliminary task and ability analysis of the tests;

2 to determine the feasibility of administering a large number of tests to the same individuals;

3 to identify the quantitative analytic procedures that would have the greatest potential for providing the kind of information that would be relevant to the objectives of the study;

4 to obtain information that would be relevant to decisions about instruments and sampling for the main study.

## Test instruments

Three test batteries were used in the pilot study. The ETS test battery consisted of the *Test of English as a Foreign Language* (TOEFL), the *Speaking Proficiency in English Assessment Kit* (SPEAK) and the *Test of English Writing* (TEW), which was a test developed for this study and closely modelled on the *Test of Written English* (TWE). Two Cambridge examinations, or test batteries, were used: the *Certificate of Proficiency in English* (CPE) and the *First Certificate in English* (FCE). These tests are described in detail in Chapter 2.

## Content analysis

A preliminary content analysis of the tasks required in the various tests was conducted, based on the frameworks of communicative language abilities and test method facets proposed by Bachman (1990). The intention of content analysis is to derive numerical values, based on expert judgment, for all of the relevant facets for each test and item. An operational instrument, developed by Swathi Vanniarajan, Antony Kunnan and Brian Lynch at UCLA, was used for these analyses, the results of which are reported in Bachman *et al.* 1988.

## Test administration and scoring

All tests were administered at three sites (UIUC, UCLA, London) during a three-week period from 14 January through 6 February 1988. Because of administrative constraints, two limitations were placed on the design of the pilot study. First, it was necessary to use students grouped in ESL classes and volunteers as subjects.

Second, it was not possible to control the order in which the tests were taken, so that different groups at the different sites took the tests in differing orders. However, given the objectives of the pilot study, this was not considered to be a problem.

The Cambridge tests were scored according to standard procedures at Cambridge, the TOEFL tests were machine-scored at UIUC, and the TEW tests were scored by a group of trained TWE readers, using standard procedures developed for this test. SPEAK tests were rated and re-rated locally at each of the three sites by two trained SPEAK raters, following standard procedures for this test.

## Subjects

Pilot study subjects were selected to represent two different levels of English proficiency. This was determined essentially by their status at their respective institutions, with students in pre-university ESL classes and students in lower level remedial ESL classes identified as the lower proficiency group, which took the FCE, and students in upper level ESL classes and international students not in ESL classes identified as the upper proficiency group, which took the CPE. Students in both the lower and upper proficiency groups also took the TOEFL, SPEAK and TEW. A total of 259 subjects participated in the pilot study, with 119 in the lower group and 140 in the upper group. Of these, complete data for all measures were obtained from 76 in the lower group and 93 in the upper group.

## Results

The results indicated that the subjects chosen (or who volunteered) for the pilot study were not particularly typical of either TOEFL or FCE/CPE test takers. The FCE group was below relevant norms on the TOEFL, while the CPE group was above. Similarly, the FCE group appeared to be considerably below norms on the FCE. This suggested that greater care needed to be taken in the sampling for the main study to ensure that the test takers in the study were closer to typical FCE/CPE and TOEFL takers.

A number of analyses were undertaken, primarily to determine their potential utility for a larger study. Because of the limited size of the sample, as well as the differences noted above between the pilot study sample and the operational populations of the FCE and the TOEFL, the results of the pilot study could be interpreted only with a great deal of caution, and no claim as to their generalizability was made. They did, however, serve to demonstrate the relative usefulness of the different analyses used.

In general, exploratory factor analyses suggested that the ETS tests of EFL are relatively unidimensional, while the Cambridge tests are factorially more complex. Furthermore, analyses across test batteries revealed both similarities and differences among the various tests. Both chi-square and regression analyses revealed important differences between the US and UK subjects. In particular, there appeared to be a sizeable difference in performance due to test preparation or familiarity with the tests, with the US subjects performing higher on the TOEFL and the UK subjects performing higher on the FCE and CPE. The regression analyses also suggested that not all of the subtests of either the FCE or the CPE are contributing unique information to their respective total scores. Finally, the regression analyses suggested that performance on either the FCE/CPE or the TOEFL predicts performance on the other test battery about equally well.

On the basis of the pilot study it was obvious that it would not be feasible to administer both the FCE and the CPE in the main study. This was because in order to address the questions of interest in the study adequately, giving both tests would effectively double the required sample size. The results of the pilot study suggested that the FCE group's performance was closer to the 480–520 "decision range" on the TOEFL than was the CPE group's. In addition, there is a much larger pool of FCE takers than CPE takers from which to sample. These considerations led us to recommend investigating only the FCE in the main study.

An additional recommendation, based on the experience of the pilot study, was that some means for examining the reliability of the Cambridge Paper 5 ratings needed to be built into the main study. The Paper 5 oral interview includes several design facets – examiner, number of candidates (ranging from one to three) and information package – which we felt had to be controlled, or at least crossed, in the design of the main study so that their individual effects and interactions as potential sources of measurement error could be examined.

Finally, specific recommendations were made regarding the sampling design and procedures for subject selection to be followed in the main study. Ideally, we wanted to sample a hypothetical bivariate population of typical Cambridge and ETS test takers. The approach planned was essentially that which was followed, as described in Chapter 2.

## Advisory Committee meeting

In the fall of 1988 the Advisory Committee held its first meeting, the purpose of which was to discuss the report on the pilot study and to provide advice to the Executive Committee on the design of the main study. The following individuals, in addition to John Reddaway, who chaired the meeting, and members of the Executive Committee, participated in this committee meeting and/or wrote reactions to the pilot study report: J. Charles Alderson, University of Lancaster; Gillian Brown, University of Cambridge; John L.D. Clark, Defense Language Institute, Monterey; Robert Kaplan, University of Southern California; Alan Maley, Bell Educational Trust; Bernard Spolsky, Bar-Ilan University; Charles Stansfield, Center for Applied Linguistics; John Upshur, Concordia University.

This meeting produced several recommendations for the structure of the main study. First, the Committee disagreed with the recommendation that only the FCE be compared to the TOEFL in the main study, and strongly recommended that the CPE be integrated into the main study design. They felt it was important for the CPE to be investigated because it is used for university entrance in the UK. As it would have been difficult at that stage in the planning to administer both the CPE and FCE at all sites, the consensus was for the CPE-TOEFL comparison to be based on smaller samples at selected sites. The Committee also recommended that a CPE and FCE administration be included in the main study to permit the investigation of the relationships between these two examinations. While these recommendations were implemented by the inclusion of additional groups of subjects at three sites, the inadequacies of the samples obtained, in terms of size and representativeness, precluded meaningful analysis, and these results are not reported here.

Second, the Committee strongly endorsed the recommendation that the main study needed to investigate the intra- and inter-rater consistency of ratings of Cambridge Papers 2 (composition) and 5 (oral interview). It was not possible to implement the investigation of rater reliability of Papers 2 and 5 in the main study, but this recommendation has been implemented in a series of follow-up studies. The committee also provided extensive input on the test content analysis, and many of these suggestions were integrated into later versions of the content analysis instruments.

Finally, throughout the meeting there was discussion of the differences between the US and UK traditions of educational measurement, and the Committee suggested that the consideration of these should inform the interpretation of the results of the main study.

## Notes

1  See Davidson and Bachman (1990) for a fuller discussion of these differences.
2  Critics have charged that US testing agencies do exert such an influence in an uncontrolled and undesirable manner, e.g., Evangelauf (1990) Fair Test Examiner 1990 (Spring) and Fair Test Examiner 1990 (Summer).

# 2 Study procedures and sample characteristics

## Test instruments

The two test batteries used in this study are described in this chapter. A list of the different tests used, their parts, numbers of items and administrative times is provided in Appendix A. Example items from the FCE are given in Appendix B, while examples from the ETS tests are given in Appendix C.

### Cambridge Examinations

FCE Paper 1 is entitled "Reading Comprehension", and includes two sections, items 1 through 25, which appear to test use or usage, and items 26 through 40, which are based on reading passages. All items follow a four-choice multiple-choice format. Example items from the two parts of this paper are provided in Appendix B.

FCE Paper 2 is entitled "Composition", and consists of five prompts, from which the candidate chooses two to answer. Candidates are requested to write 120–180 words in response to each prompt. The fifth prompt refers to several texts, from which the candidate selects one on which to write. The texts to be included in this prompt are announced two years prior to the examination, so that candidates who select this prompt will have read at least one of these prior to the test. This prompt reflects the fact that the FCE is a test which implies a course of instruction. That is, a candidate choosing prompt five could have been familiar with the texts either by virtue of his or her familiarity with FCE procedures or through a private course of study. Examples of both types of prompts are given in Appendix B.

FCE Paper 3, entitled "Use of English", includes items that appear to test various aspects of lexicon, register and other elements of English usage. The Paper 3 form used in the study had six sections. The items in Paper 3 follow a variety of formats, ranging from gap-filling to short completion to paragraph writing. Examples are provided in Appendix B.

Section 1 of Paper 3 is an open-ended gap-filling test. Section 2 is a constructed-response section involving sentence transformation. In this section, candidates are presented with a complete sentence stimulus and the beginning of a transformation, which the candidate must then complete. Sections 3 and 4 are a series of short fill-in-the-blank sentences, in each of which the fill-in requires a word or phrase. The type of word or phrase required is specified.

In Paper 3, Section 5, candidates are given a constructed-response task. This section consists of a number of prompts which together form a connected text. In the form used in the study, each prompt is a partial sentence, with elements missing or non-inflected, and the candidate has to form a correct sentence which fits with other parts of the entire text.

The last section of Paper 3 is also a constructed-response exercise, but of greater length. Candidates are given a description of a problem that a fictitious town must solve, including a brief description of the problem, five proposed solutions, a map, and some charts providing information about the town's resources, employment and population. Candidates are instructed to write two paragraphs, one discussing the solution they think is best and why, and the second discussing the solution they think should definitely not be chosen and why. No suggested length for the paragraphs is given, although there is a limit based on the lined space provided in the test booklet.

Paper 4 is a tape-plus-booklet test entitled "Listening Comprehension". The items are passage-based, with candidates listening to a tape-recorded passage and then answering several items on that passage. The test consists of several parts, each following a different item format; these formats include a variety of visual prompts, ranging from single sentences to charts, diagrams and pictures, that are to be completed on the basis of the listening passage. Candidates listen to the instructions and prompts on the tape, read the instructions in the test booklet, and respond in the test booklet.

Multiple forms of Paper 4 are used operationally at each administration of the FCE. Because of difficulties at Cambridge test centers with administering a listening test to large numbers of candidates simultaneously, Paper 4 is administered operationally to different candidates at different times, and multiple forms are produced to minimize problems with test security. Two new forms of Paper 4 are distributed worldwide for each administration. These new forms are put into the pool of available forms, and forms are usually withdrawn after they have been used in three administrations.

Some further conditions determine which centers receive which forms. If a center has had a particular test form, it generally does not receive it again in a subsequent administration. The number of forms sent to each center varies in accordance with the number of candidates and the number of rooms available at that center. If a center has a small number of candidates and one (or few) rooms that can be used simultaneously, then the center receives only one Paper 4 form, since with the test being given simultaneously to all candidates there is less risk of breach of security. At the sites used in this study, ten forms of FCE Paper 4 were administered.

Paper 5 consists of a face-to-face oral interview, the conduct of which is determined by two sets of choices. First, the number of candidates and interviewers, or examiners, may vary. Some interviews consist of one candidate and one examiner while others may include several candidates and one or two examiners. A second set of choices pertains to the "information package" that provides the content basis for the interview. For each interview, the examiner may choose one information package from among a large number of such packages that contain prompt material such as short reading passages, photographs and charts, and that determine, to a large extent, the content of the interview. Topics vary, and include areas such as holidays, sports, and food and drink. One information package is called a "set book" package, and this contains prompt material based on reading texts which the candidate can prepare before the interview, in much the same way as is done for the literary prompts for the Paper 2 composition.

Appendix B contains the instructions given to Paper 5 examiners. These instructions are taken from UCLES (1988:2–3), which is the general examiner instruction booklet for Paper 5, the instructions which were operational at the time of the study.

In general, all interviews should follow four stages:

Stage 1  general conversation (brief)
Stage 2  discussion of one or more theme (package)-related photos
Stage 3  discussion of one or more theme-related short reading passages
Stage 4  discussion task, problem-solving task, role-playing task, etc., related to the theme

The operational procedure is to send out ten new Paper 5 information packages each year, to cover the twice-yearly administrations. The December 1988 administration, on which this study was based, happened to be an exception. Several very large centers had requested Cambridge to produce more than ten information packages to provide greater flexibility in local interview administration. Cambridge agreed to send out, for the December 1988 administration only, fifteen packages, which are therefore included in this study.

## Test of English as a Foreign Language (TOEFL)

The institutional TOEFL consists of forms of the official international TOEFL that have been retired from operational use, and which are made available to institutions for their own purposes. Scores on the institutional TOEFL are not reported to other institutions by ETS; nevertheless, ETS guarantees content and statistical equivalence of the institutional and international forms of the TOEFL. There are three sections to the test, with titles and time limits as follows:

Section 1  "Listening Comprehension" (29 minutes)
Section 2  "Structure and Written Expression" (25 minutes)
Section 3  "Vocabulary and Reading Comprehension" (45 minutes)

Item types vary somewhat, but all follow a four-option multiple-choice format. Sample items taken from the instructions for each section of the institutional TOEFL are given in Appendix C.

## Speaking Proficiency in English Assessment Kit (SPEAK)

The SPEAK is a semi-direct test of oral performance, and is the institutional counterpart of the international Test of Spoken English (TSE). As with the institutional version of the TOEFL, the SPEAK consists of retired forms of the operational TSE, and is available to institutions for local use. It is a complete kit, including training materials for test administrators to learn the scoring procedure. The SPEAK is intended to measure speaking, but does not involve a live face-to-face interaction with an interlocutor. Rather, the candidate listens to a number of prompts from a cassette source tape, looks at some stimulus material in an accompanying booklet, and responds on a target cassette tape, which also records the prompts from the source tape. Examples from the SPEAK version used in the study are given in Appendix C.

## Test of English Writing (TEW)

ETS produces a centrally scored composition test called the Test of Written English (TWE), which was still considered experimental by ETS at the time the study was begun, and had no institutional counterpart. Therefore, an experienced TWE rater was asked to produce a prompt that was similar to example prompts that ETS makes available in its information to prospective test takers. This test was called the "Test of English Writing" (TEW). The prompt used for the study is given in Appendix C.

The TEW test booklet contained two typewritten sheets, on the first of which were the instructions, while the second contained the single prompt to be answered by all candidates in the study. The time limit was 30 minutes, as for the TWE, and the administrative procedures followed were the same as the operational procedures for the TWE.

# Scoring procedures

## Cambridge Examinations

All scoring procedures for the FCE at Cambridge adhere closely to the British educational measurement tradition discussed above. In subjectively marked components, considerable weight is attached to experience, seniority, and above all, to institutional memory, that is, the accumulated knowledge of "expert" individuals about how the procedure has been followed over many years. However, as might be expected in two countries "divided by a common language", there are differences in the terminology employed in the British and American measurement traditions, so before discussing the scoring procedures, it is advisable to point out some of these terminological differences. A Cambridge "examination" consists of a set of "papers", which in American measurement parlance are called a "test battery" and "tests", respectively. Cambridge papers are "marked", while in the US tests are "scored", and a UK "mark" is thus synonymous with a US "score". In the UK, "marks" also refer to the number of "points" awarded to a given question or paper. Further, the list of criteria to be used in subjectively scored papers is called a "mark-scheme" in the UK.

There are also differences in the terms that are used for the personnel involved in measurement, especially with respect to the subjective assessment of papers. An "examiner" is what would be called a "rater" or "scorer" in the US – a person who actually scores, or "marks", tests. A Chief Examiner is a subject specialist – in the case of the Cambridge EFL examinations, an EFL specialist, normally in some senior EFL teaching position in the UK, who is responsible for the overall content of the EFL exams. In addition to the examiners and Chief Examiners, there are EFL Subject Officers who work in Cambridge and oversee the year-to-year administration of the EFL tests. There were, at the time of the study, two FCE Subject Officers and four Chief Examiners for the FCE. The next level in the examiner hierarchy consists of the Team Leaders who are experienced EFL examiners who have participated in the Cambridge EFL marking system for several years. Each Team Leader in turn oversees a number of Assistant Examiners. Together, the Team Leaders and Assistant Examiners comprise the operational rater group for the papers that are subjectively rated at Cambridge (Paper 2, Composition, and Paper 3, Use of English). This operational group of raters is supervised by the Chief Examiners (who are also operational raters) and the Subject Officers, who work in Cambridge and are internally responsible for examinations.

Mark-schemes for Papers 2 and 3 are coordinated as follows. After a number of scripts have arrived at Cambridge, the Chief Examiner marks the scripts against a temporary mark-scheme. A final mark-scheme meeting is then held, attended by the Chief Examiner, the Subject Officers and examiners involved with that paper. The final mark-scheme is devised at this meeting, though facilities exist to modify it later if the Chief Examiner and Subject Officer concur.

The other EFL exams (Papers 1, 4 and 5) are marked differently. Paper 1, Reading Comprehension, uses an optically scanned multiple-choice answer sheet. Paper 4 is a constructed-response listening test, and is scored against a key by temporary clerical assistants hired during the twice-a-year exam processing. These temporary clerks are supervised by various levels of permanent Cambridge personnel who have worked in such tasks for several years. Paper 5 is an oral interview administered at the field sites. One or two candidates sit in an interview with one or two locally trained examiners. If two examiners are present, one serves to assess the candidates' performance and the other serves to conduct the interaction. If only one examiner is present, then that examiner performs both functions. The marks for Paper 5 are entered by hand onto an optical scan sheet which is then read into the computer system in Cambridge.

All papers use some sort of mark-scheme. For Paper 1, this scheme is a simple multiple-choice correct response key, applied in the computer processing. For Papers 2 and 3, these schemes are the result of the final mark-scheme meeting. The mark-scheme for Paper 4 is set much earlier in the exam development process. For Paper 5, the mark-scheme is actually a set of oral interview training materials, a rating performance guideline document, which includes a set of descriptors, training video-tapes, and materials for local examiner training at field sites.

While there is no operational re-rating of Papers 2, 3 or 5, the papers most often deemed "subjective" in Cambridge terminology, there is a system of operational checking of Papers 2 and 3, as follows. A certain percentage (5–10%) of each Assistant Examiner's work is checked by either a Team Leader or another individual called a Checker, who is also an Assistant Examiner, but with considerably more experience. The scripts which are re-marked are chosen by an expert-judgment sampling procedure. These re-marks are not done independently, that is, the re-marker can see the original mark on the test paper as he or she checks the scoring. An informal examination of the re-marks for Papers 2 and 3 in the data set for this study yielded extremely high intercorrelations between the original examiner and the re-marker, in excess of .95. However, since these re-marks are not independent of the first marks, they do not satisfy the conditions for investigating inter-rater consistency, and thus cannot be interpreted as indicators of inter-rater reliability.

Cambridge EFL paper marks are rescaled by various means during the course of exam processing in Cambridge. Papers 1, 3 and 5 are re-proportioned to a maximum of 40 possible marks, Paper 1 having originally been 55 marks, Paper 3 originally a higher number of marks (which varies from form to form) and Paper 5 originally 30 marks. Additionally, Papers 2 and 3 are scaled to the distributions of Paper 1 on an examiner-by-examiner basis. Paper 4 forms are fixed to an invariant total of 20 marks regardless of the number of items. These rescalings are intended to control sources of error in the examining process. The rescaled scores from the five papers are then added together to arrive at a total score, which is used as a basis for assigning grades.

Candidates who take the FCE receive a single letter grade of A, B, C, D or E. The first three, A, B, and C, are passing grades, D is intended to indicate a narrow failure, and E indicates a failure. Grade boundaries are established as follows. After a substantial amount of operational marking has been done, the Subject Officers and Chief Examiner study distributions of total results, as displayed in printouts of cumulative frequency distributions accompanied by normal ogive graphs. The cumulative frequency information allows the Chief Examiner and Subject Officers to determine the percentage of candidates at or below any given mark; the ogive curve is a graphic representation of the entire candidature which can be compared to similar graphs of previous years' results. Following recommendations of these individuals, the Subject Officers and Chief Examiner then fix the final grade boundaries. It should be noted that these individuals have at their disposal several sources of information to guide their judgment: knowledge of previous years' distributions and grade boundaries, recommendations from the Team Leaders, and knowledge of maintenance of standards in the test as a whole. It is also clear that *a priori* decisions on the number of candidates expected in each grade band affect this process.

## TOEFL

The institutional TOEFL is administered to examinees with a multiple-choice optically scanned answer sheet. Based on the TOEFL answer key provided by ETS, answer sheets can be either hand- or machine-scored. Given the large number of answer sheets involved in this study, these were machine-scored on an optical scanner. A correct answer is assigned a score of 1 while an incorrect answer receives a score of zero. A raw score subtotal for each of the three TOEFL sections is calculated by summing the total number of items answered correctly within each TOEFL section, while the raw score total for the TOEFL is calculated by summing the total number of items answered correctly across all three sections. Raw score subtotals and totals are converted to TOEFL standard scores via a conversion table provided with the scoring key. In the form of the institutional TOEFL used for the main study, four items, two from Section 1 and two from Section 3, were try-out items for the development of future TOEFL forms, and were not scored or counted in test takers' total scores.

## SPEAK

All SPEAK ratings are made on the basis of the tape recordings that test takers make during the SPEAK administration. The various parts of the SPEAK are rated on four scales: pronunciation, grammar, fluency and comprehensibility, each on a scale from 0 to 3. A score of 0 represents either frequent phonemic errors, no grammatical control, fragmented speech, or incomprehensible speech, while a score of 3 represents either occasional non-native pronunciation errors, minor grammatical errors, smooth speech approximating native language fluency, or completely comprehensible speech. To qualify to score the SPEAK, raters are required to complete an eight to ten-hour training program which includes the rating of training tapes to assess rater accuracy. If there is a difference in ratings greater than .95 between the norm ratings and those of the trainee on any of the SPEAK scales (i.e. pronunciation, grammar, fluency, or comprehensibility), it is suggested that the trainee complete the training course again.

In order to obtain scores for each of the four SPEAK scales (pronunciation, grammar, fluency, or comprehensibility), the ratings of the items within the SPEAK sections are averaged across all the items comprising the section. For instance, ten items are rated for grammar in Section 3, and the average rating across these items is the section score for grammar. The ratings are averaged again for each of the scales across all sections to obtain an overall rating for each scale. Averages for pronunciation, grammar, and fluency are rounded to the nearest tenth. The comprehensibility rating is multiplied by 100 and rounded to the nearest unit of 10. In accordance with the suggested scoring procedures to be found in the SPEAK administration manual (ETS 1985), each SPEAK tape was rated twice with the reported SPEAK scores based on the average of the two ratings. If the difference between any of the ratings was greater than .95, the tape was re-rated by a third rater. For those tapes requiring a third rating, examinees' scores were based on an average of the three ratings.

All SPEAK tapes for this study were rated independently twice by different trained SPEAK raters with backgrounds and training in ESL/EFL. Approximately one third of the tapes were scored by faculty and graduate teaching assistants in the Division of English as an International Language, University of Illinois at Urbana-Champaign. The rest were scored by faculty and graduate teaching assistants in the Department of English, Iowa State University in Ames. Less than 5% of the tapes required re-rating by a third rater. To facilitate scoring, a machine-scorable rating sheet was designed for the study. SPEAK raters completed this rating sheet, which was then scanned by machine, and all calculations required to obtain the SPEAK scores were carried out by computer.

## TEW

Standard scoring procedures developed for the TWE were followed in the scoring of the TEW. The TEW was rated on a global scale of writing proficiency ranging from 1 to 6. If examinees wrote off-topic, the essay was marked "Off topic" and received no score. Each essay was rated independently by two different readers, with the reported score based on the average of the two ratings. If there was more than a one point difference between the two ratings, the ratings were considered discrepant and the essay was rated by a third rater. The final rating was the average of the two ratings that were closest in magnitude, the third rating being dropped from the score calculations. All TEW scripts from the study were rated by trained TWE raters from the Language Learning Unit at the University of Toronto. Less than 1% of the TEW scripts required a third rating.

# Data preparation

The data preparation for the Cambridge examinations involved the entry of item-level test information into computer files. The vast majority of the data key-in was performed by hand using dBase III+ (Ashton-Tate 1985) on IBM PC-XTs by temporary staff who had received special training and were supervised by study staff. The machine-scorable answer sheets for the TOEFL and SPEAK were scored by Metritech Incorporated, a psychological and educational measurement firm in Champaign, using an NCS Sentry 3000 model scanner. Floppy disk files containing the scored and unscored item data, the demographic data, and so forth, from the TOEFL and the item ratings from the SPEAK were provided to the study staff. TEW scripts were counted to verify that all the scripts sent for scoring had been scored and returned. The examinee identification numbers and ratings from the TEW were manually entered into floppy disk files by project staff. All entries were checked for accuracy.

Control of candidate identification numbers is critical in a large-scale project such as this. A six-digit identification number was used: two digits to identify the site and four digits to identify candidates within sites. This six-digit number was unique for each candidate and was the number by which TOEFL and Cambridge cases were matched. The examinee identification numbers from the TOEFL answer sheet were used as the basis for the master identification list. Identification numbers were checked manually, and all duplicates were identified and checked against the identification numbers from the TEW scripts and SPEAK scoring sheets. In a few cases, site coordinators were contacted to verify or correct an examinee identification number. A master list of names and identification numbers from Cambridge was provided after data was processed in Cambridge, and the master names list from Illinois was checked and standardized to the Cambridge master list. However, any individuals who completed only the ETS tests were also included in the final data sets.

# Sampling procedures

The sampling procedures for the study reflect several major concerns, some of which were identified in the original project plan, and some of which were identified during the first Advisory Committee meeting, discussed above. This section of the report describes these procedures and highlights the major considerations underlying them. These considerations can be summarized as follows:

1  Select sites and subjects that reflect a sample of the operational worldwide populations of the TOEFL and FCE.
2  Administer both the Cambridge and ETS tests under conditions as near to normal operations as possible.
3  At each site, select subjects that reflect a cross-section of relevant test taker characteristics (e.g., age, prior training).
4  Control the study for prior test-specific preparedness, so that each candidate takes both an unfamiliar test, i.e. that test which the candidate would not normally have taken; and a familiar test, i.e. one which the candidate would normally have taken.
5  Include groups that would permit the comparison of FCE with TOEFL.

## Characteristics of typical FCE takers

Typical candidates for the FCE represent a widely varied population. They have many reasons for seeking the certification provided by the FCE. For example, a candidate might be in a business where English proficiency is required, such as in the airline industry, or in a diplomatic position which requires English, and a certificate might be one criterion for employment, promotion or salary increase.

The usual FCE population also includes wide variation in background variables. The 1988 Cambridge EFL Survey (UCLES 1989) reports that the FCE was administered to 123,282 candidates in 68 countries. Data on native language background, educational status, age, sex, and amount of non-FCE prior English study are not available.

It is possible to assume that candidates have extensive familiarity with the examination they register to take since the vast majority of candidates taking the FCE have undergone some sort of prior course aimed directly at the test. Furthermore, the specifications for the examination in fact comprise a course of instruction, which reflects the British testing philosophy of maximizing the link between teaching and testing. While exact figures on the amount of FCE preparation in the operational population are not available, there are, to be sure, some candidates without this preparation.

## Characteristics of typical TOEFL takers

Extensive information about test performance of the operational TOEFL population is provided in the *TOEFL Test and Score Manual* (ETS 1987), while detailed information on test taker characteristics is available in two TOEFL research reports: *A comparative analysis of TOEFL examinee characteristics, 1977–1979* (Wilson 1982) and *patterns of test-taking and score change for examinees who repeat the Test of English as a Foreign Language* (Wilson 1987). Wilson (1982) examined the records of over 280,000 individuals from more than 160 countries who took the TOEFL from September 1977 through August 1979, while Wilson (1987) examined the records of test takers who had taken the TOEFL at least twice between July 1984 and August 1985. Both studies report findings for the entire sample as well as for separate countries. In summary, the majority of the test takers described in these studies (80%) are "degree planners" (individuals planning to enter a college or university degree program in the US or Canada), male (72%), and have median ages of 20.6 and 25.4 for undergraduate- and graduate-level degree planners respectively. Furthermore, 28% of individuals who took the TOEFL for the first time in 1977 and 1978 had two or more test records by 1982, with much higher percentages, between 40% and 50%, being reported for three of the countries in which the study sites were located: Hong Kong, Thailand and Japan. The test taker characteristics described in these two studies are discussed further under *Characteristics of the study sample.*

## Site selection

Several key elements were involved in selecting study sites. First, there was the need to balance sites with respect to geographic region and native language. Based on the geographic distributions of the Cambridge and TOEFL operational populations, we decided to include sites in the Far East, Middle East, Europe and South America. Within each of these regions we attempted to obtain representative samples of different language groups: Chinese, Japanese and Thai for the Far East, Arabic for the Middle East, Spanish, French and German for Europe, and Spanish and Portuguese for South America.

Second, there was the question of test preparation. It was acknowledged from the outset that the majority of the FCE operational population would have attended a specific course of instruction for the examination, while it could not be assumed that the TOEFL population had attended a TOEFL-specific course of instruction prior to taking the test. Thus, there appeared to be an inherent imbalance in the two operational populations, with typical Cambridge takers being prepared for the examination, and typical TOEFL takers being largely unprepared. While there is a growing demand for the independent TOEFL preparation courses that are increasingly available to the TOEFL candidature worldwide, these courses vary widely with respect to their length and curricula, so that it was not possible to consider them systematically in the design of the study. We did, however, survey the candidates about their prior TOEFL exposure and training.

Because of this inherent difference in test preparation between the two operational populations, we felt that it was necessary to try to control for this in the research design as much as possible, since to compare unprepared TOEFL takers only with prepared FCE takers could introduce bias into our data. If we could have two types of FCE taker (prepared and unprepared) and adequately survey TOEFL takers regarding prior TOEFL-specific training, we hoped to be able to either control for or investigate the effects of test preparation on test performance.

In considering possible sites, we learned that in general a site with a large TOEFL presence, based on reported numbers of test takers by country (ETS 1987), did not necessarily have a large FCE candidature, and vice versa. We therefore identified two types of sites, represented by typical numbers of operational test takers, as "Cambridge-dominant" and "TOEFL-dominant". The former type was identified from Cambridge records as having large numbers of FCE candidates, while the latter type was identified on the basis of typically small numbers of FCE candidates and relatively large numbers of TOEFL test takers. We assumed that the "Cambridge-dominant" sites would have test takers who were largely prepared for the Cambridge tests, while at the "TOEFL-dominant" sites, test takers would not have prior FCE-specific courses, and that this would provide some control with respect to test preparedness.

Finally, the availability of local contact persons, their ability and willingness to administer both sets of tests under operational conditions, and the availability of adequate numbers of subjects, obviously had to be taken into account. We considered many sites which roughly satisfied the two criteria discussed above, and then narrowed this list to those sites where known local personnel were available to participate in the study. One person in each site eventually became the site coordinator. These local personnel were to prove invaluable in the implementation of the study.

After lengthy discussions revolving around these areas of concern, and considerable negotiation, eight sites were agreed upon, local site coordinators identified and contacted, and formal participation arrangements finalized. These were as follows:

1 *TOEFL-dominant sites*
   a) Thailand
   b) Egypt
   c) Japan
   d) Hong Kong
2 *Cambridge-dominant sites*
   a) Spain
   b) Brazil
   c) France
   d) Switzerland

These eight sites provided a total sample size of approximately 1,450 subjects.

# Administrative procedures

## Site coordinators

At the Cambridge-dominant sites, the site coordinator was the examinations officer in charge of Cambridge EFL tests at that site. The site coordinator at the TOEFL-dominant sites was an individual who was a staff member of an institution of higher education, who was familiar with the local population of "typical" TOEFL takers, and who had access to adequate numbers of these individuals from which to draw a sample. This individual generally worked closely with the local Cambridge examinations officer in arranging the schedule for test administration. In October 1988 a member of the study staff visited each site to assist in the local arrangements.

## Subject selection procedures

The selection of subjects at each site was intended to ensure a representative sample of the operational candidate population at that site. That is, for the TOEFL-dominant sites, we wanted a cross-section of candidates for variables such as age, prior English training, previous exposure to TOEFL and so on. The same was true at the Cambridge sites, except that it was in fact often necessary to select from the pool of available candidates from the known Cambridge entry candidature. Various procedures were followed to implement this selection, including random selection and expert judgment. Although minor difficulties emerged in subject selection as the project progressed, every effort was made at every juncture to ensure that a representative sample of the TOEFL or Cambridge candidature at that site was obtained.

## Test administration

At all sites, the joint administration of the FCE with the TOEFL occurred during the normal operational schedule for the Cambridge tests, which are given twice yearly, in June and December. Papers 1, 2 and 3 (Reading Comprehension, Composition, and Use of English) were administered as normal. Paper 4 (Listening Comprehension) and Paper 5 (Oral Interview), were administered as normal, within a five-week period centered on the date of the other three papers.

From very early in the study it was obvious that we would not be able to synchronize the Cambridge examinations with an operational administration of the international TOEFL, and we therefore decided to use the institutional TOEFL, which could be administered during the same period as the operational Cambridge examinations. We thus used the operational Cambridge schedule as the schedule for the entire project, and dovetailed the ETS tests into the Cambridge administration. Most typically this meant that candidates took the Cambridge and TOEFL pencil-and-paper sections (i.e. everything except Cambridge Papers 4 and 5 and the SPEAK) on adjacent days. The oral measures were administered within the five weeks centered on Cambridge Papers 1, 2 and 3, as required for the Cambridge interview. At many sites the SPEAK test was actually given in the same two-day period as the pencil-and-paper tests, by use of a rotating schedule in language laboratories. All tests were administered in strict accordance with the operational procedures prescribed for each. In addition, a background questionnaire that included a self-rating of EFL proficiency was administered during the typical two-day sequence.

A major administrative problem that affected an important objective of the study was the inability to tape-record the Cambridge oral interviews. We had intended, following the recommendation of the pilot study and the Advisory Committee, to implement a generalizability study to investigate inter-rater reliability. However, it was not possible for Cambridge to implement this part of the design at the study sites. Had we known of the severe difficulty we would meet in trying to implement interview recording, we could have begun to plan for it much earlier. It is clear, however, that Cambridge did not at that time have the control of local site personnel necessary to request interview taping within a time frame such as that of the study. This was a serious and damaging alteration to the study design.

# Characteristics of the study sample

## Test performance

Summary descriptive statistics for test or paper scores for the entire study sample are given in Table 1. Inspection of the score distributions indicated that all the measures are reasonably normally distributed, and that the distributional assumptions for parametric statistical analyses are warranted.

**Table 1**

**Score distributions, all measures**

| Variable | Mean | Std dev | Min | Max | N | Label |
|---|---|---|---|---|---|---|
| TOEFL1 | 49.619 | 6.665 | 29 | 68 | 1,448 | TOEFL 1: Listening standard score |
| TOEFL2 | 51.118 | 6.900 | 25 | 68 | 1,448 | TOEFL 2: Struct and written expression standard score |
| TOEFL3 | 51.489 | 6.696 | 28 | 66 | 1,448 | TOEFL 3: Vocab and reading standard score |
| TOEFL TOT | 507.427 | 58.863 | 310 | 647 | 1,448 | TOEFL Standard score total |
| TEW | 3.926 | .891 | 1 | 6 | 1,398 | Test of English Writing rating |
| SPK GRAM | 1.934 | .454 | 0 | 3 | 1,304 | SPEAK: Grammar rating |
| SPK PRON | 2.134 | .380 | 0 | 3 | 1,314 | SPEAK: Pronunciation rating |
| SPK FLCY | 1.945 | .440 | 0 | 3 | 1,304 | SPEAK: Fluency rating |
| SPK COMP | 201.572 | 40.906 | 50 | 300 | 1,304 | SPEAK: Comprehensibility rating |
| FCE1 SCA | 25.945 | 4.896 | 10 | 40 | 1,359 | FCE PAPER 1: Cambridge scaled score total |
| FCE2 SCA | 24.303 | 6.043 | 0 | 40 | 1,357 | FCE PAPER 2: Cambridge scaled score total |
| FCE3 SCA | 24.861 | 5.706 | 1 | 40 | 1,353 | FCE PAPER 3: Cambridge scaled score total |
| FCE4 SCA | 13.600 | 3.175 | 4 | 20 | 1,344 | FCE PAPER 4: Cambridge scaled score total |
| FCE5 SCA | 27.203 | 5.951 | 1 | 40 | 1,381 | FCE PAPER 5: Cambridge scaled score total |
| FCESCTOT[1] | 116.186 | 20.567 | 34 | 172 | 1,332 | |
| FCEGRADE[2] | 2.596 | 1.167 | 1 | 5 | 1,353 | FCE grade |

Descriptive statistics for the eight sites are given in Table 2.

**Table 2**

**Score distributions, all measures by site**

| | | Thailand | | | |
|---|---|---|---|---|---|
| **Variable** | **Mean** | **Std dev** | **Min** | **Max** | **N** |
| TOEFL1 | 45.728 | 6.529 | 29 | 66 | 169 |
| TOEFL2 | 47.657 | 6.649 | 26 | 65 | 169 |
| TOEFL3 | 47.379 | 6.294 | 30 | 63 | 169 |
| TOEFL TOT | 469.219 | 56.312 | 337 | 630 | 169 |
| TEW | 3.105 | .760 | 1 | 5 | 171 |
| SPK GRAM | 1.605 | .432 | 1 | 3 | 163 |
| SPK PRON | 1.804 | .408 | 1 | 3 | 165 |
| SPK FLCY | 1.623 | .434 | 1 | 3 | 163 |
| SPK COMP | 171.411 | 41.646 | 50 | 300 | 163 |
| FCE1 SCA | 21.842 | 4.877 | 11 | 33 | 171 |
| FCE2 SCA | 18.935 | 5.580 | 1 | 31 | 171 |
| FCE3 SCA | 19.845 | 5.798 | 6 | 33 | 171 |
| FCE4 SCA | 10.306 | 3.040 | 5 | 19 | 170 |
| FCE5 SCA | 24.046 | 7.838 | 1 | 40 | 171 |
| FCESCTOT | 95.100 | 22.786 | 34 | 150 | 170 |
| FCEGRADE | 1.535 | .986 | 1 | 5 | 170 |

| | | Egypt | | | |
|---|---|---|---|---|---|
| **Variable** | **Mean** | **Std dev** | **Min** | **Max** | **N** |
| TOEFL1 | 49.045 | 6.221 | 35 | 62 | 89 |
| TOEFL2 | 46.180 | 6.222 | 33 | 62 | 89 |
| TOEFL3 | 44.562 | 6.000 | 31 | 64 | 89 |
| TOEFL TOT | 465.978 | 53.080 | 347 | 620 | 89 |
| TEW | 3.330 | .804 | 2 | 5 | 91 |
| SPK GRAM | 1.925 | .455 | 1 | 3 | 80 |
| SPK PRON | 2.141 | .348 | 1 | 3 | 80 |
| SPK FLCY | 1.944 | .493 | 1 | 3 | 80 |
| SPK COMP | 204.177 | 42.505 | 110 | 290 | 79 |
| FCE1 SCA | 24.551 | 6.262 | 10 | 37 | 91 |
| FCE2 SCA | 23.373 | 5.897 | 9 | 36 | 90 |
| FCE3 SCA | 23.005 | 5.968 | 8 | 35 | 88 |
| FCE4 SCA | 13.303 | 3.442 | 5 | 19 | 89 |
| FCE5 SCA | 25.720 | 6.174 | 9 | 39 | 89 |
| FCESCTOT | 109.812 | 22.870 | 44 | 156 | 85 |
| FCEGRADE | 2.267 | 1.269 | 1 | 5 | 86 |

$\Rightarrow$

| Japan | | | | | |
|---|---|---|---|---|---|
| **Variable** | **Mean** | **Std dev** | **Min** | **Max** | **N** |
| TOEFL1 | 44.360 | 6.882 | 32 | 66 | 189 |
| TOEFL2 | 47.407 | 7.070 | 26 | 65 | 189 |
| TOEFL3 | 45.386 | 6.970 | 28 | 63 | 189 |
| TOEFL TOT | 457.196 | 61.741 | 310 | 620 | 189 |
| TEW | 3.297 | .882 | 2 | 5 | 128 |
| SPK GRAM | 1.928 | .524 | 0 | 3 | 114 |
| SPK PRON | 1.855 | .499 | 0 | 3 | 116 |
| SPK FLCY | 1.702 | .483 | 0 | 3 | 114 |
| SPK COMP | 189.386 | 46.130 | 50 | 290 | 114 |
| FCE1 SCA | 23.033 | 4.970 | 12 | 34 | 106 |
| FCE2 SCA | 19.503 | 7.759 | 0 | 38 | 105 |
| FCE3 SCA | 18.624 | 6.958 | 1 | 35 | 104 |
| FCE4 SCA | 10.640 | 3.314 | 5 | 18 | 89 |
| FCE5 SCA | 23.425 | 5.750 | 4 | 39 | 116 |
| FCESCTOT | 95.148 | 24.645 | 35 | 148 | 88 |
| FCEGRADE | 1.642 | 1.044 | 1 | 5 | 106 |

| Hong Kong | | | | | |
|---|---|---|---|---|---|
| **Variable** | **Mean** | **Std dev** | **Min** | **Max** | **N** |
| TOEFL1 | 51.964 | 4.497 | 43 | 66 | 196 |
| TOEFL2 | 53.036 | 6.125 | 37 | 65 | 196 |
| TOEFL3 | 53.663 | 4.901 | 40 | 66 | 196 |
| TOEFL TOT | 528.878 | 44.056 | 427 | 647 | 196 |
| TEW | 4.260 | .715 | 3 | 6 | 196 |
| SPK GRAM | 1.902 | .436 | 1 | 3 | 190 |
| SPK PRON | 2.106 | .279 | 1 | 3 | 194 |
| SPK FLCY | 1.955 | .386 | 1 | 3 | 190 |
| SPK COMP | 201.895 | 37.930 | 100 | 300 | 190 |
| FCE1 SCA | 26.898 | 4.011 | 15 | 40 | 195 |
| FCE2 SCA | 26.372 | 4.481 | 14 | 39 | 195 |
| FCE3 SCA | 26.620 | 4.225 | 15 | 40 | 195 |
| FCE4 SCA | 14.159 | 2.206 | 9 | 20 | 195 |
| FCE5 SCA | 27.384 | 5.079 | 16 | 40 | 204 |
| FCESCTOT | 121.361 | 14.473 | 89 | 172 | 194 |
| FCEGRADE | 2.846 | .998 | 1 | 5 | 195 |

$\Rightarrow$

| Spain | | | | | |
|---|---|---|---|---|---|
| **Variable** | **Mean** | **Std dev** | **Min** | **Max** | **N** |
| TOEFL1 | 46.750 | 5.668 | 33 | 63 | 196 |
| TOEFL2 | 51.883 | 6.846 | 25 | 68 | 196 |
| TOEFL3 | 54.719 | 5.354 | 38 | 65 | 196 |
| TOEFL TOT | 511.184 | 51.493 | 357 | 640 | 196 |
| TEW | 3.882 | .697 | 2 | 6 | 195 |
| SPK GRAM | 1.903 | .451 | 1 | 3 | 196 |
| SPK PRON | 2.175 | .294 | 1 | 3 | 196 |
| SPK FLCY | 1.911 | .398 | 1 | 3 | 195 |
| SPK COMP | 196.888 | 35.863 | 100 | 290 | 196 |
| FCE1 SCA | 27.331 | 4.000 | 15 | 35 | 190 |
| FCE2 SCA | 25.884 | 4.795 | 15 | 39 | 190 |
| FCE3 SCA | 26.914 | 4.189 | 16 | 37 | 190 |
| FCE4 SCA | 14.026 | 2.651 | 4 | 20 | 194 |
| FCE5 SCA | 27.776 | 4.205 | 13 | 37 | 194 |
| FCESCTOT | 121.953 | 14.140 | 75 | 152 | 190 |
| FCEGRADE | 2.879 | .998 | 1 | 5 | 190 |

| Brazil | | | | | |
|---|---|---|---|---|---|
| **Variable** | **Mean** | **Std dev** | **Min** | **Max** | **N** |
| TOEFL1 | 51.348 | 4.984 | 36 | 66 | 207 |
| TOEFL2 | 52.101 | 5.572 | 30 | 65 | 207 |
| TOEFL3 | 52.812 | 4.544 | 39 | 64 | 207 |
| TOEFL TOT | 520.865 | 43.241 | 360 | 637 | 207 |
| TEW | 3.995 | .651 | 2 | 6 | 211 |
| SPK GRAM | 1.916 | .319 | 1 | 3 | 184 |
| SPK PRON | 2.259 | .287 | 1 | 3 | 184 |
| SPK FLCY | 2.026 | .325 | 1 | 3 | 184 |
| SPK COMP | 206.413 | 31.986 | 140 | 290 | 184 |
| FCE1 SCA | 26.517 | 3.586 | 11 | 36 | 204 |
| FCE2 SCA | 26.138 | 3.916 | 18 | 40 | 204 |
| FCE3 SCA | 27.432 | 3.618 | 13 | 36 | 204 |
| FCE4 SCA | 14.461 | 2.543 | 5 | 20 | 204 |
| FCE5 SCA | 26.388 | 4.538 | 16 | 40 | 204 |
| FCESCTOT | 120.946 | 12.321 | 77 | 157 | 204 |
| FCEGRADE | 2.819 | .843 | 1 | 5 | 204 |

$\Rightarrow$

| | | France | | | |
|---|---|---|---|---|---|
| **Variable** | **Mean** | **Std dev** | **Min** | **Max** | **N** |
| TOEFL1 | 50.716 | 5.273 | 36 | 63 | 197 |
| TOEFL2 | 55.086 | 5.482 | 37 | 68 | 197 |
| TOEFL3 | 56.015 | 4.583 | 41 | 66 | 197 |
| TOEFL TOT | 539.386 | 43.395 | 407 | 633 | 197 |
| TEW | 4.714 | .800 | 3 | 6 | 199 |
| SPK GRAM | 1.933 | .387 | 1 | 3 | 172 |
| SPK PRON | 2.218 | .338 | 1 | 3 | 175 |
| SPK FLCY | 1.976 | .393 | 1 | 3 | 173 |
| SPK COMP | 202.832 | 36.306 | 90 | 290 | 173 |
| FCE1 SCA | 25.653 | 4.227 | 12 | 36 | 196 |
| FCE2 SCA | 23.616 | 6.471 | 1 | 40 | 196 |
| FCE3 SCA | 24.749 | 4.997 | 11 | 40 | 196 |
| FCE4 SCA | 14.179 | 2.688 | 5 | 19 | 196 |
| FCE5 SCA | 28.880 | 5.951 | 12 | 40 | 196 |
| FCESCTOT | 117.087 | 16.907 | 68 | 158 | 196 |
| FCEGRADE | 2.602 | 1.139 | 1 | 5 | 196 |

| | | Switzerland | | | |
|---|---|---|---|---|---|
| **Variable** | **Mean** | **Std dev** | **Min** | **Max** | **N** |
| TOEFL1 | 55.624 | 5.090 | 41 | 68 | 205 |
| TOEFL2 | 52.166 | 6.550 | 41 | 68 | 205 |
| TOEFL3 | 52.659 | 5.176 | 38 | 64 | 205 |
| TOEFL TOT | 534.854 | 49.179 | 410 | 643 | 205 |
| TEW | 4.174 | .645 | 3 | 6 | 207 |
| SPK GRAM | 2.276 | .375 | 1 | 3 | 205 |
| SPK PRON | 2.358 | .278 | 1 | 3 | 204 |
| SPK FLCY | 2.260 | .357 | 1 | 3 | 205 |
| SPK COMP | 230.098 | 34.285 | 110 | 300 | 205 |
| FCE1 SCA | 28.997 | 4.221 | 15 | 37 | 206 |
| FCE2 SCA | 27.029 | 4.583 | 15 | 38 | 206 |
| FCE3 SCA | 26.975 | 4.194 | 15 | 38 | 205 |
| FCE4 SCA | 15.386 | 2.546 | 7 | 20 | 207 |
| FCE5 SCA | 31.064 | 4.479 | 19 | 40 | 207 |
| FCESCTOT | 129.507 | 14.531 | 86 | 166 | 205 |
| TEST GRADE | 3.374 | .958 | 1 | 5 | 206 |

In order to examine the extent to which the subjects were typical of their respective operational populations, the sample means were compared with those of relevant norm groups. For the ETS tests, these were the norm groups reported in the most recent editions of the *TOEFL Test and Score Manual* (ETS 1987), the *Test of Spoken English: Manual for Score Users* (ETS 1982) and the *Test of Written English Guide* (ETS 1989), while for the FCE, the norm group was all individuals who took the FCE in December 1988 (UCLES 1989). The means and standard deviations of measures and those of their FCE and ETS norm groups are presented in Tables 3 through 6. While virtually all of the differences between the study and norm group means are statistically significant, this is primarily a function of the large sample sizes, and it thus makes more sense to consider the "practical importance" of the differences. Looking at Table 3, we see that all of the differences between the study group and FCE norm group means are less than two scaled score points, and that these differences amount to only a fraction of the standard deviation of the FCE norm group. This pattern of similar scores is also seen across countries, as shown in Table 4, with the single exception of Egypt, where the means are consistently lower than those of the FCE group.

**Table 3**

**Differences between means and standard deviations and FCE norms, December 1989**

| Test | N | $\overline{X}$ | S |
|---|---|---|---|
| **Paper 1** | | | |
| STUDY | 1,359 | 25.95 | 4.90 |
| FCE | 30,816 | 27.19 | 5.19 |
| **Paper 2** | | | |
| STUDY | 1,357 | 24.30 | 6.04 |
| FCE | 30,818 | 26.07 | 5.22 |
| **Paper 3** | | | |
| STUDY | 1,353 | 24.86 | 5.71 |
| FCE | 30,805 | 26.30 | 5.26 |
| **Paper 4** | | | |
| STUDY | 1,344 | 13.60 | 3.18 |
| FCE | 30,936 | 14.47 | 3.25 |
| **Paper 5** | | | |
| STUDY | 1,381 | 27.20 | 5.95 |
| FCE | 31,040 | 28.04 | 5.72 |
| **FCE grade[2]** | | | |
| STUDY | 1,353 | 2.60 | 1.17 |
| FCE | 30,725 | 2.89 | 1.18 |

## Table 4

## Differences between means and FCE norms, by country

|  | Paper 1 | | Paper 2 | | Paper 3 | | Paper 4 | | Paper 5 | | FCE Grade* | |
|---|---|---|---|---|---|---|---|---|---|---|---|---|
|  | N | $\overline{X}$ | N | $\overline{X}$ | N | $\overline{X}$ | N | $\overline{X}$ | N | $\overline{X}$ | N | $\overline{X}$ |
| **Thailand** | | | | | | | | | | | | |
| STUDY | 171 | 21.8 | 171 | 18.9 | 171 | 19.8 | 170 | 10.3 | 171 | 24.0 | 170 | 1.5 |
| FCE | 186 | 21.8 | 186 | 18.8 | 186 | 19.6 | 184 | 10.2 | 207 | 23.7 | 184 | 1.5 |
| **Egypt** | | | | | | | | | | | | |
| STUDY | 91 | 24.6 | 90 | 23.4 | 88 | 23.0 | 89 | 13.0 | 89 | 25.7 | 86 | 2.3 |
| FCE | 147 | 22.3 | 146 | 21.0 | 145 | 20.2 | 160 | 11.4 | 160 | 23.3 | 185 | 2.8 |
| **Japan** | | | | | | | | | | | | |
| STUDY | 106 | 23.0 | 105 | 19.5 | 104 | 18.6 | 89 | 10.6 | 116 | 23.4 | 106 | 1.6 |
| FCE | 106 | 23.0 | 105 | 19.5 | 104 | 18.6 | 89 | 10.6 | 116 | 23.4 | 403 | 2.1 |
| **Hong Kong** | | | | | | | | | | | | |
| STUDY | 195 | 26.9 | 195 | 26.4 | 195 | 26.6 | 195 | 14.2 | 204 | 27.4 | 195 | 2.8 |
| FCE | 218 | 27.1 | 218 | 26.2 | 218 | 26.5 | 221 | 13.9 | 229 | 27.4 | 218 | 2.8 |
| **Spain** | | | | | | | | | | | | |
| STUDY | 190 | 27.3 | 190 | 25.9 | 190 | 26.9 | 194 | 14.0 | 194 | 27.8 | 190 | 2.9 |
| FCE | 999 | 26.5 | 997 | 25.6 | 997 | 25.9 | 1,008 | 14.2 | 1,008 | 27.3 | 3,269 | 2.8 |
| **Brazil** | | | | | | | | | | | | |
| STUDY | 204 | 26.5 | 204 | 26.1 | 204 | 27.4 | 204 | 14.5 | 204 | 26.4 | 204 | 2.8 |
| FCE | 752 | 26.0 | 751 | 25.7 | 751 | 26.6 | 749 | 14.0 | 745 | 26.3 | 1,764 | 2.7 |
| **France** | | | | | | | | | | | | |
| STUDY | 196 | 25.7 | 196 | 23.6 | 196 | 24.7 | 196 | 14.2 | 196 | 28.9 | 196 | 2.6 |
| FCE | 222 | 25.4 | 222 | 23.2 | 222 | 24.3 | 222 | 14.1 | 222 | 28.5 | 1,499 | 2.6 |
| **Switzerland** | | | | | | | | | | | | |
| STUDY | 206 | 29.0 | 206 | 27.0 | 205 | 27.0 | 207 | 15.4 | 207 | 31.1 | 206 | 3.4 |
| FCE | 634 | 27.9 | 634 | 26.4 | 631 | 25.9 | 641 | 15.0 | 640 | 29.8 | 1,191 | 3.0 |

* Scaled scores for papers are from study sites only; grades are for entire country.

## Table 5

## Differences between study means and standard deviations and ETS norms*: Total group

| Test | N | $\overline{X}$ | S |
|------|---|---|---|
| **TOEFL1** | | | |
| ETS | 714,731 | 51.2 | 6.9 |
| Group A | 1,448 | 49.6 | 6.7 |
| **TOEFL2** | | | |
| ETS | 714,731 | 51.3 | 7.7 |
| Group A | 1,448 | 51.1 | 6.9 |
| **TOEFL3** | | | |
| ETS | 714,731 | 51.1 | 7.3 |
| Group A | 1,448 | 51.5 | 6.7 |
| **TOEFL TOT** | | | |
| ETS | 714,731 | 51.1 | 7.3 |
| Group A | 1,448 | 507.4 | 58.9 |
| **TWE/TEW** | | | |
| ETS | 230,921 | 3.64 | 0.99 |
| Group A | 1,398 | 3.93 | 0.89 |
| **TSE/SPK GRAM** | | | |
| ETS | 3,500 | 2.43 | 0.39 |
| Group A | 1,304 | 1.93 | 0.45 |
| **TSE/SPK PRON** | | | |
| ETS | 3,500 | 2.10 | 0.49 |
| Group A | 1,314 | 2.13 | 0.38 |
| **TSE/SPK FLCY** | | | |
| ETS | 3,500 | 2.15 | 0.45 |
| Group A | 1,304 | 1.95 | 0.44 |
| **TSE/SPK COMP** | | | |
| ETS | 3,500 | 221.00 | 45.00 |
| Group A | 1,304 | 201.57 | 40.91 |

*TOEFL norms are from examinees tested from July 1984 through June 1986 (ETS 1987); TWE norms are from examinees tested from July 1986 through May 1987 (ETS 1989); TSE norms are from examinees tested from November 1981 through June 1986 (ETS 1982).

## Table 6

## Differences between study means and ETS norms by country

| | TOEFL | | | | | TWE/TEW | | TSE/SPEAK | | | | |
|---|---|---|---|---|---|---|---|---|---|---|---|---|
| | N | LC | SW | VR | Tot | N | $\overline{X}$ | N | G | P | F | Comp |
| **Thailand** | | | | | | | | | | | | |
| Group A | 169 | 46 | 48 | 47 | 469 | 171 | 3.11 | 163 | 1.6 | 1.8 | 1.6 | 171 |
| ETS | 22,471 | 48 | 48 | 48 | 480 | 4,968 | 3.45 | 77 | 2.2 | 1.8 | 1.9 | 200 |
| **Egypt** | | | | | | | | | | | | |
| Group A | 89 | 49 | 46 | 45 | 466 | 91 | 3.33 | 80 | 1.9 | 2.1 | 1.9 | 204 |
| ETS | 6,544 | 49 | 50 | 49 | 491 | 1,679 | 3.66 | 56 | 2.4 | 2.0 | 2.1 | 219 |
| **Japan** | | | | | | | | | | | | |
| Group A | 189 | 44 | 47 | 45 | 457 | 128 | 3.30 | 114 | 1.9 | 1.9 | 1.7 | 189 |
| ETS | 62,659 | 49 | 50 | 49 | 496 | 31,859 | 3.58 | 93 | 2.3 | 2.0 | 2.0 | 207 |
| **Hong Kong** | | | | | | | | | | | | |
| Group A | 196 | 52 | 53 | 54 | 529 | 196 | 4.26 | 190 | 1.9 | 2.1 | 2.0 | 202 |
| ETS | 64,417 | 52 | 50 | 51 | 510 | 14,158 | 3.89 | 134 | 2.4 | 2.0 | 2.1 | 214 |
| **Spain** | | | | | | | | | | | | |
| Group A | 196 | 47 | 52 | 55 | 511 | 195 | 3.88 | 196 | 1.9 | 2.2 | 1.9 | 197 |
| ETS | 3,031 | 55 | 55 | 56 | 553 | 1,889 | 4.15 | 20 | 2.5 | 2.1 | 2.2 | 224 |
| **Brazil** | | | | | | | | | | | | |
| Group A | 207 | 51 | 52 | 53 | 521 | 211 | 4.00 | 184 | 1.9 | 2.3 | 2.0 | 206 |
| ETS | 4,424 | 52 | 52 | 54 | 528 | 1,901 | 3.86 | 19 | 2.7 | 2.3 | 2.4 | 245 |
| **France** | | | | | | | | | | | | |
| Group A | 197 | 51 | 55 | 56 | 539 | 199 | 4.71 | 173 | 1.9 | 2.2 | 2.0 | 203 |
| ETS | 9,578 | 54 | 56 | 56 | 554 | 4,905 | 4.16 | 35 | 2.5 | 2.3 | 2.3 | 233 |
| **Switzerland** | | | | | | | | | | | | |
| Group A | 205 | 56 | 52 | 53 | 535 | 207 | 4.17 | 205 | 2.3 | 2.4 | 2.3 | 230 |
| ETS | 1,920 | 58 | 57 | 56 | 570 | 1,112 | 4.35 | 9 | 2.6 | 2.3 | 2.4 | 246 |

The differences between the study group and ETS norm group means presented in Table 5 are also small, relative to the standard deviations of the ETS norm group. For all the ETS measures, with one exception, the mean differences are a fraction of the norm group's standard deviation, and for that exception, the TSE/SPEAK Grammar rating, the mean difference is less than one score point. As with the FCE scores, the differences between the study group and ETS norm group means across countries, presented in Table 6, are also small. Thus, although the study group means tend to be slightly lower than those of the FCE and ETS norm groups, both overall and by country, these differences are too small to be of practical importance, and it can be concluded that the study subjects constitute a representative sample of the FCE and ETS operational populations with respect to their test performance.

To examine differences in test performance across the eight sites, a canonical discriminant analysis (CDA) was conducted. CDA is a multivariate dimension reduction technique similar to principal components analysis, but whereas principal components analysis focuses on summarizing total variation, CDA focuses on summarizing the between-class variation represented by different groups. In applying CDA, a combination of variables (in this case, test scores) that has the highest possible multiple correlation with the group (in this case, site) variable is derived to form the first canonical variate. Subsequent canonical variates are derived from combinations of test scores that have the next highest possible correlations with the sites, but which are uncorrelated with prior canonical variates. The number of canonical variates extracted is limited to either the number of tests or the number of groups in the class variable minus one, whichever is smaller.

In interpreting the results of CDA, one first determines, through both statistical significance and amount of variance in the group variable accounted for, how many canonical variates will yield the most parsimonious interpretation of the data. In order to interpret the canonical variates, the canonical structure coefficients or the correlations between the tests and the canonical variates are examined. In order to infer differences across sites, both the magnitude and the directionality of their means on the canonical variates are examined.

The three standardized TOEFL section scores, the TEW score, the four SPEAK scores and the scaled scores of the five FCE papers were used as the predictors to test the hypothesis that there were no differences in test perform-ance across the eight sites. Test takers were grouped by site for the analysis. All of the seven possible canonical correlations were statistically significant, but only the first two, which accounted for 68% of the variation in sites, were clearly interpretable. Looking at Table 7, we can see that the first canonical variate, which had a canonical correlation with site membership of .67, accounted for 38% of the variation among sites, and was statistically significant at p < .0001. The second canonical variate, which had a canonical correlation of .63, ac-counted for 30% of the variation across sites, and was also statistically significant at p < .0001.

The TOEFL vocabulary and reading test (TOEFL1), the TEW, and FCE

## Table 7

**Canonical structure coefficients, for tests: Means on canonical variates, for sites**

|  | Canonical can1 | Variates can2 |
|---|---|---|
| Canonical correlation | 0.67 | 0.63 |
| % of variation in sites | | |
| accounted for | 38.0 | 30.0 |
| F – ratio | 26.99 | 21.47 |
| df | 91/7,526.0 | 72/6,573.0 |
| Significance | < 0.0001 | < 0.0001 |

**Canonical structure coefficients: tests**

|  | Canonical can1 | Variates can2 |
|---|---|---|
| TOEFL1 | .21 | .59 |
| TOEFL2 | .47 | -.02 |
| TOEFL3 | .75 | -.07 |
| TEW | .66 | .14 |
| SPK GRAM | .17 | .46 |
| SPK PRON | .46 | .50 |
| SPK FLCY | .29 | .53 |
| SPK COMP | .23 | .50 |
| FCE1 SCA | .46 | .44 |
| FCE2 SCA | .52 | .48 |
| FCE3 SCA | .63 | .47 |
| FCE4 SCA | .57 | .54 |
| FCE5 SCA | .33 | .32 |

**Means on canonical variates: sites**

|  | Canonical can1 | Variates can2 |
|---|---|---|
| Thailand (1) | -1.30 | -.88 |
| Egypt (2) | -1.30 | 1.20 |
| Japan (3) | -1.60 | -1.00 |
| Hong Kong (4) | .34 | .18 |
| Spain (5) | 1.00 | -.42 |
| Brazil (6) | .30 | .50 |
| France (7) | .98 | -.86 |
| Switzerland (8) | -.12 | 1.20 |

Papers 2, 3 and 4 (FCE2 SCA, FCE3 SCA and FCE4 SCA) all have high correlations with the first canonical variate, which most clearly separates the Thailand, Egypt and Japan sites from the others, as indicated by their respective means on this canonical variate: -1.3 (Thailand), -1.3 (Egypt), and -1.6 (Japan). As can be seen in Table 2, the score means for these sites on TOEFL3, TEW, FCE2 SCA, FCE3 SCA and FCE4 SCA are considerably lower than those for the other sites.

The TOEFL listening comprehension subtest, the four SPEAK ratings and the FCE listening paper (FCE4 SCA) all have high correlations with the second canonical variate, which most clearly distinguishes Thailand and Japan, with means of -.88 and -1.0, from the other sites at the low end, and Switzerland, with a mean of 1.2, at the high end. As can be seen in Table 7, the score means on TOEFL1 and the four SPEAK ratings are lower than those of the rest of the sites, while the means on these tests for Switzerland are the highest of all the sites.

These results indicate considerable differences in test performance across the sites, with individuals in three non-Indo-European language background groups performing worst on the tests of reading and writing, and individuals in two of these groups performing worst on the listening and speaking measures. These results are consistent with the findings of other studies which also suggest that mother tongue and culture affect performance on EFL proficiency tests (e.g., Angoff and Sharon 1972; Swinton and Powers 1980; Alderman and Holland 1981).

## Test takers' characteristics

Information on subjects' age, sex and the number of times they had previously taken the TOEFL was obtained from responses to questions on their TOEFL answer sheets, while information on their current educational status, TOEFL and FCE preparation was obtained from responses to questions on the background questionnaire (Appendix D, items 1–4). The descriptive statistics for the test takers' current educational status, age, sex and the test preparation variables are given in Table 8. The majority of the test takers were enrolled as students, either at the secondary school level (21.3 %), or at the college level (full-time, 27.6%, part-time, 10.4 %) or in a language institute or other English course (17%), while 23.7% indicated that they were not enrolled as students. Their median age was 21, with the youngest test taker 14 years of age and the oldest 58. Slightly over half (59.4 %) were female. Only 9.6% indicated that they had or were currently taking a course to prepare for the TOEFL, and only 7.4% said that they had taken the TOEFL at least once before. Approximately half (50.5 %) indicated that they had taken or were currently taking a course to prepare for the FCE.

Wilson (1982) provides information on characteristics of TOEFL examinees from 1977 to 1979, and these were used as a basis for comparing the study sample with the operational TOEFL population. No such information is available for the operational FCE population, so it was not possible to analyse the study sample in this regard. Wilson did not report information on current educational status.

However, he does report information on several of the other variables included in the study. The mean age for his population was 21.4% for undergraduate-level degree planners and 26.3% for graduate-level planners, as compared to 22.7% for the study group. A larger difference between the operational TOEFL population and the study sample can be seen in the sex of the test takers, with Wilson reporting that 72% of his group were male, compared to about 41% for the study. Similarly, Wilson reports that 32% of his group were repeat takers of TOEFL, compared with only about 7% for the study sample.

**Table 8**

**Test takers' characteristics**

| Current educational status | |
|---|---|
| Secondary school | 21.3% |
| Part-time college | 10.4% |
| Full-time college | 27.6% |
| Language institute or English course | 17.0% |
| Not enrolled as a student | 23.7% |

**Current age**

| Mean | Median | Min | Max |
|---|---|---|---|
| 22.7 | 21.0 | 14.0 | 58.0 |

**Sex**

| Male | 40.6% |
|---|---|
| Female | 59.4% |

**TOEFL preparation course**

| Yes | 9.6% |
|---|---|
| No | 90.4% |

**Times previously taken TOEFL**

| None | 92.7% |
|---|---|
| One | 4.8% |
| Two or more | 2.6% |

**FCE preparation course**

| Yes | 50.5% |
|---|---|
| No | 49.5% |

## Table 9

## Test takers' characteristics, by site

| Current educational status | | | | | | | | |
|---|---|---|---|---|---|---|---|---|
| | | | | Site | | | | |
| Status | Thai'd | Egypt | Japan | Hong K'g | Spain | Brazil | France | Switz'd |
| Secondary school | 3.5% | 3.5% | 0.0% | 86.5% | 15.8% | 26.0% | NA* | 0.0% |
| Part-time college | 5.3% | 3.5% | 0.8% | 1.1% | 9.3% | 41.2% | NA | 2.0% |
| Full-time college | 32.7% | 19.8% | 86.4% | 5.6% | 53.0% | 9.8% | NA | 4.9% |
| Language institute | 4.1% | 24.4% | 3.2% | 2.9% | 13.7% | 10.8% | NA | 54.0% |
| Not enrolled | 54.4% | 48.8% | 9.6% | 3.4% | 8.2% | 12.3% | NA | 39.0% |

| Current age | | | | |
|---|---|---|---|---|
| Site | Mean | Median | Min | Max |
| Thailand | 27.1 | 26.0 | 16 | 58 |
| Egypt | 29.2 | 28.0 | 16 | 55 |
| Japan | 21.6 | 21.0 | 19 | 52 |
| Hong Kong | 19.1 | 18.0 | 16 | 47 |
| Spain | 22.5 | 22.0 | 14 | 45 |
| Brazil | 21.0 | 19.0 | 14 | 43 |
| France | 20.9 | 20.0 | 14 | 36 |
| Switzerland | 24.5 | 23.0 | 16 | 56 |

| Sex | | |
|---|---|---|
| Site | Male | Female |
| Thailand | 39.6% | 60.4% |
| Egypt | 59.6% | 40.4% |
| Japan | 41.5% | 58.5% |
| Hong Kong | 45.5% | 54.5% |
| Spain | 39.0% | 61.0% |
| Brazil | 29.3% | 70.7% |
| France | 44.4% | 55.6% |
| Switzerland | 36.5% | 63.5% |

* Because of a clerical error, the background questionnaire administered in France did not include items pertaining to educational status and test preparation.

These patterns of difference can also be seen across the study sites, as shown in Table 9. The mean ages for all the sites are fairly close to those for students planning to take the TOEFL, with the exception of Thailand and Egypt, where the mean is closer to that of the TOEFL graduate planners. At all sites there were lower proportions of males than reported for the TOEFL population. Finally, there were generally smaller proportions of TOEFL-repeaters at all sites than reported for the TOEFL population, with the TOEFL-dominant sites reporting between 7.9% and 20.7% TOEFL-repeaters and the Cambridge-dominant sites reporting fewer than 3% TOEFL-repeaters.

In summary, the study sample was similar to the operational populations of both the TOEFL and the FCE in terms of their test performance. With respect to test taker characteristics, the study sample was quite close in age to TOEFL undergraduate degree planners, has a higher proportion of females, and a much smaller proportion of TOEFL-repeaters than the TOEFL operational population.

## Notes

1 A number of grades are reported in the FCE examination ranging from A to F. In the December 1989 administration, the grade boundaries were established with respect to total score range, and were as follows:
A: 146–180
B: 134–145
C: 113–133
D: 107–112
F: 106 or less
In relation to Table 1 therefore, the mean score for the examination as an overall score for the study sample was 116.186. In effect this is equivalent to a low grade C.

2 In the study, the grades were coded in the following way: A=5, B=4, C=3, D=2, F=1. To interpret the average grade meaningfully the reader should use the conversion table below:
A: 4–5
B: 3–4
C: 2–3
D: 1–2
F: 0–1

# 3 Reliability of the two test batteries

Reliability is an essential test quality that can be thought of as the degree to which test scores are free from measurement error. In a language test, any factor other than the ability being measured that affects the test score is a potential source of measurement error.

There are several potential sources of measurement error in both test batteries. For the discrete-item tests – FCE Papers 1, parts of Papers 3 and 4 and the TOEFL – inconsistency across items is a potential source of measurement error. For those papers that are scored subjectively – parts of FCE Paper 3, and Papers 2 and 5, the TEW and the SPEAK – inconsistency within and across raters is a potential source of error.

In addition to the above sources of error, equivalence was a concern for FCE Papers 1, 2, 4 and 5. Although only one form of FCE Paper 1 is normally used for each operational administration, two separate forms of this paper were erroneously sent out to and administered at study sites, so that non-equivalence of forms for this paper became a potential source of error. For FCE Paper 2, composition, candidates write on two topics which they choose from among five, so that non-equivalence of topics is a potential source of error. Multiple forms of Paper 4 are used routinely for FCE for reasons of test security. The FCE Paper 5 oral interview is based on an information package, and since examiners may choose from among a large number of such packages, non-equivalence of information packages is a potential source of error. Furthermore, the oral interview is administered with different grouping patterns; some are conducted with one examinee per examiner, while in other cases several examinees interact with each other and the examiner in a group interview. Thus, differences across grouping patterns, as well as differential interactions between candidates and examiners and among candidates in the group interview, are also potential sources of measurement error. These potential sources of measurement error are summarized in Table 10.

While we had hoped to investigate all of these potential sources of error, this was not possible, for reasons that are discussed below.

**Table 10**

**Potential sources of measurement error**

| Potential source of error | FCE papers | ETS tests |
|---|---|---|
| Inter-item inconsistencies | 1, 3, 4 | TOEFL 1, 2, 3 |
| Intra- and inter-rater inconsistencies | 2, 3, 5 | TEW<br>SPEAK |
| Lack of equivalence | 1: forms<br>2: topics<br>4: forms<br>5: information<br>   packages<br>5: grouping<br>   patterns | N/A |

## Internal consistency and consistency of ratings

Classical internal consistency estimates (coefficient $\alpha$) were calculated for the discrete-item tests (FCE Papers 1, 3 and 4 and the TOEFL). Since two forms of FCE Paper 1 and ten forms of FCE Paper 4 were administered in the study, the internal consistency reliability estimates reported for these papers are the weighted averages (using Fisher's Z transformation) of the coefficient alphas for the different forms of each paper.

Consistency of ratings for the TEW and SPEAK was estimated through the application of generalizability theory, using a single-facet random design with raters as the facet. We would note that using generalizability coefficients in this manner represents a departure from common practice in language testing, in which inter-rater correlations are typically reported as estimates of rater consistency. However, scores on the TEW and SPEAK (and also their operational counterparts, the TWE and TSE, respectively) are in fact composites of two or more ratings, so that it is the reliability of these composite ratings, rather than agreement among raters, that is of primary interest. Since generalizability coefficients are computed from the variance components associated with the composite ratings, these are, we believe, a more direct estimate of the consistency of the TEW and SPEAK ratings. Because multiple independent ratings are not routinely done as part of the operational FCE, the consistency of ratings for Papers 2 and 5 could not be estimated.

Reliability estimates for the study sample, along with the reported norms for the FCE Papers reported for 164,256 examinees who took the FCE in the December 1988 and December 1989 operational administrations world-wide, are given in Table 11. The norm for Paper 3 is the average KR–20 (using Fisher's Z transformation) for three random samples of 300 each drawn from the December 1988 and December 1989 operational administrations, while the norm for Paper 4 is the average KR–20 (using Fisher's Z transformation) for random samples of 300 examinees per reported form. Scores for all three TOEFL sections, as well as for the TOEFL total, for the TEW and for four scales of the SPEAK, are reported. In order to provide comparable information, we have reported reliabilities that could be estimated for the FCE papers and for the comparable tests in the ETS battery.

## Table 11

### Reliability estimates 1

| Test | k | N | Study | Norm |
|---|---|---|---|---|
| FCE Paper 1 | 40 | 1,394 | .791 | .901 |
| FCE Paper 2 | | 1,357 | NA | NA |
| FCE Paper 3 | 52 | 995 | .847 | .870 |
| FCE Paper 4 | 27 | 759 | .616 | .705 |
| FCE Paper 5 | | 1,381 | NA | NA |
| TOEFL 1 | 50 | 1,467 | .889 | .90 |
| TOEFL 2 | 38 | 1,467 | .834 | .86 |
| TOEFL 3 | 58 | 1,467 | .874 | .90 |
| TEW | | 1,318 | .896 | .86 |
| SPEAK COMP | | 1,318 | .970 | .88 |

Notes on Table 11:
1  This study and Cambridge norm reliabilities are given to three decimals of precision. ETS reliabilities are given to two decimals in the published ETS reports. No k-sizes are given for any of the composition or speaking tests because they do not contain items.
2  The version of the institutional TOEFL used in the study contained two experimental/non-scored items in TOEFL2.
3  Weighted average coefficient alphas across more than one test form are given for Papers 4 and 1.
4  Generalizability coefficients are reported for Paper 2, TEW and SPEAK.
5  Subjects on which reliabilities are calculated are as follows:
    FCE Paper 1, for 164,256 examinees who took the FCE from December 1988 through December 1989, inclusive;

FCE Paper 3, for three random samples of 300 examinees each, from the June 1989 FCE administration;

FCE Paper 4, for random samples of approximately 300 examinees per form from the June 1989 FCE administration;

TOEFL, for examinees tested in the US and Canada between December 1984 and February 1986 (ETS 1987);

TWE, for examinees tested from July 1986 through May 1988 (ETS 1989);

TSE, for 134 examinees tested in the fall of 1979 (Clark and Swinton 1980; ETS 1982).

In general, the FCE reliabilities for our sample were slightly lower than those typically obtained operationally by Cambridge and somewhat below the reliabilities reported for the ETS tests.

## Equivalence of FCE Paper 1 forms

Owing to an error in the distribution of examination materials, two different forms of FCE Paper 1 were administered to study subjects. Both of these forms were normal operational forms. One form was designated "old" and the other "new". In order to decide whether scores from both forms could be used, or whether it would be possible to equate scores from one form to those from the other, a classical true-score equating design was used. In retrospect, it would also have been appropriate to use item response theory (IRT) equating procedures for this task, but at the time we were not sure whether the IRT assumptions could be met by these data.

The design used for equating was that of non-random groups with a common equating test administered to both groups (Levine 1955; Angoff 1971, 1982; Peterson *et al*. 1989). In this design, two different groups of individuals take two different forms to be equated, as well as a single "anchor test" that forms the basis of the equating. In our case, Section 3 of the TOEFL served as the anchor test. In general terms, the procedure was to relate scores from FCE1 "old" and FCE1 "new" to scores on TOEFL Section 3, and then use these relationships to equate scores from the two FCE1 forms.

Before attempting an equating procedure, we first examined the equivalence of the two tests. We examined the content and format of the items of the two forms, and judged them to be comparable. We also compared their means, variances, reliabilities and correlations with other measures. These comparisons are presented in Table 12.

As can be seen, the two forms are very nearly parallel; the differences between their means and reliabilities are non-significant, and although the difference between their variances is significant, the F-ratio is quite small. Looking at the correlations of the "old" and "new" scores with the parts of the TOEFL, we can see that the difference between correlations is significant in only one of four cases.

## Table 12

## FCE 1 Forms "Old" and "New": Means, standard deviations, reliabilities and correlations with other measures

|  | "Old" | "New" | |
|---|---|---|---|
| N | 1,068 | 310 | |
| X | 26.71 | 26.97 | z=0.738 (NS) |
| $s^2$ | 24.02 | 28.96 | $F_{(311,1087)}$=1.21 (p<.05) |
| Range | 10-38 | 10-40 | |
| Kurtosis | -.044 | 0.114 | |
| Skewness | -.496 | -.450 | |
| α | 0.712 | 0.745 | z=1.10 (NS) |
| **Correlations** | | | |
| TOEFL 1 | 0.589 | 0.674 | z=2.20 (p=.014) |
| TOEFL 2 | 0.632 | 0.606 | z=0.65 (NS) |
| TOEFL 3 | 0.653 | 0.658 | z=1.40 (NS) |
| TOEFL TOT | 0.708 | 0.721 | z=0.42 (NS) |

The next step was to determine if linear equating was justified, and this was done by regressing the scores from the "old" and "new" forms separately on TOEFL 3 and examining the plots of the residuals. The statistics for these two regression equations are given in Table 13.

## Table 13

## Regression statistics, with TOEFL Section 3 as predictor

| Dependent | α | B | ß | F | p | $R^2$ |
|---|---|---|---|---|---|---|
| Observed "Old" | 11.87 | .374 | .653 | 791.02 | .0000 | .425 |
| Observed "New" | 11.76 | .407 | .656 | 234.66 | .0000 | .431 |
| Estimated "Old" | 13.22 | .339 | .658 | 234.66 | .0000 | .431 |

The normal probability plots of the standardized residuals were examined to determine whether the distributions of the observed and expected scores were identical. These plots are given in Figure 1, where the dots describe a perfect linear relationship as a reference, while the asterisks represent the standardized residuals (the difference between observed scores and the predicted or expected scores, divided by the standard deviation of the residuals).

# Figure 1

## Normal probability plots of standardized residuals

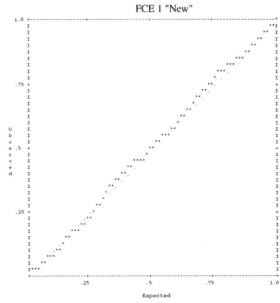

As can be seen from these plots, the residuals fall very nearly on a straight line, with virtually no tendency to trail off at either end, suggesting that linear equating would provide a reasonably good fit.

Having determined that linear equating was justified, we then followed Tucker's model (Angoff 1971) to estimate the regression coefficients for estimating "old" scores from observed "new" scores. Using these coefficients, estimated "old" scores were computed and these were then regressed on TOEFL3. The statistics for this regression equation, along with those from the obtained "old" and "new" scores, are given in Table 13. As can be seen, the three regression equations are very similar, differing only in the intercept ($\alpha$), for the estimated "old" scores (13.22) two points larger than those for the observed "old" (11.87) and "new" (11.76) scores.

Because of the similarities in the regressions, we decided to determine whether transforming observed "new" scores to "old" scores would make a difference. The means and standard deviations of the total group, for the observed "old" and estimated "old" scores, were computed and compared. The difference between the means for the observed "old" scores (26.82) and estimated "old" scores (26.58) was not significant ($z = 1.27$). The variance for the observed "old" scores was 24.92 and for estimated "old" scores 22.94, and the difference between these was not significant ($F_{(1378,1378)} = 1.08$). Furthermore, since the observed "new" scores were perfectly correlated with the estimated "old" scores, we decided not to transform the "new" scores to "old" scores, but to treat the two sets of scores as equivalent.

## Equivalence of FCE Paper 2 forms

For FCE Paper 2, each test taker wrote two compositions and received a score for each. Distribution summary statistics for all five FCE Paper 2 topics are presented in Table 14.

**Table 14**

**Descriptive statistics for FCE Paper 2 topics**

| Topic | N | Mean | Std dev | Min | Max |
|-------|-----|-------|---------|-----|-----|
| 1 | 688 | 10.96 | 2.93 | 4 | 18 |
| 2 | 301 | 10.15 | 3.31 | 1 | 18 |
| 3 | 798 | 10.50 | 3.04 | 1 | 19 |
| 4 | 843 | 10.24 | 2.95 | 1 | 18 |
| 5 | 49 | 10.82 | 3.34 | 5 | 19 |

The equivalence of the first four Paper 2 topics was examined with a single-facet g-study with topic as a facet. This yielded a generalizability coefficient of .899, which can be interpreted as an intra-class correlation coefficient between the scores on test takers' first and second topics, irrespective of which of the four topics was chosen. This suggests a high degree of consistency of scores across the two topics chosen. Although this single-facet design essentially ignores inconsistencies across the four topics, such inconsistencies do, in fact, contribute to the variance component for topic in this design. The high coefficient obtained thus implies a high degree of consistency across all four topics, and it was therefore concluded that further investigation of inconsistencies across the four individual topics was unnecessary.

## Equivalence of FCE Paper 4 forms

FCE Paper 4, listening comprehension, is operationally administered separately from the other papers, generally in smaller groups. For reasons of test security, different forms are routinely used with different test takers. Distribution summary statistics and reliabilities for the ten forms of FCE Paper 4 that were administered in the study are presented in Table 15.

**Table 15**

**Descriptive statistics for FCE Paper 4 forms**

| Form | N | Mean | Std dev | Min | Max | α |
|------|-----|-------|---------|-----|------|------|
| 16 Tot | 107 | 13.44 | 2.88 | 7 | 19.5 | .616 |
| 17 Tot | 147 | 16.09 | 2.21 | 8 | 20 | .569 |
| 18 Tot | 57 | 16.48 | 1.80 | 13 | 19.5 | |
| 20 Tot | 56 | 16.77 | 2.63 | 7.5 | 20 | |
| 21 Tot | 54 | 16.44 | 2.46 | 6 | 19.5 | |
| 22 Tot | 61 | 14.74 | 2.60 | 8 | 19 | |
| 23 Tot | 97 | 13.96 | 3.10 | 5 | 20 | .658 |
| 24 Tot | 622 | 11.37 | 3.02 | 4.5 | 19 | .643 |
| 25 Tot | 118 | 16.25 | 2.23 | 7.5 | 20 | .513 |
| 26 Tot | 80 | 15.59 | 2.36 | 9.5 | 20.5 | |
| TAF* | 1,399 | 13.62 | 3.51 | 4.5 | 20.5 | |

* Total for all forms

Because of the considerable differences in both test content and test format across the different forms of Paper 4, as well as the sizeable differences in their means, standard deviations and reliabilities, the equating procedure used for the two forms of Paper 1 was not justified for Paper 4. Furthermore, because of the differences in the numbers of test takers who were administered the different forms of Paper 4, we could not utilize generalizability theory, which is based on the standard ANOVA assumptions, one of which is orthogonality. Thus, we employed multiple linear regression analysis with Paper 4 score as the criterion, with a dummy variable for form, and the TOEFL listening comprehension score as predictors. This enabled us to estimate the differences in Paper 4 score that were due to the particular form taken, controlling for differences in listening ability. With FCE Paper 4 scaled score as a criterion variable, the predictors were entered into the regression equation sequentially, following a hierarchical step-down procedure. Thus, the covariate, TOEFL listening comprehension test score (TOEFL1), was entered first, dummy variables for FCE Paper 4 form second, and the variable term for the listening ability by form interaction entered last. The results of the regression analysis are presented in Table 16.

**Table 16**

**Results of regression analyses of Paper 4 forms**

| Variable entered | $R^2$ | $R^2$ change | F-value |
|---|---|---|---|
| TOEFL1 | .37 | .37 | 781.94* |
| Paper 4 Form | .45 | .08 | 107.71* |
| Form by TLCSTD | .48 | .03 | 62.55* |

*(p < .0001)

As can be seen in Table 16, listening ability, represented by TOEFL1, accounted for 37% of the variance in FCE Paper 4 performance. After controlling for listening ability, Paper 4 form accounted for an additional 8% of the variance, indicating that the particular form test takers completed had a significant impact on their test performance. The interaction term (Form by TOEFL1) accounted for an additional 3% of the variance and was also statistically significant, which indicates an interaction between form and ability. In other words, the form that test takers completed produced a differential advantage or disadvantage on test performance depending on test takers' listening ability. Together, test form and the interaction between test form and listening ability accounted for 11% of the variance in Paper 4 test performance, which is a considerable source of measurement error. Thus, in spite of the fact that the Paper 4 scaling procedure is intended to take into account the use of different forms, this approach is not particularly successful in eliminating this source of measurement error.

# Equivalence of FCE Paper 5 information packages

Distribution summary statistics for the fifteen FCE Paper 5 information packages
are presented in Table 17.

**Table 17**

**Distribution statistics for FCE Paper 5 information packages**

| Package | N | Mean | Std dev | Min | Max |
|---------|-----|-------|---------|-----|-----|
| 1 | 155 | 20.16 | 4.49 | 8 | 30 |
| 2 | 143 | 21.46 | 4.22 | 11 | 30 |
| 3 | 111 | 20.87 | 3.75 | 12 | 30 |
| 4 | 90 | 21.10 | 4.86 | 3 | 30 |
| 5 | 67 | 20.49 | 4.17 | 9 | 29 |
| 6 | 108 | 20.74 | 4.13 | 9 | 30 |
| 7 | 137 | 21.19 | 4.66 | 7 | 30 |
| 8 | 68 | 20.40 | 3.69 | 13 | 29 |
| 9 | 110 | 19.59 | 3.86 | 13 | 29 |
| 10 | 37 | 19.57 | 2.36 | 16 | 26 |
| 11 | 26 | 21.15 | 2.78 | 14 | 26 |
| 12 | 7 | 19.43 | 2.80 | 16 | 25 |
| 13 | 21 | 19.05 | 3.38 | 10 | 26 |
| 14 | 25 | 20.00 | 3.03 | 14 | 28 |
| 15 | 21 | 21.05 | 3.34 | 13 | 28 |
| m* | 253 | 19.57 | 5.45 | 1 | 30 |
| Total | 1,379 | 20.43 | 4.43 | 1 | 30 |

m*=package number missing

There were relatively small differences in means across the different packages,
with the difference between the highest (21.46 for Package 2) and lowest (19.05
for Package 13) less than the standard deviation of any one package.

The equivalence of the fifteen information packages was investigated following the same procedure described above for the multiple forms of Paper 4, using
dummy variables for information packages and the SPEAK comprehensibility
rating (SPEAK4) as a covariate. The results of the regression analysis are
presented in Table 18.

**Table 18**

**Results of regression analyses of Paper 5 information packages**

| Variable entered | $R^2$ | $R^2$ change | F-value |
|---|---|---|---|
| SPEAK4 | .30 | .30 | 452.93* |
| Paper 5 Form | .31 | .01 | 31.58* |
| Form by SPEAK4 | .32 | .01 | 17.47* |

* ($p < .0001$)

Speaking ability, represented by SPEAK4, accounts for 30% of the variance in the Paper 5 test scores (FCE5 SCA). The different Paper 5 forms and the interaction between speaking ability and form account for only 2% of the variance in Paper 5 test scores after controlling for speaking ability. Thus, although the effects due to different information packages and interactions between test takers' speaking ability were both statistically significant, the practical importance of these differences is negligible. The 2% of the variation on FCE Paper 5 scaled scores accounted for by information package and the package by ability interaction is not large and suggests that these are not major sources of measurement error. However, variation in scores due to inconsistencies across different grouping patterns and different examiners' ratings could not be examined in this design. That is, even though the proportion of score variation due to form and the interaction between form and speaking ability may contain grouping pattern and examiner variation, the predictors that were included account for only 32% of the score variance, so that a significant portion of error due to grouping pattern and examiner variation may remain undetected and undifferentiated in the error term of this regression.

## Discussion

Of the various potential sources of measurement error in the FCE, all but three were investigated. Internal consistency estimates for the FCE range from a low of .602 for Paper 4 to a high of .847 for Paper 3. The equivalence of the two FCE Paper 1 forms that were administered was very good, suggesting that Paper 1 scores from one FCE operational administration to another may be equivalent. FCE Paper 2 composition topics and Paper 5 information packages also appear to be equivalent. The lack of equivalence among the various FCE Paper 4 forms, however, constitutes a potential problem to the interpretation of scores from this paper. It is clear that a given test taker's score on this paper was partly a function of the particular form he or she happened to receive. While the low internal consistency and lack of equivalence of forms of Paper 4 mark this paper as problematic, the fact that scores for this paper are not reported, but are added to those of the other papers to arrive at an overall score, lessens, to some extent, the potential effect of the unreliability of this paper on the test taker's grade. The inability to estimate the degree of consistency across grouping patterns and raters in the Paper 5 oral interview, and across raters for the Paper 2 composition, represented an inadequacy in the study.

Largely because the ETS tests are considerably less complex in their structure, administration and scoring procedures than are the Cambridge examinations, there are fewer potential sources of measurement error to contend with. Furthermore, the operational procedures of the ETS tests facilitate the estimation of internal consistencies among items and consistencies among raters. Internal consistencies among TOEFL items are regularly within acceptable ranges, and consistencies of TEW and SPEAK ratings are uniformly high.

# 4 Comparability of abilities measured

In order to determine whether, and to what extent, the two test batteries (FCE and ETS) might be comparable, it was first necessary to investigate the extent to which patterns of performance support interpretations of similar abilities. This was done by examining the patterns of correlations within each of the two test batteries and across the two batteries using exploratory factor analysis. Three correlation matrices were analysed:

1  intercorrelations among the scaled scores for the five FCE papers;
2  intercorrelations among the standardized scores for eight ETS measures;
3  intercorrelations among all thirteen of these measures.

These correlation matrices are presented in Appendix E. Since the FCE grade and TOEFL total score are combinations of the individual paper or test scores, they were not included in the factor analyses. The matrix of product-moment correlations among the various test scores to be analyzed was examined for appropriateness of the common factor model in several ways: demonstration that the determinant of the matrix was positive and non-zero, and that values for Bartlett's test of sphericity and Kaiser's revised measures of sampling adequacy were above acceptable limits. All three of the correlation matrices examined satisfied these criteria. Principal axes were extracted with squared multiple correlations on the diagonal as initial communality estimates. The eigenvalues, or characteristic roots, obtained from the initial extraction were plotted on a scree plot, an examination of which, along with differences between successive eigenvalues, led to an initial decision about the appropriate number of factors to extract. The number of roots by the Montanelli-Humphreys parallel analysis criterion was obtained as an additional check on the number of factors (Montanelli and Humphreys 1976). Then, depending on the number of factors decided upon for a given correlation matrix, specified numbers of principal axes were successively extracted. The principal axes for each correlation matrix were then rotated to three factor structure matrices, or "solutions":

1  an orthogonal solution with the normal varimax procedure;
2  an oblique solution with the direct oblimin procedure; and
3  an oblique solution with Tucker and Finkbeiner's (1981) least-squares hyperplane fitting ("DAPPFR").

The final determination of the number of factors and the "best" solution was made on the basis of simplicity and interpretability, these qualities being judged subjectively. Simplicity was evaluated by examining the patterns of loadings for the orthogonal and oblique solutions and the scatter plots of loadings on the rotated axes. Interpretability was evaluated with reference to the nature of the tasks and abilities thought to be operationalized in the different measures. Exploratory factor analyses were performed with SPSS-PC (SPSS 1988) and with programs written for the IBM-PC by John B. Carroll (Carroll 1989).

## Within test battery factor structures

The results of the exploratory factor analysis for the FCE scaled paper scores are given in Table 19, while those for the ETS test scores are in Table 20.

The scree plots and the parallel analyses suggested that two factors underlay each set of test scores. Furthermore, as can be seen from the factor correlations in Tables 19 and 20, oblique solutions were the "best" (i.e., maximized the criteria of simplicity and interpretability) for both. In the DAPPFR solution for the FCE, Papers 1, 2 and 3 loaded most heavily on the first factor, while Papers 4 and 5 loaded most heavily on the second, and the two factors were highly correlated (.826). This solution suggests that the first factor is a "structure, reading and writing" factor, while the second is a "speaking and listening" factor. In the solution for the ETS tests, TOEFL Section 1 and the SPEAK ratings load most heavily on the first factor, while TOEFL Sections 2 and 3 and the TEW rating load most heavily on the second, and the factors were also highly correlated (.601). This suggests that the first factor is a "speaking and listening" factor, while the second is a "structure, reading and writing" factor, although the relatively high loading of TOEFL Section 1, listening, clouds this interpretation slightly.

Since both of these factor solutions were highly oblique, a Schmid-Leiman transformation to orthogonal primary factors with a second-order general factor was performed on each (Schmid and Leiman 1957). In the case of the FCE papers, all loaded most heavily on the general factor, which accounted for slightly over half of the total variance in the tests. The loadings on the first-order factors follow the pattern that was observed in the DAPPFR solution, with Papers 3 and 5 retaining sizeable loadings on their respective first-order factors. This suggests that the FCE Papers all tend to measure a single language ability, with specific abilities being measured by Papers 3 and 5 and, to a lesser degree, by Papers 1, 2 and 4.

The ETS tests also loaded most heavily on a general factor, which accounted for about 43% of the total variance. All of the ETS tests, with perhaps the exception of TOEFL Section 1, retained high loadings on the two primary factors, and the pattern of these loadings follows that seen in the oblique factor solution. This suggests that the ETS tests also tend to measure a single language ability, with specific abilities also being measured by the different tests.

## Table 19

## Exploratory factor analysis of FCE scaled scores

| | Variable | Communality |
|---|---|---|
| | Paper 1 | .54835 |
| | Paper 2 | .48888 |
| | Paper 3 | .62272 |
| | Paper 4 | .41468 |
| | Paper 5 | .32595 |

| Factor | Eigenvalue | % of var* | Cum % of var** |
|---|---|---|---|
| 1 | 3.18529 | 63.7 | 63.7 |
| 2 | .63769 | 12.8 | 76.5 |
| 3 | .48866 | 9.8 | 86.2 |
| 4 | .41719 | 8.3 | 94.6 |
| 5 | .27117 | 5.4 | 100.0 |

**DAPPFR rotated reference vector (factor) matrix**

| | Factor 1 | Factor 2 |
|---|---|---|
| Paper 1 | .37149 | .08358 |
| Paper 1 | .35106 | .07660 |
| Paper 3 | .58443 | -.08216 |
| Paper 4 | .09591 | .32561 |
| Paper 5 | -.03288 | .41892 |

**Factor correlation matrix**

| | Factor 1 | Factor 2 |
|---|---|---|
| Factor 1 | 1.00000 | |
| Factor 2 | 0.82578 | 1.00000 |

**Orthogonalized factor matrix with second-order general factor**

| | General factor | Factor 1 | Factor 2 | Communality |
|---|---|---|---|---|
| Paper 1 | .733 | .275 | .062 | .617 |
| Paper 2 | .689 | .260 | .057 | .546 |
| Paper 3 | .809 | .433 | .061 | .846 |
| Paper 4 | .679 | .071 | .241 | .524 |
| Paper 5 | .622 | .024 | .310 | .484 |
| Eigenvalue | 2.514 | .336 | .165 | |
| % variance | 50.3 | 6.7 | 3.3 | 60.3 |

* Percentage of variance
** Cumulative percentage of variance

## Table 20

### Exploratory factor analysis of ETS test scores

| Variable | Communality |
|----------|-------------|
| TOEFL1 | .53783 |
| TOEFL2 | .57999 |
| TOEFL3 | .57389 |
| TEW | .37555 |
| SPK GRAM | .80099 |
| SPK PRON | .60725 |
| SPK FLCY | .77096 |
| SPK COMP | .89596 |

| Factor | Eigenvalue | % of var* | Cum % of var** |
|--------|-----------|-----------|----------------|
| 1 | 4.93914 | 61.7 | 61.7 |
| 2 | 1.17112 | 14.6 | 76.4 |
| 3 | .55103 | 6.9 | 83.3 |
| 4 | .39869 | 5.0 | 88.2 |
| 5 | .38118 | 4.8 | 93.0 |
| 6 | .28032 | 3.5 | 96.5 |
| 7 | .20493 | 2.6 | 99.1 |
| 8 | .07357 | .9 | 100.0 |

**DAPPFR rotated reference vector (factor) matrix**

|  | Factor 1 | Factor 2 |
|--|----------|----------|
| TOEFL1 | .34760 | .32641 |
| TOEFL2 | -.00549 | .67358 |
| TOEFL3 | -.04562 | .70738 |
| TEW | .11923 | .43109 |
| SPK GRAM | .72887 | -.04008 |
| SPK PRON | .51106 | .16001 |
| SPK FLCY | .71783 | -.01195 |
| SPK COMP | .82199 | -.04844 |

**Factor correlation matrix**

|  | Factor 1 | Factor 2 |
|--|----------|----------|
| Factor 1 | 1.00000 | |
| Factor 2 | .60090 | 1.00000 |

$\Rightarrow$

**Orthogonalized factor matrix with second-order general factor**

|  | General factor | Factor 1 | Factor 2 | Communality |
|---|---|---|---|---|
| TOEFL1 | .654 | .275 | .258 | .569 |
| TOEFL2 | .648 | -.004 | .532 | .703 |
| TOEFL3 | .642 | -.036 | .559 | .726 |
| TEW | .534 | .094 | .341 | .410 |
| SPK GRAM | .668 | .576 | -.032 | .779 |
| SPK PRON | .651 | .404 | .126 | .603 |
| SPK FLCY | .684 | .567 | -.009 | .791 |
| SPK COMP | .750 | .650 | -.038 | .986 |
| Eigenvalue | 3.445 | 1.325 | .797 | |
| % variance | 43.1 | 16.6 | 9.9 | 69.6 |

\* Percentage of variance
\*\* Cumulative percentage of variance

These two sets of test scores show remarkable similarities in their factor structures. A higher-order general factor accounts for a large proportion of the variance in each of the two test batteries, with relatively more of the variance being accounted for by primary factors in the ETS tests (about 57%) than in the FCE papers (about 50%). This suggests that while each test battery appears to measure a single language ability, the ETS tests provide relatively more information about specific language abilities than do the FCE papers. While these similarities in factor structures would appear to reflect similarities in the abilities of the study's subjects, they also suggest that these two sets of tests measure these abilities in much the same way.

## Across test battery factor structures

In order to examine the relationships between scores from the two test batteries, the correlations among the scaled scores for the five FCE Papers and for the eight ETS test scores were analyzed with exploratory factor analysis, using the procedures described above. Although the scree test suggested that only two or three factors should be extracted, the parallel analyses criterion indicated five. Therefore, solutions with two, three, four and five principal axes were examined. Each of these was rotated to orthogonal and oblique solutions. The solution that appeared to maximize the simplicity and interpretability criteria was a four-factor oblique solution, the results of which are presented in Table 21.

Looking at the DAPPFR solution, we can see that the first factor is defined almost exclusively by the SPEAK ratings, the second by salient loadings for

TOEFL Sections 2 and 3 and the TEW, the third by loadings for FCE Papers 1, 2 and 3, and the fourth by loadings on FCE Papers 4 and 5 and TOEFL Section 1.

**Table 21**

**Exploratory factor analysis of FCE paper scores and ETS test scores**

| Variable | Communality (h²) |
|---|---|
| FCE1 | .58958 |
| FCE2 | .52228 |
| FCE3 | .66459 |
| FCE4 | .48009 |
| FCE5 | .42786 |
| TOEFL1 | .59892 |
| TOEFL2 | .60101 |
| TOEFL3 | .61938 |
| TEW | .39597 |
| SPK GRAM | .80465 |
| SPK PRON | .62949 |
| SPK FLCY | .77734 |
| SPK COMP | .89563 |

| Factor | Eigenvalue | % of var | Cum % of var |
|---|---|---|---|
| 1 | 7.48415 | 57.6 | 57.6 |
| 2 | 1.32523 | 10.2 | 67.8 |
| 3 | .65258 | 5.0 | 72.8 |
| 4 | .57734 | 4.4 | 77.2 |
| 5 | .55311 | 4.3 | 81.5 |
| 6 | .50183 | 3.9 | 85.3 |
| 7 | .38833 | 3.0 | 88.3 |
| 8 | .37212 | 2.9 | 91.2 |
| 9 | .34312 | 2.6 | 93.8 |
| 10 | .27587 | 2.1 | 96.0 |
| 11 | .25262 | 1.9 | 97.9 |
| 12 | .20044 | 1.5 | 99.4 |
| 13 | .07325 | .6 | 100.0 |

⇒

## DAPPFR rotated reference vector (factor) matrix

|         | Factor 1 | Factor 2 | Factor 3 | Factor 4 |
|---------|----------|----------|----------|----------|
| FCE1    | -.02936  | .07424   | .22534   | .14376   |
| FCE2    | .06990   | -.02149  | .34866   | .00239   |
| FCE3    | -.02482  | .02652   | .43943   | -.00484  |
| FCE4    | -.00383  | -.04553  | .06807   | .32530   |
| FCE5    | .16311   | -.02695  | .01953   | .22664   |
| TOEFL1  | .05520   | .05610   | -.05553  | .39100   |
| TOEFL2  | .04659   | .54607   | -.00476  | .01384   |
| TOEFL3  | -.08041  | .39974   | .04126   | .13982   |
| TEW     | .06944   | .21260   | .12569   | .01632   |
| SPK GRAM| .58579   | .01391   | -.00018  | -.00059  |
| SPK PRON| .31411   | -.02522  | .16952   | .04140   |
| SPK FLCY| .52355   | -.01975  | .00876   | .06202   |
| SPK COMP| .67897   | .03786   | .01395   | -.04700  |

## Factor correlation matrix

|          | Factor 1 | Factor 2 | Factor 3 | Factor 4 |
|----------|----------|----------|----------|----------|
| FACTOR 1 | 1.00000  |          |          |          |
| FACTOR 2 | .45129   | 1.00000  |          |          |
| FACTOR 3 | .63365   | .75098   | 1.00000  |          |
| FACTOR 4 | .74285   | .66075   | .82447   | 1.00000  |

## Orthogonalized factor matrix with second-order general factor

|          | General factor | Factor 1 | Factor 2 | Factor 3 | Factor 4 | $h^{2*}$ |
|----------|----------------|----------|----------|----------|----------|----------|
| FCE1     | .754           | -.031    | .078     | .175     | .104     | .617     |
| FCE2     | .711           | .074     | -.023    | .270     | .002     | .584     |
| FCE3     | .820           | -.026    | .028     | .341     | -.004    | .789     |
| FCE4     | .704           | -.004    | -.048    | .053     | .236     | .556     |
| FCE5     | .621           | .173     | -.028    | .015     | .165     | .443     |
| TOEFL1   | .776           | .058     | .059     | -.043    | .284     | .692     |
| TOEFL2   | .680           | .049     | .573     | -.004    | .010     | .793     |
| TOEFL3   | .711           | -.085    | .419     | .032     | .102     | .699     |
| TEW      | .581           | .074     | .223     | .097     | .012     | .402     |
| SPK GRAM | .642           | .621     | .015     | -.000    | -.000    | .798     |
| SPK PRON | .707           | .333     | -.026    | .131     | .030     | .630     |
| SPK FLCY | .676           | .555     | -.021    | .007     | .045     | .767     |
| SPEAK4   | .705           | .719     | .040     | .011     | -.034    | 1.018    |
| Eigenvalue | 6.401        | 1.377    | .571     | .252     | .189     |          |
| % variance | 49.2         | 10.6     | 4.4      | 1.9      | 1.5      | 67.6     |

* Communality

This solution suggests that the first factor can be interpreted as a "SPEAK" factor, the second an "ETS structure, reading and writing" factor, the third an "FCE structure, writing and reading" factor, and the fourth a "listening and interactive speaking" factor. Since Factors 2 and 3 appear to be associated with similar abilities but different test formats, these factors may also be interpreted to some degree as test method factors. That is, the second factor may be an "ETS-type written test" factor, while the third factor may be an "FCE-type written test" factor.

Because all four factors were highly correlated with each other, a Schmid-Leiman transformation was performed. As would be expected with very high correlations among the first-order factors, all of the measures had high salient loadings on the second-order general factor, which accounted for about 49% of the total variance. The first-order factors can be characterized as follows: Factor 1 (10.6% of variance) – SPEAK ratings and FCE Paper 5; Factor 2 (4.4% of variance) – TOEFL Sections 2 and 3 and the TEW; Factor 3 (1.9 % of variance) – FCE Papers 1, 2, and 3; and Factor 4 (1.5% of variance) – FCE Paper 4 and TOEFL Section 1.

These loadings suggest that all of these tests measure, to a considerable degree, a common portion of the language abilities that characterize the test takers in the study sample. After this general, or common, ability, the next largest component appears to be associated with speaking ability. This is followed by two components that appear to be combinations of ability (reading, structure and writing) and test method ("ETS test method" and "FCE test method"). Finally, there is a relatively small component associated with listening ability.

The fact that all of the measures examined loaded most heavily on a higher-order general factor, and that two of the first-order factors appear to be associated with aspects of language ability – speaking and listening – across both tests, suggests that these tests do, in general, measure the same abilities. The fact that two of the factors appear to be associated in part with specific tests suggests that some of the observed differences in performance across the two test batteries are attributable to differences in the methods used in testing.

## Discussion

The factor structure of any given set of test scores will be a function of both the profile of language abilities of the specific groups of individuals tested and the characteristics of the specific tests used. The large portions of variance accounted for by the general factors in our analyses suggest that the FCE papers and ETS tests administered in this study appear to measure, to a large degree, the same common aspect of the language proficiency of the subjects in our sample. We feel that at present there is no basis for interpreting this general factor as anything other than a common aspect of language proficiency shared by these subjects as measured by these tests. That is, this general factor does not necessarily represent the same aspect of language proficiency as do the general factors that have been found in other sets of language tests with other groups of subjects (e.g., Oller 1979; Carroll 1983; Bachman and Palmer 1982a, Sang *et al.* 1986).

In addition to a common, general aspect of language ability, the test batteries in this study appear to reflect shared specific abilities and different testing formats. The primary factor that accounts for the largest proportion of variance is associated with measures of speaking, especially the SPEAK. The primary factor that accounts for the least variance is associated with measures of listening. The FCE oral interview loads almost equally on both the speaking and listening factors, suggesting that it measures both these abilities to some degree. A third primary factor (associated with the ETS paper-and-pencil tests) can be identified as an "ETS written test factor", while a fourth factor (associated with the FCE pencil-and-paper tests) can be identified as an "FCE written test factor".[1]

# Note

1  It is interesting to note that the measures with the smallest communalities, or shared variances, in all the analyses were FCE Papers 4 and 5 and the TEW. One obvious explanation for this with Paper 4 is its low reliability, and as the reliability of Paper 5 could not be adequately estimated, this explanation is possible for this paper, as well. Given the high inter-rater reliability that was estimated for the TEW, however, this explanation does not seem plausible, suggesting an avenue for further research.

# 5 Effect of test preparation on test performance

The effect of test preparation on test performance has been an issue of recent concern for test developers and researchers (FTC 1979; Messick 1980; Powers 1985, 1986). One of the findings of the pilot study was that there might be a difference in test performance on the two batteries as a function of whether or not test takers had attended a course specifically aimed at one of the batteries. That is, the results of the pilot study suggested that individuals who had undergone an FCE course did relatively better on the FCE than did individuals who had not attended such a course. Therefore, we have examined the effects of FCE preparation at two levels, with two different procedures. At the level of the paper/test, we used multiple linear regression analysis with a dummy variable for test preparation, while for tests consisting of dichotomously scored items, the Mantel-Haenszel procedure was used to identify individual items that appeared to be sensitive to differential test preparation among study subjects.

## At the paper/test level

This portion of the investigation examined whether participation in a course designed to prepare test takers to take the FCE would have a significant effect on performance on either the FCE papers or the ETS tests. Information on test takers' participation in an FCE course was obtained from the background questionnaire that was administered to all subjects. To examine the effects of an FCE course on test performance, multiple linear regression analysis, with a dummy variable for FCE preparation (0 = no, 1 = yes) and a covariate to control for differences in ability, was used. Effects were examined on a test-by-test basis. For example, to examine the effect of FCE preparation on TOEFL Section 3, FCE Paper 1 served as the ability covariate, with the dummy variable representing test preparation. Likewise, to examine preparation effects on FCE Paper 1, the TOEFL Section 3 score was the ability covariate, with the dummy again representing test preparation.

In all, ten regressions were conducted; each of the five FCE papers served as the dependent variable with the ETS test that appeared to measure similar abilities designated as the ability covariate, and vice versa, with the ETS tests as dependent variables and the corresponding FCE tests as ability covariates. The results of these analyses are presented in Table 22.

## Table 22

## Results of regression analyses with FCE preparation as a dummy variable

| Variables included | ß | $R^2$ | $R^2$ change | F-ratio |
|---|---|---|---|---|
| **Dependent: FCE1** | | | | |
| TOEFL3 | .70 | .45 | .45 | 858.96* |
| Test preparation | .60 | .47 | .02 | 470.82* |
| PREP*TOEFL3 | -.46 | .47 | .002 | 317.01* |
| **Dependent: FCE2** | | | | |
| TEW | .57 | .28 | .28 | 398.79* |
| Test preparation | .61 | .33 | .05 | 253.74* |
| PREP*TEW | -.40 | .34 | .01 | 175.05* |
| **Dependent: FCE3** | | | | |
| TOEFL2 | .75 | .43 | .43 | 793.57* |
| Test preparation | 1.23 | .50 | .07 | 529.54* |
| PREP*TOEFL2 | -.99 | .52 | .02 | 375.08* |
| **Dependent: FCE4** | | | | |
| TOEFL1 | .75 | .40 | .40 | 699.33* |
| Test preparation | 1.35 | .44 | .04 | 408.84* |
| PREP*TOEFL1 | -1.20 | .46 | .02 | 297.31* |
| **Dependent: FCE5** | | | | |
| SPEAK4 | .65 | .35 | .35 | 547.06* |
| Test preparation | .51 | .35 | .002 | 276.25* |
| PREP*SPCOMP | -.49 | .36 | .007 | 194.57* |
| **Dependent: TOEFL1** | | | | |
| FCE4 | .66 | .40 | .40 | 699.32* |
| Test preparation | .03 | .40 | .002 | 352.75* |
| PREP*FCE4 | -.09 | .40 | .0003 | 235.24* |
| **Dependent: TOEFL2** | | | | |
| FCE3 | .70 | .43 | .43 | 793.57* |
| Test preparation | -.22 | .45 | .02 | 430.44* |
| PREP*FCE3 | .07 | .45 | .0002 | 286.94* |
| **Dependent: TOEFL3** | | | | |
| FCE1 | .71 | .45 | .45 | 858.96* |
| Test preparation | .19 | .45 | .0006 | 430.11* |
| PREP*FCE1 | -.23 | .45 | .002 | 288.3 |
| **Dependent: TEW** | | | | |
| FCE2 | .59 | .28 | .28 | 398.79* |
| Test preparation | .31 | .28 | .0009 | 200.02* |
| PREP*FCE2 | -.37 | .28 | .005 | 136.83* |
| **Dependent: SPEAK4** | | | | |
| FCE5 | .59 | .35 | .35 | 547.06* |
| Test preparation | .27 | .36 | .01 | 291.04* |
| PREP*FCE5 | -.15 | .36 | .0008 | 194.57* |

\* ($p < .0001$)

The test preparation variable and the attendant interaction term (test preparation by ability covariate) were statistically significant in all ten of the regression analyses. However, for seven of these analyses (FCE Papers 1 and 5 and the five ETS tests) the combined effects of the test preparation variable and the interaction term accounted for less than 3% of the variation in dependent variable. Although these effects are statistically significant because of the large sample size, we believe they are of little practical importance. In other words, participation in an FCE preparation course has very little impact on performance on either FCE Papers 1 and 5 or the ETS tests.

For FCE Papers 2, 3 and 4, however, the combined effects of test preparation and the interaction between FCE preparation and the ability covariate are, we believe, large enough to warrant discussion. These effects accounted for 6% of the variation in test scores on FCE Paper 2, 9% on FCE Paper 3, and 6% on FCE Paper 4. Translating these into predicted raw score differences, we can say that on the average, participating in an FCE preparation course increased test takers' scores on Paper 2 by 2.5 points, Paper 3 by 2.6 points, and Paper 4 by 1.4 points, in comparison to test takers who did not participate in an FCE preparation course. (While the regression weights for the interaction terms indicate that FCE preparation tended to favour slightly individuals of low ability, these differences are so small as not to be of practical importance.) These results indicate that FCE preparation did have an impact on test takers' scores for these three tests, particularly for FCE Paper 3.

## At the item level

The individual test item is the building block of test development (Wainer 1989). At test development institutions in the US, item analyses are routinely carried out to ensure that each item is psychometrically sound individually, and in relationship to the other items and to the test itself. As the technical aspects in measurement have developed over the past 30 years, interest in how items function has continued to grow. One aspect of this research is differential item functioning (DIF), which examines the effects of factors such as sex, race and ethnicity on performance at the item level. Guiding these investigations is the question of whether individuals of equal ability who are members of different groups have equal probabilities of answering items in a test correctly, or whether a larger proportion of one of the groups answers the item(s) correctly than would be expected from their ability level. For example, if, after controlling for ability, twice as many males answer an item correctly as do a comparable group of females, such an item would be considered to function differentially, unduly favouring male test takers.

Numerous methods, including those based on IRT procedures, have been proposed for investigating DIF (Shepard *et al.* 1985; Linn *et al.* 1981), and the Mantel-Haenszel (MH) procedure (Mantel and Haenszel 1959) has been suggested as an alternative procedure to IRT methods in investigating DIF (Holland and Thayer 1986; McPeek and Wild 1986). We used the MH procedure to examine whether any items favoured test takers who had participated in an FCE test preparation course over those who had not participated in such a course.

The MH procedure was originally devised for retrospective epidemiological studies to investigate the relationship between the presence or absence of a potential risk factor and the occurrence of a disease (Mantel and Haenszel 1959). Individuals were categorized as having the risk factor or not and were further classified into subgroups (strata) on the basis of "nuisance" variables, such as the number of packs of cigarettes smoked per day. For the study, test takers were classified as having participated in an FCE preparation course or not, and to avoid confounding genuine group differences in ability with differential item functioning, test takers are further classified on the basis of their ability, as represented by test performance. Thus, on a 29-item test such as the TOEFL vocabulary part, for example, there are potentially 30 score groups (0 to 29). On a given item, the performance of FCE-prepared test takers who received a score of, say, 21 is compared to that of unprepared test takers who also received a score of 21.

The responses of test takers from FCE-prepared and unprepared groups to the items of interest were compared on the basis of two indices. The Mantel-Haenszel common-odds ratio (MHODDS) indicates the degree to which a given item functions differentially. The MHODDS may be interpreted as the average amount by which the probability ("odds") that the responses of reference group members to a given item will be correct is larger than the odds for comparable members of the focal group (Holland and Thayer 1986). For the study sample, an MHODDS greater than 1.0 for an item indicates that, on average, the members of a reference group (FCE-prepared test takers) performed better than did comparable members of the focal group (unprepared test takers). Alternatively, an MHODDS of less than 1.0 indicates that the unprepared test takers performed better than did the FCE-prepared test takers. The Mantel-Haenszel chi-square (MHCHIX) indicates whether there is a statistically significant difference in item functioning between the two groups. The MHCHIX has one degree of freedom, and will identify items which function differentially for either subgroup. A computer program written in Fortran (Ryan 1988) was used to calculate the MHCHIX, MHODDS, and the standard error of the MHODDS for every item in the Mantel-Haenszel analyses (Phillips and Holland 1987). Any item with an MHCHIX greater than 3.84 (p > .05 for a chi-square with 1 degree of freedom) and an MHODDS greater than 1.6 (favouring FCE-prepared test takers) or less than .625 (favouring unprepared test takers), was flagged as a differentially functioning item. These criteria were selected because previous research has shown that differences in item functioning of this magnitude have practical significance for test development (Holland 1985).

**Table 23**

**Numbers and percentages of items that function differentially, favouring either FCE-prepared or unprepared test takers, detected in FCE Paper 1 and the TOEFL**

| | Dif items | | | | | | No dif | | Total |
|---|---|---|---|---|---|---|---|---|---|
| | FCE prep | | No prep | | Total dif | | | | |
| Test | N | % | N | % | N | % | N | % | |
| FCE Paper 1 | | | | | | | | | |
| Section A | 6 | 24 | 8 | 32 | 14 | 56 | 11 | 44 | 25 |
| Section B | 2 | 13 | 2 | 13 | 4 | 27 | 11 | 73 | 15 |
| FCE Paper 1 total | 8 | 20 | 10 | 25 | 18 | 45 | 22 | 55 | 40 |
| TOEFL Section 1 | | | | | | | | | |
| Part A | 2 | 10 | 2 | 10 | 4 | 20 | 16 | 80 | 20 |
| Part B | 2 | 10 | 1 | 7 | 3 | 20 | 12 | 80 | 15 |
| Part C | 2 | 13 | 0 | 0 | 2 | 13 | 13 | 87 | 15 |
| TOEFL Section 2 | | | | | | | | | |
| Structure | 0 | 0 | 0 | 0 | 0 | 0 | 14 | 100 | 14 |
| Written Exp. | 8 | 33 | 6 | 25 | 14 | 58 | 10 | 42 | 24 |
| TOEFL Part 3 | | | | | | | | | |
| Vocabulary | 8 | 28 | 6 | 21 | 14 | 48 | 15 | 52 | 29 |
| Reading | 4 | 14 | 3 | 10 | 7 | 24 | 22 | 76 | 29 |
| TOEFL total | 26 | 18 | 18 | 12 | 44 | 30 | 102 | 70 | 146 |

The MH procedure is appropriate for dichotomously scored items only. The tests examined include the three sections of the TOEFL and the two sections of FCE Paper 1. Table 23 indicates the numbers of items detected as differentially functioning ("Dif") that favour either the FCE-prepared test takers ("FCE prep") or unprepared test takers ("No prep"), the numbers of items not favouring either group ("No dif") and the total numbers of items in the subparts of these tests. As shown in Table 23, considerable numbers of items were found to be differentially functioning. For the TOEFL, on average, the FCE-prepared test takers were more likely to answer 18% of the test items correctly than unprepared test takers of equal ability, while 12% of the TOEFL items favoured the unprepared test takers. Oddly enough, the advantage is reversed for FCE Paper 1, where 20% of the items favoured the FCE-prepared test takers and 25% of the items actually favoured the unprepared test takers.

Although the advantages of the FCE-prepared and unprepared test takers may appear to cancel one another out for the most part, it should be noted that, by current testing standards, an enormous number of items were found to be differentially functioning. On the TOEFL, 30% of the items favoured one group or the other, while 45% of the items were identified as differentially functioning on FCE Paper 1. The highest proportion of differentially functioning items was from the TOEFL written expression subtest (58%), followed by FCE Paper 1 (56%) and the TOEFL vocabulary subtest (48%), the latter two of which are quite similar in both content and format. The TOEFL structure subtest, on the other hand, which is also similar to FCE Paper 1 Section A in many respects, had no differentially functioning items. If these analyses were being carried out at the test development stage, the test would be "purified" by dropping out all the items that had been identified as differentially functioning, and then adding these items back one at a time, recomputing the MHODDS and MHCHIX as they are added back, to determine which, if any, could be retained. This could not be done in this case because after dropping all the differentially functioning items there were not enough items left to carry out the analyses again.

In addition to the large numbers of differentially functioning items detected, the chi-square statistics and the MHODDS ratios associated with these differentially functioning items were extreme values. Several of the chi-square statistics were well over 100, which cannot be explained by the large sample size alone, and is unusual for analyses of this type. The MHODDS indices for the FCE preparation analysis were as large as 5.3 and as low as .231 and frequently over 2.0 and .500, values which indicate that the members of one group are twice as likely to answer the item correctly as are members of the other group with equal ability. Thus, several of the items distinctly favoured one group or the other.

While the MH analyses clearly indicate large numbers of differentially functioning items, a qualification regarding the interpretation of these results must be pointed out. The study design for examining the effect of FCE preparation was potentially confounded with language background, since it turned out that the FCE-prepared test takers were largely from Indo-European language backgrounds, while the unprepared test takers were largely from non-Indo-European language backgrounds. This confound was unavoidable, given the other considerations in the sampling design, in that it reflects the characteristics of the operational distributions of the FCE and the ETS tests. That is, the Cambridge examinations, which candidates generally take after attending an FCE preparation course, are widely taken in Europe and South America, while the ETS tests, for which candidates obviously do not take an FCE preparation course, are also widely administered in Asia and the Middle East. Clearly there are differentially functioning items in both the TOEFL and FCE Paper 1, based on what was specified as an FCE test preparation factor. However, whether the test preparation factor has been specified unequivocally or is confounded by language background has not been resolved in this investigation.

## Discussion

Two different types of analyses were conducted to examine the effect of FCE test preparation on test performance:

1 multiple linear regression on test scores with a dummy variable for test preparation and a covariate for language ability, and

2 the Mantel-Haenszel procedure for the tests with dichotomously scored items.

The regression analyses indicated that FCE preparation has little effect on any of the ETS test scores, or on marks for FCE Papers 1 and 5. And even for those papers where the effect was noteworthy – FCE Papers 2, 3 and 4 – the predicted scaled score differences were all less than one half of their respective standard deviations, which is a relatively small effect size.

In contrast, while the regression analyses suggest that FCE preparation had no significant effect on performance on the ETS tests and FCE Papers 1 and 5, the results of the Mantel-Haenszel analyses with the three sections of the TOEFL and the two parts of FCE Paper 1 suggest that this issue should be considered further. Although the regressions suggest that the FCE preparation factor is effectively cancelled out, with about equal numbers of items favouring the FCE-prepared and unprepared groups, there is no assurance that this type of pattern is present on all forms. Furthermore, if some combination of test preparation and cultural and linguistic background affects so many of the dichotomously scored items so strongly, we would expect that this source of bias may be even stronger in the items that require completion responses, such as in FCE Papers 3 and 4. We also believe that the Mantel-Haenszel procedure provides a valuable tool for investigating other potential sources of item bias, such as sex and item content.

Due to an unavoidable confound in the study sampling design between FCE preparedness and cultural background, the results that were obtained cannot be attributed uniquely to test preparation.[1] The Mantel-Haenszel procedure did detect very large proportions of items in both FCE Paper 1 and the TOEFL that were functioning differentially, and for many of these differentially functioning items the chances of one subgroup of test takers answering them correctly were twice as large as were those of the other subgroup. Given what is known about the effects of mother tongue and cultural background on foreign language learning, it is reasonable to expect that much of the observed *dif* in both the FCE and TOEFL is attributable to differences in test takers' mother tongues and cultural backgrounds. We feel that this level of item bias should be of concern to developers of both these tests, and that further research should be conducted in order to achieve a better understanding of its causes, whether these are prior test preparation, mother tongue/culture background, or some combination of these.

# Note

1 In a follow-up study Ryan and Bachman (1992) have attempted to resolve this confound by examining the effects both within and across Indo-European and non-Indo-European language background groups, and across pairs (Cambridge-TOEFL) of study sites.

# 6 Interchangeability of FCE and ETS test scores

The results of exploratory factor analyses indicated that all of the five FCE paper scores and eight ETS test scores load most heavily on a higher-order general factor that accounts for nearly half of the total variance of these measures. As indicated above, these results suggest that these tests measure, to a large degree, a similar aspect of EFL proficiency. In addition, two pairs of tests of similar abilities (listening and speaking) across test batteries share salient loadings on first-order factors. These results suggest that the interchangeability of scores from pairs of tests across test batteries may be meaningfully examined. Furthermore, since test preparation was found to have virtually no effect on performance on the ETS test scores, and very little effect on performance on the FCE papers, it was not necessary to consider this as a factor in these analyses. The interchangeability of scores from pairs of tests of similar abilities across the two test batteries was examined in two ways:

1 through an IRT equating procedure, and
2 through multiple linear regression analysis.

## IRT modeling and equating

Three pairs of tests of similar abilities are composed of individual test items, and their comparability could thus potentially be investigated at the item level. These pairs of measures are FCE Paper 1 and TOEFL Section 3 (reading), FCE Paper 3 (usage) and TOEFL Section 2 (structure) and FCE Paper 4 and TOEFL Section 1 (listening). One approach to comparability is empirically to relate observed scores on similar tests to ability levels on a common ability scale through IRT modeling. However, since any IRT-based approach requires the satisfaction of strong assumptions about the nature of the data, before attempting to apply this approach to item scores from the above tests, the tenability of these assumptions needs to be demonstrated.

The primary assumption upon which most currently available IRT models depend is that of unidimensionality, which means that all the items in a given test measure a single ability or trait. A second set of assumptions is associated with specific IRT models. These generally have to do with

1 the nature of the relationship between the test taker's ability, $\theta$, and the probability, "p", of getting a given item right, and
2 the number of characteristics, or parameters, required to model that probability adequately.

Although the relationship between θ and "p" has been characterized in a number of ways, most currently available IRT models employ a logistic function, which is curvilinear. There is less agreement on the question of the number of parameters required to represent this logistic function adequately. The most general model in current use is the three-parameter logistic (3PL) model (Birnbaum 1968), which estimates three characteristics of items:

1 item discriminating power, represented by the "a" parameter,
2 item difficulty, represented by the "b" parameter, and
3 the probability of a correct response by test takers of very low ability, represented by the "c" parameter, sometimes referred to as the "guessing parameter".

Two other commonly used models are the two-parameter logistic (2PL) model, which assumes that the "c" parameter is zero and estimates only the "a" and "b" parameters, and the one-parameter logistic (1PL), or Rasch, model, which assumes that the "c" parameter is zero and that the "a" parameter is equal to one, and estimates only the "b" parameter. Before attempting to model a set of test items with IRT, both the dimensionality of the items and the "goodness of fit" of the particular IRT model to the data need to be assessed.[1]

## Dimensionality assessment

Although the exploratory factor analysis of the scores from the two test batteries indicated the presence of a strong higher-order general factor, the purpose of the dimensionality check was to determine if this was reflected in unidimensionality at the level of individual test items. The question of dimensionality is a complex one, and is still largely unresolved among IRT specialists. It is now generally agreed that all tests are likely to be multidimensional to some degree, so that the question is not whether a given test is unidimensional or not, but rather whether it is sufficiently multidimensional to make IRT modeling invalid. There is a large and rapidly growing literature on the potential effects of multidimensionality on IRT item parameter and ability estimates, and several different approaches to dimensionality assessment have been developed (cf. Hattie 1985 for an extensive review). To date, the most commonly used approaches with language tests have been item-level exploratory factor analysis (e.g., Davidson 1988) and Bejar's approach (Bejar 1980; Henning *et al.* 1985; Henning 1988).

For the purposes of a preliminary investigation of dimensionality, we chose the two measures that appeared to be the best candidates for IRT equating, in that we felt they were the most likely to be unidimensional, a view based both on the abilities they purport to measure and on the similarities among the item types. These two tests were FCE Paper 1 and TOEFL Section 3, each with two subtests which appear to measure vocabulary and reading comprehension. Since the IRT procedure for relating FCE and TOEFL scores to a common scale requires that item scores from these two tests be analysed in a single IRT model, we investigated the dimensionality of all of the items in each of these tests, as well as that of similar subsets of items from both tests: vocabulary items and reading items.

## Table 24

## Eigenvalues greater than 1 from each principal components extraction

### FCE vocabulary items

| Factor | Eigenvalue | % of var* | Cum % of var** |
|--------|-----------|-----------|----------------|
| 1 | 10.105 | 40.4 | 40.4 |
| 2 | 1.787 | 7.1 | 47.6 |
| 3 | 1.498 | 6.0 | 53.6 |
| 4 | 1.026 | 4.1 | 57.7 |

### FCE reading items

| Factor | Eigenvalue | % of var | Cum % of var |
|--------|-----------|----------|--------------|
| 1 | 6.084 | 40.6 | 40.6 |
| 2 | 1.390 | 9.3 | 49.8 |
| 3 | 1.105 | 7.4 | 57.2 |

### FCE vocabulary and reading items

| Factor | Eigenvalue | % of var | Cum % of var |
|--------|-----------|----------|--------------|
| 1 | 15.277 | 38.2 | 38.2 |
| 2 | 2.287 | 5.7 | 43.9 |
| 3 | 1.794 | 4.5 | 48.4 |
| 4 | 1.488 | 3.7 | 52.1 |
| 5 | 1.144 | 2.9 | 55.0 |
| 6 | 1.046 | 2.6 | 57.6 |
| 7 | 1.035 | 2.6 | 60.2 |
| 8 | 1.011 | 2.5 | 62.7 |
| 9 | 1.001 | 2.5 | 65.2 |

### TOEFL vocabulary items

| Factor | Eigenvalue | % of var | Cum % of var |
|--------|-----------|----------|--------------|
| 1 | 9.136 | 31.5 | 31.5 |
| 2 | 2.220 | 7.7 | 39.2 |
| 3 | 1.582 | 5.5 | 44.6 |
| 4 | 1.320 | 4.6 | 49.2 |
| 5 | 1.181 | 4.1 | 53.2 |
| 6 | 1.027 | 3.5 | 56.8 |

⇒

| TOEFL reading items | | | |
|---|---|---|---|
| Factor | Eigenvalue | % of var* | Cum % of var** |
| 1 | 10.614 | 36.6 | 36.6 |
| 2 | 1.736 | 6.0 | 42.6 |
| 3 | 1.425 | 4.9 | 47.5 |
| 4 | 1.208 | 4.2 | 51.7 |
| 5 | 1.065 | 3.7 | 55.3 |
| 6 | 1.024 | 3.5 | 58.9 |

| TOEFL vocabulary and reading items | | | |
|---|---|---|---|
| Factor | Eigenvalue | % of var | Cum % of var |
| 1 | 18.246 | 31.5 | 31.5 |
| 2 | 2.952 | 5.1 | 36.5 |
| 3 | 2.215 | 3.8 | 40.4 |
| 4 | 1.799 | 3.1 | 43.5 |
| 5 | 1.551 | 2.7 | 46.1 |
| 6 | 1.469 | 2.5 | 48.7 |
| 7 | 1.372 | 2.4 | 51.0 |
| 8 | 1.310 | 2.3 | 53.3 |
| 9 | 1.206 | 2.1 | 55.4 |
| 10 | 1.195 | 2.1 | 57.4 |
| 11 | 1.105 | 1.9 | 59.3 |
| 12 | 1.039 | 1.8 | 61.1 |
| 13 | 1.015 | 1.7 | 62.9 |

\* Percentage of variance
\*\* Cumulative percentage of variance

A traditional approach to IRT dimensionality assessment is the exploratory factor analysis of the inter-item tetrachoric correlation matrix (Lord and Novick 1968; Lord 1980), and this was utilized in our investigation. The eigenvalues greater than one and percentages of variance accounted for from the principal components analysis of the matrix of inter-item tetrachoric correlations for each of the FCE Paper 1 and TOEFL Section 3 tests and subtests (vocabulary, reading) are presented in Table 24.

As can be seen in Table 24, the percentage of variance accounted for by the first factor in all six sets was more than 30%, well above the criterion of 20% that has been suggested by Reckase (1979) as a criterion for unidimensionality. Furthermore, for the combined FCE Paper 1 and TOEFL Section 3 vocabulary items, the first factor accounted for 25% of the variance, while for the combined reading items the first factor accounted for 31% of the variance. These results suggest that these two tests are essentially unidimensional.

A more recent approach to IRT dimensionality assessment is that of Stout (1987), who has proposed a non-parametric model to produce a statistical index, "t", which indicates the extent of departure from unidimensionality in a given set of test items. This index is calculated on the basis of two separate subtests formed from the test under investigation. These analyses were computed with programs written by Junker (1988), the results of which are given in Table 25.

**Table 25**

**Investigation of dimensionality: Stout's t-test**

| Test/item set | t | p | $H_o$ (a = .05) |
|---|---|---|---|
| FCE Voc | -1.41120 | .48006 | accept: unidimensional |
| FCE Read | 1.70854 | .04377 | reject: multidimensional |
| FCE1 Tot | -.16721 | .48006 | accept: unidimensional |
| TOEFL Voc | .51774 | .30232 | accept: unidimensional |
| TOEFL Read | 3.97816 | .00003 | reject: multidimensional |
| TOEFL3 Tot | 5.23227 | .00000 | reject: multidimensional |
| F1 and T3 Voc | 1.17652 | .11969 | accept: unidimensional |
| F1 and T3 Read | 1.16324 | .12237 | accept: unidimensional |

These results indicate that the individual vocabulary tests appear to be essentially unidimensional, while the individual reading tests appear to be multidimensional. At the level of the total tests, FCE Paper 1 appears to be essentially unidimensional, while TOEFL appears to be multidimensional. These differences in apparent dimensionality are not reflected in results obtained for the combined vocabulary and reading tests, which were found to be essentially unidimensional.[2]

## Assessment of model fit

Although there was some ambiguity in the results of our dimensionality checks for the combined item sets, the majority of the evidence supported the interpretation that these tests were essentially unidimensional. This being so, along with the fact that there is not, as yet, either a commonly accepted test for multidimensionality or a clear understanding of how multidimensional a measure must be before IRT estimates are invalid, we proceeded to investigate the relative fit of the 1PL, 2PL and 3PL models to the data. We employed four different approaches that are currently in common use for assessing IRT model fit:
1 the BILOG fit statistic (Mislevy and Bock 1986);
2 the number of misfitting items;

3  the examination of residuals (Hambleton and Swaminathan 1985); and
4  Bejar's (1980) approach to estimating the invariance of item parameters.

## BILOG fit statistic

BILOG uses a marginal maximum likelihood estimation procedure for estimating item parameters, and this procedure provides a fit statistic (-2 times the log likelihood function). For samples with large numbers of subjects, the likelihood function is distributed approximately as a chi-square, and can be used to test the relative fit of different IRT models (Hambleton and Swaminathan 1985: 154). The fit statistics of the 1PL, 2PL and 3PL models to the data for the six tests of vocabulary and reading were compared, and the results are presented in Table 26.

**Table 26**

**BILOG fit statistics for 1PL, 2PL and 3PL IRT models and differences (Diff) among IRT models**

|  | 1PL | 2PL | 3PL | Diff(1–2) | Diff(2–3) | Diff(1–3) |
|---|---|---|---|---|---|---|
| FCE Voc | 29436.18 | 29326.19 | 29306.21 | 109.99* | 19.98 | 129.97* |
| FCE Read | 17103.87 | 16841.32 | 16848.24 | 262.56* | -6.92 | 255.64* |
| FCE1 Tot | 46381.68 | 45917.25 | 45920.89 | 464.43* | -3.63 | 460.79* |
| TOEFL Voc | 45580.56 | 44947.12 | 44865.18 | 633.44* | 81.94* | 715.37* |
| TOEFL Re | 45692.07 | 45073.88 | 45037.28 | 618.20* | 36.60** | 654.80* |
| TOEFL3 Tot | 90775.69 | 89301.00 | 89148.97 | 1474.73* | 151.99* | 1626.72* |

  * Significant at p = .05
 ** Significant at p = .01

With all the datasets, there were statistically significant differences in model fit between the 1PL and 2PL models, and between the 1PL and 3PL models. But with only the TOEFL vocabulary, TOEFL reading and TOEFL total datasets there were significant differences in model fit between the 2PL and 3PL models. It should be noted that with FCE reading and total datasets the 2PL model provides a slightly better fit than does the 3PL model, although the difference in fit is not statistically significant. These results indicate that both the 2PL and 3PL models provide significantly better fits to these data than does the 1PL model.

## Analysis of misfitting items

Model fit can also be assessed by examining a simple count of the number of significantly (p < .01) misfitting items, as identified by BILOG. The numbers of significantly misfitting items for the six tests, for all three IRT models, are given in Table 27.

**Table 27**

**Numbers of misfitting items (p < .01)**

|              | 1PL | 2PL | 3PL |
|--------------|-----|-----|-----|
| TOEFL3 Vocab | 14  | 0   | 0   |
| TOEFL3 Read  | 8   | 2   | 1   |
| TOEFL3 Total | 27  | 3   | 1   |
| FCE Vocab    | 4   | 0   | 0   |
| FCE Vocab    | 5   | 0   | 0   |
| FCE Total    | 9   | 1   | 1   |

As can be seen, the number of misfitting items is much larger for the 1PL than for either the 2PL or 3PL models. These results again indicate that both the 2PL and 3PL models provide better fits to these datasets than does the 1PL model.

## Analysis of residuals

Another way of assessing model fit is to compute a standardized residual (SR) for each item and to tabulate the percentages of items with differing sizes of SRs. The SR is a function of the difference between the observed item facility at a given ability level and the estimated item facility at that ability level, which is estimated from both the item and ability parameters. The SR thus provides a global index of model fit. Assuming the approximately normal distribution of the SRs within the framework of regression theory, these SRs are scaled with a mean of zero and standard deviation of one. Thus, when a given IRT model fits the data, the SRs are expected to be small and randomly distributed around zero. The numbers and percentages of items in different SR ranges for the 1PL, 2PL and 3PL models for the six tests are given in Table 28.

These results indicate that for all six tests, for the 1PL model, the majority of the items have SRs of 3 or more, while for both the 2PL and 3PL models the majority of the items have SRs of 1 or less. That is, the 1PL parameters provide very poor estimates of observed item facilities for the majority of the items, while the 2PL and 3PL parameters provide reasonably good estimates. These results are consistent with the earlier analyses, and again indicate the inadequacy of the 1PL model for these tests.

## Table 28

## Percentages of standardized residuals

### TOEFL3 vocabulary items

|  | 1PL | 2PL | 3PL |
|---|---|---|---|
| 0 <= SR < 1 | 12 | 60 | 63 |
| 1 <= SR < 2 | 9 | 30 | 29 |
| 2 <= SR < 3 | 6 | 9 | 7 |
| 3 <= SR | 73 | 0 | 1 |

### TOEFL3 reading items

|  | 1PL | 2PL | 3PL |
|---|---|---|---|
| 0 <= SR < 1 | 18 | 67 | 64 |
| 1 <= SR < 2 | 12 | 27 | 30 |
| 2 <= SR < 3 | 13 | 6 | 4 |
| 3 <= SR | 57 | 1 | 2 |

### TOEFL3 total

|  | 1PL | 2PL | 3PL |
|---|---|---|---|
| 0 <= SR < 1 | 18 | 66 | 64 |
| 1 <= SR < 2 | 8 | 26 | 30 |
| 2 <= SR < 3 | 8 | 7 | 6 |
| 3 <= SR | 66 | 1 | 0 |

### FCE1 vocabulary

|  | 1PL | 2PL | 3PL |
|---|---|---|---|
| 0 <= SR < 1 | 8 | 61 | 61 |
| 1 <= SR < 2 | 9 | 30 | 30 |
| 2 <= SR < 3 | 9 | 7 | 7 |
| 3 <= SR | 73 | 1 | 2 |

### FCE1 reading

|  | 1PL | 2PL | 3PL |
|---|---|---|---|
| 0 <= SR < 1 | 9 | 58 | 58 |
| 1 <= SR < 2 | 7 | 26 | 26 |
| 2 <= SR < 3 | 7 | 9 | 9 |
| 3 <= SR | 76 | 7 | 8 |

### FCE1 total

|  | 1PL | 2PL | 3PL |
|---|---|---|---|
| 0 <= SR < 1 | 10 | 65 | 67 |
| 1 <= SR < 2 | 6 | 27 | 24 |
| 2 <= SR < 3 | 5 | 7 | 8 |
| 3 <= SR | 79 | 1 | 1 |

## Invariance of item parameters

Bejar (1980) proposed an approach to dimensionality assessment that is based on the examination of the invariance of item parameter estimates. According to this approach, test items are divided into subtests according to content. Item difficulty "b" parameters for the total test and for content subtests are then estimated separately. In our application, we estimated the difficulty parameters for items in a homogeneous subtest, and for the same items as part of the total test, and then compared these. For example, difficulty parameters were estimated for the FCE Paper 1 vocabulary items as a homogeneous subtest. Difficulty parameters for these same vocabulary items were then estimated as part of the FCE Paper 1 total test. Differences between the difficulty parameter estimates based on the homogeneous vocabulary subtest and those based on the total test provided the basis for comparisons with Bejar's method.

Bejar's method provides a t-test and associated probability level for rejecting the hypothesis of invariance. The results of these analyses are presented in Table 29.

**Table 29**

**Bejar's t-test for item invariance**

|            | 1PL    |         | 2PL   |         | 3PL   |        |
|------------|--------|---------|-------|---------|-------|--------|
|            | t      | p       | t     | p       | t     | p      |
| FCE Vocab  | 160.76 | <<.001  | 2.85  | <.01    | 3.54  | <.002  |
| FCE Read   | 251.60 | <<.001  | 5.33  | <<.001  | 3.57  | <.01   |
| TOEFL Vocab| 155.76 | <<.001  | 0.23  | <.84    | 1.38  | <.20   |
| TOEFL Read | 309.40 | <<.001  | 2.29  | <.05    | 0.74  | <.46   |

These results indicate that the 1PL model fails to provide invariance of difficulty parameter estimates with all four datasets, while the 2PL and 3PL models fail for three and two of the datasets, respectively. It is not surprising that the 3PL model estimates are invariant for the TOEFL, given the fact that test takers are encouraged to guess when they are not sure of the correct answer, and that TOEFL items are calibrated and selected on the basis of the 3PL model (ETS 1987; Cowell 1982; Hicks 1984).

In the investigation of IRT assumptions we applied what we believe to be the best of the currently available approaches to assessing the appropriateness of three IRT models, the 1PL, or Rasch model, and the 2PL and 3PL models, to the analysis of item-level data from the FCE Paper 1 and TOEFL Section 3. Our first conclusion is that these tests do not violate the IRT unidimensionality assumption sufficiently to invalidate the use of IRT modeling as a basis for investigating the comparability of the two test batteries. Our second conclusion is that of the three models compared, the Rasch model consistently fails the tests of model fit that we have applied, while the 2PL and 3PL models provide generally acceptable fits. The differences in model fit between the 2PL and 3PL IRT models were relatively small and non-significant. Given the fact that our sample for FCE Paper 4 was limited to subjects who took a single form, we therefore took a decision to utilize the 2PL model for equating purposes, since it is much less demanding than is the 3PL model in the respect of numbers of items and subjects required, and thus could potentially be used appropriately for all of the tests.

## Appropriateness of IRT modeling for FCE Paper 4 and TOEFL Section 1

Having demonstrated that the IRT assumption of essential unidimensionality was satisfied for FCE Paper 1 and TOEFL Section 3, we proceeded to determine whether IRT modeling would be appropriate for the other two pairs of tests (FCE Paper 3 and TOEFL Section 2, FCE Paper 4 and TOEFL Section 1). Because the responses to FCE Paper 3 are not dichotomous, the Rasch partial-credit model (Wright and Mead 1976), which was the only such IRT model available at the time of the study, might have been used with this test. However, since we had already demonstrated that the Rasch model provided inadequate fits to data from the other tests, we had no reason to believe that it would provide an adequate fit to the responses for FCE Paper 3. We therefore decided to drop FCE Paper 3, and hence its closest counterpart, TOEFL Section 2, from further consideration for IRT-based equating.

For the purpose of equating the two tests of listening comprehension (FCE Paper 4 and TOEFL Section 1) we used Form 24 of FCE Paper 4, which was the form taken by the largest number of candidates (N = 622). Although the items in this form of FCE Paper 4 are intended to be scored on polychotomous scales, the majority of these scores were, in fact, dichotomous. Two items, numbers 1 and 2, that were actually scored polychotomously were eliminated from the dataset, as were items 23 and 24, which were not scored operationally. In order to assess the dimensionality of FCE Paper 4 and TOEFL Section 1, factor analysis and Stout's t-test were used, the results of which are presented in Table 30.

According to both the factor analysis and Stout's t-test, the listening tests could be considered essentially unidimensional. The first factor for each of the three item sets accounts for at least 38% of the variance, while Stout's t failed to reach significance for any of the three item sets.

Although we had decided not to use the Rasch model for equating the reading tests, in checking model-data fit for the listening tests we decided to include it, along with the 2PL model. This was largely because of the Rasch model's widespread use in language testing research, and because it had been proposed in the original project design as the model to be used in IRT-based comparisons. The results of BILOG likelihood ratios for the 1PL and 2PL models for the listening tests are presented in Table 32.

## Table 30

## Eigenvalues greater than 1 from each principal components extraction

| | FCE listening items | | |
|---|---|---|---|
| Factor | Eigenvalue | % of var* | Cum % of var** |
| 1 | 8.13383 | 38.7 | 38.7 |
| 2 | 1.81136 | 8.6 | 47.4 |
| 3 | 1.65601 | 7.9 | 55.2 |
| 4 | 1.27593 | 6.1 | 61.3 |
| 5 | 1.26849 | 6.0 | 67.4 |

| | TOEFL listening items | | |
|---|---|---|---|
| Factor | Eigenvalue | % of var | Cum % of var |
| 1 | 21.12996 | 42.3 | 42.3 |
| 2 | 2.86749 | 5.7 | 48.0 |
| 3 | 2.16230 | 4.3 | 52.3 |
| 4 | 1.96210 | 3.9 | 56.2 |
| 5 | 1.58785 | 3.2 | 59.4 |
| 6 | 1.50605 | 3.0 | 62.4 |
| 7 | 1.40428 | 2.8 | 65.2 |
| 8 | 1.32146 | 2.6 | 67.9 |
| 9 | 1.26497 | 2.5 | 70.4 |
| 10 | 1.15714 | 2.3 | 72.7 |
| 11 | 1.00498 | 2.0 | 74.7 |

| | FCE and TOEFL listening items combined | | |
|---|---|---|---|
| Factor | Eigenvalue | % of var | Cum % of var |
| 1 | 27.91446 | 39.3 | 39.3 |
| 2 | 3.29336 | 4.6 | 44.0 |
| 3 | 3.22809 | 4.5 | 48.5 |
| 4 | 2.69449 | 3.8 | 52.3 |
| 5 | 2.48950 | 3.5 | 55.8 |
| 6 | 2.06174 | 2.9 | 58.7 |
| 7 | 1.81829 | 2.6 | 61.3 |
| 8 | 1.71792 | 2.4 | 63.7 |
| 9 | 1.62217 | 2.3 | 66.0 |
| 10 | 1.59373 | 2.2 | 68.2 |
| 11 | 1.45729 | 2.1 | 70.3 |
| 12 | 1.39287 | 2.0 | 72.2 |
| 13 | 1.32303 | 1.9 | 74.1 |
| 14 | 1.22621 | 1.7 | 75.8 |
| 15 | 1.13083 | 1.6 | 77.4 |
| 16 | 1.10019 | 1.5 | 79.0 |
| 17 | 1.03052 | 1.5 | 80.4 |

\* Percentage of variance
\*\* Cumulative percentage of variance

## Table 31
### Summary results of Stout's approach

| Test | t | p | $H_o$ (a=.01) |
|------|---|---|---------------|
| FCE Listening | .85910 | .19514 | accept: unidimensional |
| TOEFL Listening | -.51309 | .48006 | accept: unidimensional |
| FCE & TOEFL Listening | -.50729 | .48006 | accept: unidimensional |

## Table 32
### BILOG -2 log likelihood ratio

| Test | 1 PL | 2 PL | Diff(1-2) |
|------|------|------|-----------|
| F4 | 13604.539 | 13445.299 | 159.240* |
| T1 | 88825.109 | 87719.800 | 1105.309* |
| T1F4 | 47545.120 | 46685.850 | 859.270* |

*Significant at a=.001

These analyses again suggest that the Rasch model is inadequate for these data. Furthermore, it was found that only two items on each of the two listening tests were identified as misfitting for the 2PL model.

## IRT score equating

On the basis of the investigation of model fit, it was decided that the two-parameter model would be used for IRT equating in the study. The two pairs of tests included in this equating procedure are FCE Paper 1 with TOEFL Section 3 and FCE Paper 4 with TOEFL Section 1. Since two different tests with no anchor test items were used for the study, an IRT true-score equating approach was employed for equating scores from the FCE and TOEFL tests of reading (FCE Paper 1 and TOEFL Section 3) and listening comprehension (FCE Paper 4 and TOEFL Section 1). The first step in the equating procedure was to obtain IRT estimates for the difficulty ("b") and discrimination ("a") parameters for the items and for the ability parameters ("θ") for test takers, on the basis of the combined items from each pair of tests. In the second step, these parameter estimates were used to compute a number-right "true score" for each test for each test taker (Lord 1980). Each of these estimated "true scores" has associated with it a standard error of estimate. After transforming the estimated number-right "true" scores for the TOEFL Section 1 to standard score equivalents for interpretability, we obtained two estimated "true" scores – one for FCE Paper 1 and one for TOEFL Section 3 – for each individual test taker.

A visual inspection of these two lists of scores indicated considerable overlap in boundaries between scores from one test to the other. That is, individuals whose "true" Paper 4 scores were 18, for example, had corresponding TOEFL Section 1 scores that ranged from 59 to 62, while individuals with TOEFL "true" scores of 37 had corresponding Paper 4 scores that ranged from 8 to 9. Because of the difficulty in interpreting these overlapping score ranges, regression analysis was employed to provide a single predicted score for each predictor. Since the relationship between the two sets of scores is not symmetrical, we regressed both ways, using each set of scores to predict the other. It should be noted that each predictor has an associated standard error of estimate, which is reflected in the standard error of estimate (SE) of the corresponding predicted score. Tables 33 and 34 contain the predictor scores, the predicted scores rounded to the nearest whole number, and the standard errors of estimate for the predicted scores, for FCE Paper 1 and TOEFL Section 3, while Tables 35 and 36 provide the same information for FCE Paper 4 and TOEFL Section 1.

**Table 33**

**IRT equated true-scores: TOEFL 3 and FCE 1 (Reading)**
**Predicted FCE 1 scores**

**(FCE 1 = .6661(TOEFL 3) - 7.9301 ± SE)**

| TOEFL 3 | Predicted FCE 1 | SE | TOEFL 3 | Predicted FCE 1 | SE |
|---|---|---|---|---|---|
| 20 | 5 | 0.435 | 44 | 21 | 0.422 |
| 21 | 6 | 0.434 | 45 | 22 | 0.422 |
| 22 | 7 | 0.433 | 46 | 23 | 0.422 |
| 23 | 7 | 0.432 | 47 | 23 | 0.423 |
| 24 | 8 | 0.431 | 48 | 24 | 0.423 |
| 25 | 9 | 0.430 | 49 | 25 | 0.423 |
| 26 | 9 | 0.429 | 50 | 25 | 0.423 |
| 27 | 10 | 0.429 | 51 | 26 | 0.424 |
| 28 | 11 | 0.428 | 52 | 27 | 0.424 |
| 29 | 11 | 0.427 | 53 | 27 | 0.424 |
| 30 | 12 | 0.427 | 54 | 28 | 0.425 |
| 31 | 13 | 0.426 | 55 | 29 | 0.425 |
| 32 | 13 | 0.425 | 56 | 29 | 0.426 |
| 33 | 14 | 0.425 | 57 | 30 | 0.427 |
| 34 | 15 | 0.424 | 58 | 31 | 0.427 |
| 35 | 15 | 0.424 | 59 | 31 | 0.428 |
| 36 | 16 | 0.424 | 60 | 32 | 0.429 |

$\Rightarrow$

| TOEFL 3 | Predicted FCE 1 | SE | TOEFL 3 | Predicted FCE 1 | SE |
|---------|-----------------|-----|---------|-----------------|-----|
| 37 | 17 | 0.423 | 61 | 33 | 0.429 |
| 38 | 17 | 0.423 | 62 | 33 | 0.430 |
| 39 | 18 | 0.423 | 63 | 34 | 0.431 |
| 40 | 19 | 0.423 | 64 | 35 | 0.432 |
| 41 | 19 | 0.422 | 65 | 35 | 0.433 |
| 42 | 20 | 0.422 | 66 | 36 | 0.434 |
| 43 | 21 | 0.422 | 67 | 37 | 0.435 |

## Table 34

### Predicted TOEFL 3 scores

### (TOEFL 3 = 1.4858 (FCE 1) + 12.3235 ± SE)

| FCE1 | Predicted TOEFL3 | SE | FCE1 | Predicted TOEFL3 | SE |
|------|------------------|-----|------|------------------|-----|
| 0 | 20 | 0.652 | 21 | 44 | 0.631 |
| 1 | 20 | 0.650 | 22 | 45 | 0.631 |
| 2 | 20 | 0.648 | 23 | 46 | 0.631 |
| 3 | 20 | 0.646 | 24 | 48 | 0.632 |
| 4 | 20 | 0.645 | 25 | 49 | 0.632 |
| 5 | 20 | 0.643 | 26 | 51 | 0.633 |
| 6 | 21 | 0.641 | 27 | 52 | 0.633 |
| 7 | 23 | 0.640 | 28 | 54 | 0.634 |
| 8 | 24 | 0.639 | 29 | 55 | 0.635 |
| 9 | 26 | 0.637 | 30 | 57 | 0.636 |
| 10 | 27 | 0.636 | 31 | 58 | 0.637 |
| 11 | 29 | 0.635 | 32 | 60 | 0.639 |
| 12 | 30 | 0.634 | 33 | 61 | 0.640 |
| 13 | 32 | 0.633 | 34 | 63 | 0.641 |
| 14 | 33 | 0.633 | 35 | 64 | 0.643 |
| 15 | 35 | 0.632 | 36 | 66 | 0.645 |
| 16 | 36 | 0.632 | 37 | 67* | 0.646 |
| 17 | 38 | 0.631 | 38 | 67* | 0.648 |
| 18 | 39 | 0.631 | 39 | 67* | 0.650 |
| 19 | 41 | 0.631 | 40 | 67* | 0.652 |
| 20 | 42 | 0.631 | | | |

* 67 is the highest possible standard score on Section 1 of this form of the institutional TOEFL.

## Table 35

## IRT equated true-scores: TOEFL 1 and FCE 4 (Listening) Predicted FCE Scores

### (FCE 4 = .4191(TOEFL 1) -7.3265 ± SE)

| TOEFL1 | Predicted FCE4 | SE | TOEFL1 | Predicted FCE4 | SE |
|--------|--------|-------|--------|--------|-------|
| 25 | 3 | 0.323 | 47 | 12 | 0.313 |
| 26 | 4 | 0.322 | 48 | 13 | 0.313 |
| 27 | 4 | 0.321 | 49 | 13 | 0.313 |
| 28 | 4 | 0.320 | 50 | 14 | 0.313 |
| 29 | 5 | 0.320 | 51 | 14 | 0.313 |
| 30 | 5 | 0.319 | 52 | 14 | 0.314 |
| 31 | 6 | 0.318 | 53 | 15 | 0.314 |
| 32 | 6 | 0.318 | 54 | 15 | 0.314 |
| 33 | 7 | 0.317 | 55 | 16 | 0.315 |
| 34 | 7 | 0.316 | 56 | 16 | 0.315 |
| 35 | 7 | 0.316 | 57 | 17 | 0.315 |
| 36 | 8 | 0.315 | 58 | 17 | 0.316 |
| 37 | 8 | 0.315 | 59 | 17 | 0.316 |
| 38 | 9 | 0.315 | 60 | 18 | 0.317 |
| 39 | 9 | 0.314 | 61 | 18 | 0.318 |
| 40 | 9 | 0.314 | 62 | 19* | 0.318 |
| 41 | 10 | 0.314 | 63 | 19* | 0.319 |
| 42 | 10 | 0.313 | 64 | 19* | 0.320 |
| 43 | 11 | 0.313 | 65 | 19* | 0.320 |
| 44 | 11 | 0.313 | 66 | 19* | 0.321 |
| 45 | 12 | 0.313 | 67 | 19* | 0.322 |
| 46 | 12 | 0.313 | 68 | 19* | 0.323 |

* 19 was the highest possible score on Form 24 of FCE Paper 4.

Table 36

Predicted TOEFL 1 scores

(TOEFL 1 = 2.3563(FCE 4) + 17.8661 ± SE)

| FCE 4 | Predicted TOEFL 1 | SE | FCE 4 | Predicted TOEFL 1 | SE |
|-------|-------------------|-------|-------|-------------------|-------|
| 0 | 20 | 0.781 | 13 | 48 | 0.742 |
| 1 | 20 | 0.775 | 14 | 51 | 0.743 |
| 2 | 23 | 0.769 | 15 | 53 | 0.744 |
| 3 | 25 | 0.764 | 16 | 56 | 0.745 |
| 4 | 27 | 0.760 | 17 | 58 | 0.747 |
| 5 | 30 | 0.756 | 18 | 60 | 0.750 |
| 6 | 32 | 0.753 | 19 | 63 | 0.753 |
| 7 | 34 | 0.750 | 20 | 65 | 0.756 |
| 8 | 37 | 0.747 | 21 | 67 | 0.760 |
| 9 | 39 | 0.745 | 22 | 68* | 0.764 |
| 10 | 41 | 0.744 | 23 | 68* | 0.769 |
| 11 | 44 | 0.743 | 24 | 68* | 0.775 |
| 12 | 46 | 0.742 | 25 | 68* | 0.781 |

* 68 is the highest possible standard score on Section 1 of this form of the institutional TOEFL.

# Regression analyses

Three of the FCE Papers – Papers 2, 3 and 5 – and two of the ETS tests – the TEW and the SPEAK – were determined not to be appropriate for IRT modeling, so the interchangeability of scores from these tests was investigated with multiple linear regression analysis. Using regression analysis, each of the three FCE papers was regressed on the corresponding ETS test, and vice versa, yielding two sets of predictions. Table 37 contains scores for FCE Papers 3, 2 and 5, with the corresponding predicted scores for TOEFL 2, the TEW and SPEAK Comprehensibility, while Table 38 contains scores for the TEW, TOEFL 2 and SPEAK Comprehensibility and the corresponding predicted scores for FCE Papers 2, 3 and 5.

**Table 37**

**Predicted ETS scores, from FCE scaled scores**

| Regression equations | r | R² |
|---|---|---|
| ˆTOEFL 2 = 32.524 + 0.761*(FCE 3) | .629 | .395 |
| ˆTEW = 2.229 + 0.069*(FCE 2) | .470 | .221 |
| ˆSPEAK4 = 91.255 + 4.021*(FCE 5) | .572 | .327 |

| FCE3 | TOEFL2 | FCE2 | TEW | FCE5 | SPEAK4 |
|---|---|---|---|---|---|
| 1 | 33 | 1 | 2 | 1 | 95 |
| 2 | 34 | 2 | 2 | 2 | 99 |
| 3 | 35 | 3 | 2 | 3 | 103 |
| 4 | 36 | 4 | 3 | 4 | 107 |
| 5 | 36 | 5 | 3 | 5 | 111 |
| 6 | 37 | 6 | 3 | 6 | 115 |
| 7 | 38 | 7 | 3 | 7 | 119 |
| 8 | 39 | 8 | 3 | 8 | 123 |
| 9 | 39 | 9 | 3 | 9 | 127 |
| 10 | 40 | 10 | 3 | 10 | 131 |
| 11 | 41 | 11 | 3 | 11 | 135 |
| 12 | 42 | 12 | 3 | 12 | 140 |
| 13 | 42 | 13 | 3 | 13 | 144 |
| 14 | 43 | 14 | 3 | 14 | 148 |
| 15 | 44 | 15 | 3 | 15 | 152 |
| 16 | 45 | 16 | 3 | 16 | 156 |
| 17 | 45 | 17 | 3 | 17 | 160 |
| 18 | 46 | 18 | 3 | 18 | 164 |
| 19 | 47 | 19 | 4 | 19 | 168 |
| 20 | 48 | 20 | 4 | 20 | 172 |
| 21 | 49 | 21 | 4 | 21 | 176 |
| 22 | 49 | 22 | 4 | 22 | 180 |
| 23 | 50 | 23 | 4 | 23 | 184 |
| 24 | 51 | 24 | 4 | 24 | 188 |
| 25 | 52 | 25 | 4 | 25 | 192 |
| 26 | 52 | 26 | 4 | 26 | 196 |
| 27 | 53 | 27 | 4 | 27 | 200 |
| 28 | 54 | 28 | 4 | 28 | 204 |
| 29 | 55 | 29 | 4 | 29 | 208 |
| 30 | 55 | 30 | 4 | 30 | 212 |
| 31 | 56 | 31 | 4 | 31 | 216 |
| 32 | 57 | 32 | 4 | 32 | 220 |
| 33 | 58 | 33 | 5 | 33 | 224 |
| 34 | 58 | 34 | 5 | 34 | 228 |
| 35 | 59 | 35 | 5 | 35 | 232 |
| 36 | 60 | 36 | 5 | 36 | 236 |
| 37 | 61 | 37 | 5 | 37 | 240 |
| 38 | 61 | 38 | 5 | 38 | 244 |
| 39 | 62 | 39 | 5 | 39 | 248 |
| 40 | 63 | 40 | 5 | 40 | 252 |

## Table 38

## Predicted FCE scaled scores, from ETS scores

| Regression equations | | | r | R² |
|---|---|---|---|---|
| ^FCE 2 = 11.962 + 3.192*(TEW) | | | .470 | .221 |
| ^FCE 3 = -1.793 + 0.519*(TOEFL 2) | | | .629 | .395 |
| ^FCE 5 = 11.039 + 0.081*(SPEAK4) | | | .572 | .327 |

| TEW | FCE2 | TOEFL2 | FCE3 | SPEAK4 | FCE5 |
|---|---|---|---|---|---|
| 1 | 15 | 25 | 11 | 50 | 15 |
| 2 | 18 | 26 | 12 | 60 | 16 |
| 3 | 22 | 27 | 12 | 70 | 17 |
| 4 | 25 | 28 | 13 | 80 | 18 |
| 5 | 28 | 29 | 13 | 90 | 18 |
| 6 | 31 | 30 | 14 | 100 | 19 |
| | | 31 | 14 | 110 | 20 |
| | | 32 | 15 | 120 | 21 |
| | | 33 | 15 | 130 | 22 |
| | | 34 | 16 | 140 | 22 |
| | | 35 | 16 | 150 | 23 |
| | | 36 | 17 | 160 | 24 |
| | | 37 | 17 | 170 | 25 |
| | | 38 | 18 | 180 | 26 |
| | | 39 | 18 | 190 | 26 |
| | | 40 | 19 | 200 | 27 |
| | | 41 | 20 | 210 | 28 |
| | | 42 | 20 | 220 | 29 |
| | | 43 | 21 | 230 | 30 |
| | | 44 | 21 | 240 | 31 |
| | | 45 | 22 | 250 | 31 |
| | | 46 | 22 | 260 | 32 |
| | | 47 | 23 | 270 | 33 |
| | | 48 | 23 | 280 | 34 |
| | | 49 | 24 | 290 | 35 |
| | | 50 | 24 | 300 | 35 |
| | | 51 | 25 | | |
| | | 52 | 25 | | |
| | | 53 | 26 | | |
| | | 54 | 26 | | |
| | | 55 | 27 | | |
| | | 56 | 27 | | |
| | | 57 | 28 | | |
| | | 58 | 28 | | |
| | | 59 | 29 | | |
| | | 60 | 29 | | |
| | | 61 | 30 | | |
| | | 62 | 30 | | |
| | | 63 | 31 | | |
| | | 64 | 31 | | |
| | | 65 | 32 | | |
| | | 66 | 32 | | |
| | | 67 | 33 | | |
| | | 68 | 34 | | |

# Discussion

We believe that the interchangeability of test scores can be discussed meaningfully only at the level of individual pairs of similar tests, since it is at this level that interpretations of specific areas of language ability can justifiably be made. It is also at this level that the predictions are the most accurate, particularly with the pairs of tests that were equated through IRT procedures. The IRT equating procedure estimates an ability level for each test taker on the basis of the combined items from a given pair of tests and then estimates equivalent scores for the two tests based on these estimates of ability. When item and ability parameters are invariant across different groups, IRT equating yields very accurate score equivalents. The results of the regression analyses are less accurate, as can be seen from the relative sizes of the coefficients of determination ($R^2$), which range from a low of .221 for the TEW-FCE Paper 2 regression, to a high of .395 for the TOEFL Section 2-FCE Paper 3 regression. Furthermore, the accuracy of predictions based on regressions will also be affected to some degree by differences in the reliabilities of the individual tests, in a way that the IRT equating procedure is not.

We would be remiss if we did not sound two additional words of caution about these results. First, because of the low reliabilities observed for some of the tests, these exact correspondences may vary with other groups of test takers. Second, the statistical correspondences between the Cambridge and ETS tests of EFL that we have discussed in this section should not be taken as sufficient evidence that they are arbitrarily interchangeable for any or all of the uses for which they are intended. Decisions regarding which test to take, or which scores to accept, for any given test-use situation should also be based on test content considerations, which are discussed in the following section.

## Notes

1 The results discussed here are, in part, from a detailed investigation of the dimensionality of FCE Paper 1 and TOEFL Section 3 items and the relative fit of three IRT models that was conducted by Choi (1992). These results are also discussed in Choi and Bachman (1992).

2 The fact that different approaches to dimensionality assessment may yield different conclusions regarding the dimensionality of a given set of test items reflects the current uncertainty in the field with regard to how to assess dimensionality and the relative effects of violations of unidimensionality on IRT item and ability parameter estimates. This is discussed at greater length with respect to these tests in Choi (1992) and Choi and Bachman (1992).

# 7 Test content analysis

## Introduction

In order to provide as broad a basis as possible for examining the comparability of the two test batteries, an essential component of the study was the description of the comparability of their content. This type of investigation was considered essential for several reasons. First, information about test content is potentially of more use to prospective test takers than the results of the analyses of test performance, in that it can provide a description of the types of tasks and areas of content that test takers are likely to encounter on the two test batteries. Such information should also provide a useful check for test designers and developers on the extent to which their tests accurately reflect their respective sets of objectives or tables of specifications. Second, we considered information about test content to be an important complement to the analyses of test performance, in helping us to understand better the abilities measured by the two test batteries. Finally, we were interested in developing a general set of procedures for conducting the content analysis of language tests, which we believe to be an area of vital concern to both language test developers and language testing researchers. The specific objectives of the study content analysis were thus as follows:

1  to provide a description of differences and similarities in content between the Cambridge and ETS test batteries that would be useful to prospective test takers;
2  to provide a description of the Cambridge test battery that would be useful for Cambridge test designers and test writers;
3  to provide a description of the content of the two test batteries that would complement the information obtained from the analysis of test performance;
4  to develop instruments and procedures for conducting content analysis that would be useful to the field of language testing at large.

The theoretical framework that provided the basis for the study content analysis is that proposed by Bachman (1990). This includes components of communicative language ability (CLA) and test method facets (TMFs) which together constitute a taxonomic framework for describing the language abilities that are intended to be measured and the content of the tasks that are employed as elicitation procedures in language tests. The components of CLA are listed in Appendix F, while test method facets associated with test "input" that were employed in the content analysis are listed in Appendix G. This framework was implemented operationally through subjective ratings by expert judges. Operational instruments for judges to employ in subjectively rating the parts (instructions, items/ questions, passages) of the Cambridge and ETS test batteries with respect to components of CLA and TMFs were developed and refined as part of the study. Since recent research has suggested that there is little agreement among "expert" judges in their ratings of test content (e.g., Alderson 1990a; Alderson 1990b; Alderson and Lukmani 1989), we therefore also addressed the question of inter-rater consistency.

## Content ratings by expert judges

The CLA and TMF instruments were developed in several stages. The first attempt at the content analysis of the two test batteries consisted essentially of counting the occurrences of items in various categories such as the number of words per clause, number of clauses per text, numbers of content and function words, numbers of simple, compound and complex sentences, numbers of academic and non-academic items, numbers of different types of discourse connectives, and the numbers of different illocutionary acts (Bachman, Kunnan, Vanniarajan and Lynch 1988). After detailed discussion at the 1988 meeting with the Advisory Committee, it was decided to adopt a less complex approach to implementing the content analysis.

We decided to operationally define the different aspects of test content – components of CLA and the TMFs – as subjective ratings by expert judges. We thus needed to develop a means for reliably quantifying the intuitions of expert judges about the content and tasks of the two test batteries, and the abilities they measure, particularly how and to what extent the two specific batteries examined were the same or different. The mechanism for doing this was an instrument that specifies a number of measures or indicators of the various abilities and test method facets. Thus, two instruments for quantifying judgments were developed, one for components of CLA and one for TMFs.

In the next stage, the project staff and several other applied linguists were asked to assist in the refinement of the two initial instruments. Each of these individuals was assigned a specific pair of tests (one from each of the two test batteries) and asked to do the following:

1 read the tests closely, and form some initial impressions about their characteristics and how they are similar and/or different;
2 familiarize themselves with the proposed rating instruments for quantifying test method facets and language abilities;
3 go through the part of the test on which they were concentrating and attempt to apply the instruments to quantify the relevant facets and abilities;
4 make notes about how well or poorly the various indicators capture their intuitions about the characteristics of the tests, and suggest revisions of the instruments.

The primary consideration at this stage was to identify a set of measures or indicators that would be the most useful for the objectives of the content analysis, specifically, for characterizing content differences between the Cambridge and ETS tests. Following further trials of facets on the structure and reading tests, additional refinements in the instruments were made (reported in Bachman *et al.* 1989). The versions of the CLA and TMF instruments that were used in the main study were completed in mid-March of 1989, and are provided in Appendices H and I, respectively. These instruments have since been revised for use in the follow-up research and development activities that are described in Chapter 8.

## CLA rating instrument

The CLA instrument consisted entirely of rating scales, which attempted to capture both the degree to which components of CLA were involved in the successful completion of a given test task, and the approximate level of ability required. Raters were asked to rate each item or passage for each of the twelve components of CLA. The rating scale was designed so that each rating included three types of information. First, the perceived degree of involvement of the ability or abilities in a given test task was reflected by the rating categories "not involved", "somewhat involved" and "critical", with the last category meaning that the examinee could not be expected to complete the task successfully if he or she did not have that ability. Second, the level of ability required was captured in the levels "basic", "intermediate" and "advanced". Finally, information about what abilities might be involved, but not critically, in completing the task, are reflected in the scale point "somewhat involved". These three types of information were combined to form a single rating scale as follows:

| Not required | Somewhat involved | Critical basic | Critical intermediate | Critical advanced |
|---|---|---|---|---|
| 0 | 1 | 2 | 3 | 4 |

## TMF rating instrument

The TMF instrument included rating scales for the TMFs associated with test input, which Bachman defines as "the information contained in a given test task, to which the test taker is expected to respond" (1990:125), as well as counts for certain specific facets. Thus, for example, the facet "grammar" was quantified with a rating on a three-point scale ranging from 0 (very simple) to 2 (very complex), while "length" was described in terms of the total number of words. Raters were asked to rate all test items and, for appropriate facets, reading passages, using a common TMF rating checklist. For certain facets the raters were asked to give separate ratings for hypothetical "prepared" and "unprepared" test takers (e.g., for the identification of problem, specification of procedures, degree of contextualization, genre). Raters were instructed to use the scales provided to assign a number that would characterize the facet for a given item or passage, and not the effect of the facet on the difficulty of the item. Based on trialling of earlier versions of the TMF instrument, one limitation on ratings was imposed: for single-sentence items, the highest possible rating for "degree of contextualization" was "1". Furthermore, the facets for grammar, sentence type, embeddings and voice were not rated for passages, since they all would have had uniformly high values.

## Implementation of the content ratings

Three pairs of test materials were examined in the content analysis:
1  FCE Paper 1 and TOEFL Section 3 booklets;
2  FCE Paper 3 and TOEFL Section 2 booklets; and
3  FCE Paper 4, form 24, and TOEFL Section 1 booklets, tapes and transcripts of tapes.

Time did not permit the examination of other parts of either test battery. The instructions, individual items and the listening and reading passages in these tests were rated on the scales for CLA and TMFs.

Individuals with extensive training and experience in EFL teaching, and who were familiar with either or both of the two test batteries, were asked to rate different pairs of tests from the two batteries, using the CLA and TMF rating instruments. The first content ratings were done with three judges – two American and one British – independently rating the vocabulary and reading tests (FCE Paper 1 and TOEFL Section 3). Generalizability studies of these ratings indicated not only a high degree of consistency among raters, but also that two ratings were essentially as consistent as were three (Bachman *et al.* 1989). Therefore, the ratings that were done subsequently involved two judges independently rating the structure tests (FCE Paper 3 and TOEFL Section 2) and the listening comprehension tests (one form of FCE Paper 4 and TOEFL Section 1). For each pair, one judge was American and one was British, so as to avoid potential bias in the ratings. Ratings of the separate judges were edited into datasets suitable for statistical analysis by PC-SAS (SAS Institute 1985) and GENOVA (Crick and Brennan 1983).

## Rater consistency

Investigating the consistency of the content ratings is different from investigating consistency of ratings of test taker performance, in that the object of measurement is the *test item*, rather than the *test taker*. For purposes of estimating inter-rater consistency in rating test takers, we generally assume that certain characteristics of test takers, such as differences in the age, sex and language background, are not related either to differences in the abilities being measured or to differences in the ratings assigned by different raters. If such characteristics do turn out to affect ratings differentially, then this would suggest bias in the ratings. Thus, to estimate the classical true-score inter-rater reliability of a set of ratings, an intraclass correlation would typically be computed among two or more raters across a group of test takers who are assumed to vary only in their levels on the ability being measured.

If we did want to determine whether differences in factors such as age, sex and native language affect ratings, we would have to design a generalizability study ("g-study") with these factors as facets. We could then determine the relative effects of these factors on ratings by examining the relative sizes of the variance components associated with them. This is analogous to the approach taken here to investigating the consistency of content ratings. Each rater rated a given set of items on all 48 facets (thirteen CLA and 35 TMF), so the g-studies we conducted used a random i x r x f design where the test item (i) was the object of measurement and the facets were raters (r), and the CLA or TMFs (f).

Since our concern was to assess consistency across raters, we were not directly interested in the values of the generalizability coefficients, which reflect the amount of variation in items, across raters and facets. Rather, we were interested in the amount of variation in ratings that was related only to differences across raters, as estimated by the g-study variance components associated with raters. With the single exception of the CLA ratings for FCE Paper 4, the estimated variance components associated with raters for all the tests were equal to zero, indicating virtually perfect agreement among raters. The variance components associated with raters for the CLA ratings for FCE Paper 4 were very small, relative to the variance components for items and facets, also indicating a high degree of rater agreement.

## Comparisons between content ratings for the FCE and the TOEFL

In order to compare the ratings for items and passages across the two test batteries, we needed single ratings for each of the facets for each test in a given pair. For items, we averaged the ratings of the two or three raters across all the items in a given test. In the case of passages, since there were relatively small numbers of passages, we used the median facet rating for each facet across all of the passages in a given test. Thus for the FCE Paper 4 listening items, for example, we computed a mean facet rating for the CLA component, "lexicon", of 2.30, while the corresponding mean facet rating for the TOEFL listening items was 2.45 (Table 39). Similarly for the FCE Paper 4 listening passages, the median and mean facet ratings for "lexicon" were 3.00 and 3.25, respectively, while the corresponding median and mean ratings for the TOEFL listening passages were 3.50 and 3.33 respectively (Table 40). These average ratings (mean facet ratings for items, median facet ratings for passages) provide an indication of the average value of a given facet for a given test, while the amount of variation in ratings across items and passages is indicated by the standard deviations (SD) and semi-interquartile ranges (Q). The average ratings for CLAs and their associated indicators of variance for the listening (FCE Paper 4 and TOEFL Section 1), structure (FCE Paper 3 and TOEFL Section 2) and vocabulary and reading (FCE Paper 1 and TOEFL Section 3) tests are given in Tables 39–44, while those for the TMFs associated with test input are given in Tables 45–50.

We compared the mean ratings for CLA and input TMFs for FCE Papers 1, 3 and 4 and TOEFL Sections 1, 2 and 3 across all items, for individual pairs of tests, and for the vocabulary and reading subtests of FCE Paper 1 and TOEFL Section 3 separately. In addition, we compared median and mean ratings for the passages for the listening and reading tests. Although many differences between the average facet ratings for the FCE papers and TOEFL sections emerged, we needed to set a criterion for interpreting a difference as meaningful. In the case of CLA, all the ratings were done on five-point scales (zero to 4), while the TMF ratings generally consisted of three-point scales (zero to 2). Furthermore, the amount of variation in ratings differed across tests and facets, as can be seen in Tables 39 through 50, so that a mean difference of, say, 1.0, or .5, for example, could not be interpreted as equally meaningful for all facets. We therefore decided to interpret any difference between the mean ratings for the FCE and the TOEFL items on a given facet as "meaningful" if that difference was greater than the standard deviations of the ratings for that facet on either of the two tests. For the listening and reading passages, we used this criterion, along with a similar criterion based on median differences and semi-interquartile ranges: a difference between median facet ratings for FCE and TOEFL passages was considered "meaningful" if it was greater than the semi-interquartile ranges of the ratings for that facet on either of the two tests. The differences that satisfied the criteria for meaningfulness are summarized in Table 51 for the CLA ratings and in Table 52 for the TMF ratings.

## Table 39

## Comparison of mean facet ratings for CLA:
## Listening items (FCE4* and TOEFL1)

|  | FCE4* | | | TOEFL1 | | |
|---|---|---|---|---|---|---|
|  | #Items | Mean | Std dev | #Items | Mean | Std dev |
| Lexicon | 25 | 2.30 | 1.11 | 50 | 2.45 | 0.70 |
| Morphology | 25 | 0.00 | 0.00 | 50 | 0.25 | 0.56 |
| Syntax | 25 | 0.54 | 0.68 | 50 | 2.37 | 0.60 |
| Phonology/Graphology | 25 | 2.00 | 0.00 | 50 | 2.00 | 0.00 |
| Cohesion | 25 | 0.64 | 0.83 | 50 | 0.24 | 0.47 |
| Ideation | 25 | 1.02 | 1.57 | 50 | 1.43 | 0.69 |
| Manipulative | 25 | 0.32 | 0.82 | 50 | 0.21 | 0.50 |
| Heuristic | 25 | 0.96 | 1.54 | 50 | 0.06 | 0.24 |
| Imaginative | 25 | 0.12 | 0.59 | 50 | 0.06 | 0.28 |
| Dialect | 25 | 0.00 | 0.00 | 50 | 0.00 | 0.00 |
| Register | 25 | 0.78 | 1.40 | 50 | 0.31 | 0.56 |
| Strategic Competence | 25 | 1.50 | 1.62 | 50 | 1.10 | 0.33 |

* Test form 24

## Table 40

## Comparison of mean and median facet ratings for CLA:
## Listening passages (FCE4* and TOEFL1)

|  | FCE4* | | | | | TOEFL1 | | | | |
|---|---|---|---|---|---|---|---|---|---|---|
|  | #Pass | Med | Mean | Q** | Std dev | #Pass | Med | Mean | Q** | Std dev |
| Lexicon | 4 | 3.00 | 3.25 | 0.50 | 0.71 | 3 | 3.50 | 3.33 | 0.50 | 0.82 |
| Morphology | 4 | 0.50 | 0.50 | 0.50 | 0.53 | 3 | 1.00 | 1.33 | 0.50 | 0.52 |
| Syntax | 4 | 1.50 | 1.75 | 0.75 | 1.28 | 3 | 3.00 | 2.83 | 0.50 | 0.75 |
| Phonology/ Graphology | 4 | 2.00 | 2.00 | 0.00 | 0.00 | 3 | 2.00 | 2.00 | 0.00 | 0.00 |
| Cohesion | 4 | 2.00 | 2.12 | 0.25 | 1.13 | 3 | 1.50 | 1.50 | 0.50 | 0.55 |
| Ideation | 4 | 2.00 | 2.25 | 0.75 | 1.04 | 3 | 1.50 | 1.67 | 0.50 | 0.82 |
| Manipulative | 4 | 0.00 | 0.50 | 0.50 | 0.76 | 3 | 0.00 | 0.33 | 0.50 | 0.52 |
| Heuristic | 4 | 0.50 | 1.25 | 1.25 | 1.58 | 3 | 1.00 | 0.67 | 0.50 | 0.52 |
| Imaginative | 4 | 0.00 | 0.63 | 0.50 | 1.06 | 3 | 0.00 | 0.00 | 0.00 | 0.00 |
| Dialect | 4 | 0.00 | 0.50 | 0.50 | 0.76 | 3 | 0.00 | 0.00 | 0.00 | 0.00 |
| Register | 4 | 1.00 | 1.25 | 0.25 | 0.89 | 3 | 0.00 | 0.33 | 0.50 | 0.52 |
| Strategic Competence | 4 | 1.50 | 1.62 | 1.50 | 1.77 | 3 | 0.50 | 0.67 | 0.50 | 0.82 |

* Test form number 24
** Semi-interquartile range

## Table 41

### Comparison of mean facet ratings for CLA: Structure items (FCE3 and TOEFL2)

|  | FCE3 | | | TOEFL2 | | |
|---|---|---|---|---|---|---|
|  | #Items | Mean | Std dev | #Items | Mean | Std dev |
| Lexicon | 50 | 2.71 | 0.74 | 40 | 2.20 | 1.05 |
| Morphology | 50 | 0.99 | 0.97 | 40 | 1.05 | 1.21 |
| Syntax | 50 | 2.52 | 1.12 | 40 | 2.84 | 0.51 |
| Phonology/Graphology | 50 | 2.00 | 0.00 | 40 | 2.00 | 0.00 |
| Cohesion | 50 | 1.29 | 1.37 | 40 | 0.46 | 0.89 |
| Ideation | 50 | 0.06 | 0.42 | 40 | 0.50 | 0.50 |
| Manipulative | 50 | 0.00 | 0.00 | 40 | 0.00 | 0.00 |
| Heuristic | 50 | 0.00 | 0.00 | 40 | 0.00 | 0.00 |
| Imaginative | 50 | 0.00 | 0.00 | 40 | 0.00 | 0.00 |
| Dialect | 50 | 0.00 | 0.00 | 40 | 0.00 | 0.00 |
| Register | 50 | 0.02 | 0.14 | 40 | 0.00 | 0.00 |
| Strategic Competence | 50 | 2.00 | 0.00 | 40 | 1.00 | 1.01 |

## Table 42

### Comparison of mean facet ratings for CLA: Vocabulary items (FCE1 and TOEFL3)

|  | FCE1 | | | TOEFL3 | | |
|---|---|---|---|---|---|---|
|  | #Items | Mean | Std dev | #Items | Mean | Std dev |
| Lexicon | 25 | 2.25 | 0.74 | 30 | 3.24 | 0.61 |
| Morphology | 25 | 0.47 | 0.78 | 30 | 0.36 | 0.61 |
| Syntax | 25 | 1.91 | 0.84 | 30 | 1.81 | 0.98 |
| Phonology/Graphology | 25 | 2.00 | 0.00 | 30 | 2.00 | 0.00 |
| Cohesion | 25 | 0.28 | 0.61 | 30 | 0.29 | 0.59 |
| Ideation | 25 | 0.61 | 0.61 | 30 | 0.81 | 0.70 |
| Manipulative | 25 | 0.16 | 0.47 | 30 | 0.00 | 0.00 |
| Heuristic | 25 | 0.00 | 0.00 | 30 | 0.02 | 0.15 |
| Imaginative | 25 | 0.00 | 0.00 | 30 | 0.10 | 0.52 |
| Dialect | 25 | 0.04 | 0.20 | 30 | 0.00 | 0.00 |
| Register | 25 | 0.00 | 0.00 | 30 | 0.01 | 0.11 |
| Strategic Competence | 25 | 0.00 | 0.00 | 30 | 0.04 | 0.26 |

**Table 43**

**Comparison of mean facet ratings for CLA:
Reading items (FCE1 and TOEFL3)**

| | FCE1 | | | TOEFL3 | | |
|---|---|---|---|---|---|---|
| | #Items | Mean | Std dev | #Items | Mean | Std dev |
| Lexicon | 15 | 2.44 | 0.59 | 30 | 3.07 | 0.61 |
| Morphology | 15 | 0.38 | 0.61 | 30 | 0.27 | 0.56 |
| Syntax | 15 | 2.49 | 0.73 | 30 | 2.59 | 0.79 |
| Phonology/Graphology | 15 | 2.00 | 0.00 | 30 | 2.00 | 0.00 |
| Cohesion | 15 | 1.44 | 1.29 | 30 | 1.17 | 0.97 |
| Ideation | 15 | 1.13 | 0.92 | 30 | 0.96 | 0.92 |
| Manipulative | 15 | 0.18 | 0.61 | 30 | 0.00 | 0.00 |
| Heuristic | 15 | 0.02 | 0.15 | 30 | 0.18 | 0.53 |
| Imaginative | 15 | 0.00 | 0.00 | 30 | 0.27 | 0.65 |
| Dialect | 15 | 0.02 | 0.15 | 30 | 0.00 | 0.00 |
| Register | 15 | 0.02 | 0.15 | 30 | 0.03 | 0.23 |
| Strategic Competence | 15 | 0.00 | 0.00 | 30 | 0.92 | 1.18 |

**Table 44**

**Comparison of mean facet ratings for CLA:
Reading passages (FCE1 and TOEFL3)**

| | FCE1 | | | | | TOEFL3 | | | | |
|---|---|---|---|---|---|---|---|---|---|---|
| | #Pass | Med | Mean | Q | Std dev | #Pass | Med | Mean | Q | Std dev |
| Lexicon | 3 | 3.00 | 3.00 | 0.00 | 0.00 | 5 | 4.00 | 3.53 | 0.50 | 0.52 |
| Morphology | 3 | 1.00 | 0.67 | 0.50 | 0.50 | 5 | 1.00 | 1.33 | 0.50 | 0.49 |
| Syntax | 3 | 3.00 | 2.89 | 0.50 | 0.33 | 5 | 3.00 | 3.20 | 0.00 | 0.41 |
| Phonology/ Graphology | 3 | 2.00 | 2.00 | 0.00 | 0.00 | 5 | 2.00 | 2.00 | 0.00 | 0.00 |
| Cohesion | 3 | 3.00 | 2.33 | 0.50 | 1.00 | 5 | 2.00 | 2.07 | 1.00 | 0.80 |
| Ideation | 3 | 2.00 | 2.00 | 1.50 | 1.66 | 5 | 1.00 | 1.00 | 1.00 | 0.85 |
| Manipulative | 3 | 0.00 | 0.44 | 0.00 | 0.88 | 5 | 0.00 | 0.00 | 0.00 | 0.00 |
| Heuristic | 3 | 0.00 | 0.44 | 0.00 | 0.88 | 5 | 0.00 | 0.27 | 0.50 | 0.46 |
| Imaginative | 3 | 0.00 | 0.78 | 1.00 | 1.20 | 5 | 1.00 | 0.80 | 0.50 | 0.94 |
| Dialect | 3 | 0.00 | 0.00 | 0.00 | 0.00 | 5 | 0.00 | 0.00 | 0.00 | 0.00 |
| Register | 3 | 0.00 | 0.89 | 0.50 | 1.27 | 5 | 0.00 | 0.07 | 0.00 | 0.26 |
| Strategic Competence | 3 | 0.00 | 0.67 | 0.00 | 1.32 | 5 | 0.00 | 0.00 | 0.00 | 0.00 |

**Table 45**

**Comparison of mean facet ratings for TMF:**
**Listening items (FCE4* and TOEFL1)**

| | FCE4* | | | TOEFL1 | | |
|---|---|---|---|---|---|---|
| | #Items | Mean | Std dev | #Items | Mean | Std dev |
| Length: #Words | 25 | 9.42 | 9.35 | 50 | 37.62 | 12.37 |
| Vocabulary: Infrequent | 25 | 1.84 | 0.37 | 50 | 1.39 | 0.60 |
| Vocabulary: Specialized | 25 | 1.82 | 0.49 | 50 | 1.59 | 0.53 |
| Vocabulary: Ambiguous | 25 | 1.91 | 0.36 | 50 | 1.86 | 0.43 |
| Context: American | 25 | 0.34 | 0.69 | 50 | 0.15 | 0.39 |
| Context: British | 25 | 0.56 | 0.79 | 50 | 0.01 | 0.10 |
| Context: Other | 25 | 0.24 | 0.66 | 50 | 0.01 | 0.10 |
| Context: Academic | 25 | 0.24 | 0.66 | 50 | 0.37 | 0.53 |
| Context: Non-Academic | 25 | 0.40 | 0.70 | 50 | 0.00 | 0.00 |
| Relation to passage | 25 | 2.00 | 0.00 | 15** | 2.50 | 0.68 |
| Distribution of Info | 25 | 0.04 | 0.20 | 50 | 0.61 | 0.65 |
| Type Info: Abstract | 25 | 1.76 | 0.61 | 50 | 1.92 | 0.27 |
| Type Info: Negative | 25 | 1.89 | 0.38 | 50 | 1.65 | 0.59 |
| Type Info: Counterfactual | 25 | 2.00 | 0.00 | 50 | 1.75 | 0.52 |
| Topic: American | 25 | 0.38 | 0.70 | 50 | 0.19 | 0.44 |
| Topic: British | 25 | 0.60 | 0.76 | 50 | 0.04 | 0.20 |
| Topic: Academic | 25 | 0.00 | 0.00 | 50 | 0.35 | 0.50 |
| Topic: Technical | 25 | 0.30 | 0.61 | 50 | 0.13 | 0.42 |
| Genre/item type: Prep | 25 | 2.00 | 0.00 | 50 | 2.00 | 0.00 |
| Genre/item type: Unprep | 25 | 1.50 | 0.51 | 50 | 0.64 | 0.48 |
| Grammar: Rating | 25 | 0.36 | 0.48 | 50 | 0.71 | 0.62 |
| Grammar: Sentence type | 25 | 1.33 | 0.93 | 50 | 1.78 | 0.50 |
| Grammar: Embeddings | 25 | 0.31 | 0.56 | 50 | 0.52 | 0.72 |
| Grammar: Voice | 25 | 0.11 | 0.38 | 50 | 0.15 | 0.44 |
| Cohesion: Reference | 25 | 0.52 | 0.79 | 50 | 0.94 | 0.76 |
| Cohesion: Substitution | 25 | 0.00 | 0.00 | 50 | 0.16 | 0.37 |
| Cohesion: Adversatives | 25 | 0.02 | 0.15 | 50 | 0.05 | 0.22 |
| Cohesion: Causals | 25 | 0.00 | 0.00 | 50 | 0.04 | 0.20 |
| Cohesion: Temporals | 25 | 0.18 | 0.39 | 50 | 0.01 | 0.10 |
| Cohesion: Lexical | 25 | 0.00 | 0.00 | 50 | 0.97 | 0.85 |
| Illocution: Directness | 25 | 2.00 | 0.00 | 50 | 1.50 | 0.63 |
| Illocution: Number | 25 | 2.00 | 0.00 | 50 | 1.58 | 0.50 |
| Illocution: Variety | 25 | 2.00 | 0.00 | 50 | 1.78 | 0.42 |
| Sociolinguistic: Dialect | 25 | 2.00 | 0.00 | 50 | 2.00 | 0.00 |
| Sociolinguistic: Variety | 25 | 0.00 | 0.00 | 50 | 0.19 | 0.39 |
| Sociolinguistic: Register | 25 | 0.24 | 0.44 | 50 | 0.92 | 0.27 |

* Test form number 24
** Only 15 of the 50 TOEFL listening items are based on passages, so "relation to passage" was rated for only these 15.

## Table 46

## Comparison of mean facet ratings for TMFs: Listening passages (FCE4* and TOEFL1)

| | | FCE4* | | | | | TOEFL1 | | | |
|---|---|---|---|---|---|---|---|---|---|---|
| | #Pass | Med | Mean | Q | Std dev | #Pass | Med | Mean | Q | Std dev |
| Length: #Words | 4 | 422.50 | 388.30 | 66.30 | 99.91 | 3 | 129.00 | 159.50 | 47.00 | 48.81 |
| Vocabulary: Infrequent | 4 | 1.50 | 1.50 | 0.50 | 0.53 | 3 | 1.00 | 0.83 | 0.50 | 0.75 |
| Vocabulary: Specialized | 4 | 2.00 | 1.62 | 0.50 | 0.52 | 3 | 1.00 | 1.17 | 0.50 | 0.75 |
| Vocabulary: Ambiguous | 4 | 2.00 | 1.75 | 0.25 | 0.46 | 3 | 2.00 | 2.00 | 0.00 | 0.00 |
| Context: American | 4 | 1.50 | 1.25 | 0.75 | 0.89 | 3 | 1.00 | 1.33 | 0.50 | 0.52 |
| Context: British | 4 | 2.00 | 1.62 | 0.50 | 0.52 | 3 | 0.00 | 0.00 | 0.00 | 0.00 |
| Context: Other | 4 | 0.00 | 0.50 | 0.50 | 0.76 | 3 | 0.00 | 0.00 | 0.00 | 0.00 |
| Context: Academic | 4 | 0.00 | 0.63 | 0.75 | 0.92 | 3 | 1.00 | 1.17 | 0.50 | 0.75 |
| Context: Non-Academic | 4 | 0.50 | 0.75 | 0.75 | 0.89 | 3 | 0.00 | 0.00 | 0.00 | 0.00 |
| Relation to passage | | [Not relevant] | | | | | [Not relevant] | | | |
| Distribution of Info | 4 | 0.00 | 0.38 | 0.50 | 0.52 | 3 | 1.00 | 1.00 | 0.00 | 0.00 |
| Type Info: Abstract | 4 | 2.00 | 1.25 | 1.00 | 1.04 | 3 | 2.00 | 2.00 | 0.00 | 0.00 |
| Type Info: Negative | 4 | 1.00 | 1.00 | 1.00 | 1.07 | 3 | 2.00 | 2.00 | 0.00 | 0.00 |
| Info: Counterfactual | 4 | 2.00 | 1.75 | 0.00 | 0.71 | 3 | 2.00 | 2.00 | 0.00 | 0.00 |
| Topic: American | 4 | 0.50 | 0.63 | 0.50 | 0.74 | 3 | 1.50 | 1.33 | 0.50 | 0.82 |
| Topic: British | 4 | 1.00 | 1.25 | 0.50 | 0.71 | 3 | 0.00 | 0.00 | 0.00 | 0.00 |
| Topic: Academic | 4 | 0.00 | 0.00 | 0.00 | 0.00 | 3 | 1.00 | 1.00 | 0.00 | 0.63 |
| Topic: Technical | 4 | 0.50 | 0.63 | 0.50 | 0.74 | 3 | 2.00 | 2.00 | 0.00 | 0.00 |
| Genre: Prep | 4 | 2.00 | 2.00 | 0.00 | 0.00 | 3 | 2.00 | 2.00 | 0.00 | 0.00 |
| Genre: Unprep | 4 | 1.50 | 1.50 | 0.50 | 0.53 | 3 | 1.00 | 0.83 | 0.00 | 0.41 |
| Grammar: Rating | | [Not rated**] | | | | | [Not rated**] | | | |
| Grammar: Sentence type | | [Not rated**] | | | | | [Not rated**] | | | |
| Grammar: Embeddings | | [Not rated**] | | | | | [Not rated**] | | | |
| Grammar: Voice | | [Not rated**] | | | | | [Not rated**] | | | |
| Cohesion: Reference | | 2.00 | 2.00 | 0.00 | 0.00 | 3 | 2.00 | 2.00 | 0.00 | 0.00 |
| Cohesion: Substitution | | 0.00 | 0.63 | 0.75 | 0.92 | 3 | 0.00 | 0.33 | 0.50 | 0.52 |
| Cohesion: Adversatives | 4 | 1.50 | 1.12 | 1.00 | 0.99 | 3 | 1.00 | 0.83 | 0.50 | 0.75 |
| Cohesion: Causals | 4 | 1.00 | 1.00 | 1.00 | 1.07 | 3 | 0.00 | 0.67 | 1.00 | 1.03 |
| Cohesion: Temporals | 4 | 2.00 | 1.75 | 0.00 | 0.71 | 3 | 2.00 | 1.50 | 0.50 | 0.84 |
| Cohesion: Lexical | 4 | 2.00 | 1.75 | 0.00 | 0.71 | 3 | 2.00 | 2.00 | 0.00 | 0.00 |
| Illocution: Directness | 4 | 2.00 | 2.00 | 0.00 | 0.00 | 3 | 2.00 | 2.00 | 0.00 | 0.00 |
| Illocution: Number | 4 | 1.00 | 0.88 | 0.75 | 0.83 | 3 | 2.00 | 2.00 | 0.00 | 0.00 |
| Illocution: Variety | 4 | 2.00 | 1.50 | 0.50 | 0.76 | 3 | 2.00 | 2.00 | 0.00 | 0.00 |
| Sociolinguistic: Dialect | 4 | 2.00 | 2.00 | 0.00 | 0.00 | 3 | 2.00 | 2.00 | 0.00 | 0.00 |
| Sociolinguistic: Variety | 4 | 2.00 | 2.00 | 0.00 | 0.00 | 3 | 0.50 | 0.50 | 0.50 | 0.55 |
| Sociolinguistic: Register | 4 | 1.00 | 0.88 | 0.75 | 0.83 | 3 | 1.00 | 0.67 | 0.50 | 0.52 |

* Test form number 24
** The facets for grammar, sentence type, embeddings and voice were not rated for passages, since they all would have had uniformly high values.

## Table 47

### Comparison of mean facet ratings for TMF:
### Structure items(FCE3 and TOEFL2)

| | FCE3 | | | TOEFL2 | | |
|---|---|---|---|---|---|---|
| | #Items | Mean | Std dev | #Items | Mean | Std dev |
| Length: #Words* | 50 | 18.13 | 33.43 | 40 | 19.75 | 7.67 |
| Vocabulary: Infrequent | 50 | 1.96 | 0.20 | 40 | 1.12 | 0.80 |
| Vocabulary: Specialized | 50 | 1.89 | 0.35 | 40 | 1.52 | 0.73 |
| Vocabulary: Ambiguous | 50 | 1.92 | 0.27 | 40 | 1.90 | 0.34 |
| Context: American | 50 | 0.70 | 0.46 | 40 | 0.65 | 0.64 |
| Context: British | 50 | 0.78 | 0.44 | 40 | 0.51 | 0.50 |
| Context: Other | 50 | 0.70 | 0.46 | 40 | 0.53 | 0.50 |
| Context: Academic | 50 | 0.56 | 0.56 | 40 | 0.95 | 0.61 |
| Context: Non-Academic | 50 | 0.72 | 0.55 | 40 | 0.65 | 0.48 |
| Relation to passage | [Not relevant] | | | [Not relevant] | | |
| Distribution of Info | 50 | 0.52 | 0.50 | 40 | 0.50 | 0.50 |
| Type Info: Abstract | 50 | 1.87 | 0.42 | 40 | 1.40 | 0.74 |
| Type Info: Negative | 50 | 1.81 | 0.53 | 40 | 1.89 | 0.42 |
| Type Info: Counterfactual | 50 | 1.94 | 0.24 | 40 | 1.95 | 0.22 |
| Topic: American | 50 | 0.53 | 0.50 | 40 | 0.35 | 0.73 |
| Topic: British | 50 | 0.55 | 0.50 | 40 | 0.03 | 0.16 |
| Topic: Academic | 50 | 0.07 | 0.26 | 40 | 0.57 | 0.79 |
| Topic: Technical | 50 | 0.07 | 0.26 | 40 | 0.64 | 0.80 |
| Genre/item type: Prep | 50 | 2.00 | 0.00 | 40 | 2.00 | 0.00 |
| Genre/item type: Unprep | 50 | 0.85 | 0.36 | 40 | 0.69 | 0.47 |
| Grammar: Rating | 50 | 0.98 | 0.59 | 40 | 0.96 | 0.68 |
| Grammar: Sentence type | 50 | 0.65 | 0.88 | 40 | 0.82 | 0.92 |
| Grammar: Embeddings | 50 | 0.15 | 0.36 | 40 | 0.46 | 0.57 |
| Grammar: Voice | 50 | 0.18 | 0.41 | 40 | 0.34 | 0.59 |
| Cohesion: Reference | 50 | 0.59 | 0.53 | 40 | 0.21 | 0.52 |
| Cohesion: Substitution | 50 | 0.04 | 0.20 | 40 | 0.03 | 0.16 |
| Cohesion: Adversatives | 50 | 0.04 | 0.20 | 40 | 0.03 | 0.16 |
| Cohesion: Causals | 50 | 0.06 | 0.24 | 40 | 0.01 | 0.11 |
| Cohesion: Temporals | 50 | 0.03 | 0.17 | 40 | 0.05 | 0.22 |
| Cohesion: Lexical | 50 | 0.26 | 0.48 | 40 | 0.36 | 0.51 |
| Illocution: Directness | 50 | 2.00 | 0.00 | 40 | 2.00 | 0.00 |
| Illocution: Number | 50 | 2.00 | 0.00 | 40 | 2.00 | 0.00 |
| Illocution: Variety | 50 | 2.00 | 0.00 | 40 | 2.00 | 0.00 |
| Sociolinguistic: Dialect | 50 | 2.00 | 0.00 | 40 | 2.00 | 0.00 |
| Sociolinguistic: Variety | 50 | 1.00 | 1.01 | 40 | 0.50 | 0.50 |
| Sociolinguistic: Register | 50 | 0.15 | 0.36 | 40 | 0.01 | 0.11 |

* FCE3 Item word count average includes section six, producing this skewed distribution.

## Table 48

### Comparison of mean facet ratings for TMFs:
### Vocabulary items (FCE1 and TOEFL3)

| | FCE1 | | | TOEFL3 | | |
|---|---|---|---|---|---|---|
| | #Items | Mean | Std dev | #Items | Mean | Std dev |
| Length: #Words | 25 | 16.31 | 2.83 | 30 | 21.66 | 4.86 |
| Vocabulary: Infrequent | 25 | 1.93 | 0.25 | 30 | 0.81 | 0.52 |
| Vocabulary: Specialized | 25 | 2.00 | 0.00 | 30 | 1.28 | 0.76 |
| Vocabulary: Ambiguous | 25 | 1.95 | 0.28 | 30 | 2.00 | 0.00 |
| Context: American | 25 | 0.99 | 0.81 | 30 | 0.62 | 0.49 |
| Context: British | 25 | 1.00 | 0.82 | 30 | 0.46 | 0.50 |
| Context: Other | 25 | 0.95 | 0.79 | 30 | 0.40 | 0.49 |
| Context: Academic | 25 | 0.99 | 0.81 | 30 | 0.70 | 0.46 |
| Context: Non-Academic | 25 | 0.99 | 0.81 | 30 | 0.38 | 0.49 |
| Relation to passage | [Not relevant] | | | [Not relevant] | | |
| Distribution of Info | 25 | 0.36 | 0.48 | 30 | 0.33 | 0.47 |
| Type Info: Abstract | 25 | 1.84 | 0.44 | 30 | 1.08 | 0.81 |
| Type Info: Negative | 25 | 1.72 | 0.56 | 30 | 1.90 | 0.34 |
| Type Info: Counterfactual | 25 | 1.85 | 0.43 | 30 | 1.96 | 0.26 |
| Topic: American | 25 | 0.01 | 0.12 | 30 | 0.60 | 0.75 |
| Topic: British | 25 | 0.08 | 0.27 | 30 | 0.08 | 0.27 |
| Topic: Academic | 25 | 0.03 | 0.16 | 30 | 0.74 | 0.68 |
| Topic: Technical | 25 | 0.01 | 0.12 | 30 | 0.33 | 0.60 |
| Genre/item type: Prep | 25 | 1.99 | 0.12 | 30 | 2.00 | 0.00 |
| Genre/item type: Unprep | 25 | 0.96 | 0.20 | 30 | 1.54 | 0.58 |
| Grammar: Rating | 25 | 0.85 | 0.54 | 30 | 0.98 | 0.67 |
| Grammar: Sentence type | 25 | 1.36 | 0.90 | 30 | 1.51 | 0.82 |
| Grammar: Embeddings | 25 | 0.57 | 0.52 | 30 | 0.52 | 0.50 |
| Grammar: Voice | 25 | 0.17 | 0.38 | 30 | 0.28 | 0.54 |
| Cohesion: Reference | 25 | 0.65 | 0.71 | 30 | 0.57 | 0.62 |
| Cohesion: Substitution | 25 | 0.00 | 0.00 | 30 | 0.00 | 0.00 |
| Cohesion: Adversatives | 25 | 0.01 | 0.12 | 30 | 0.01 | 0.11 |
| Cohesion: Causals | 25 | 0.05 | 0.23 | 30 | 0.01 | 0.11 |
| Cohesion: Temporals | 25 | 0.04 | 0.20 | 30 | 0.01 | 0.11 |
| Cohesion: Lexical | 25 | 0.00 | 0.00 | 30 | 0.09 | 0.29 |
| Illocution: Directness | 25 | 2.00 | 0.00 | 30 | 1.93 | 0.25 |
| Illocution: Number | 25 | 1.97 | 0.16 | 30 | 2.00 | 0.00 |
| Illocution: Variety | 25 | 2.00 | 0.00 | 30 | 2.00 | 0.00 |
| Sociolinguistic: Dialect | 25 | 2.00 | 0.00 | 30 | 2.00 | 0.00 |
| Sociolinguistic: Variety | 25 | 0.69 | 0.96 | 30 | 0.44 | 0.50 |
| Sociolinguistic: Register | 25 | 0.64 | 0.48 | 30 | 0.00 | 0.00 |

**Table 49**

**Comparison of mean facet ratings for TMFs:**
**Reading items (FCE1 and TOEFL3)**

| | FCE1 | | | TOEFL3 | | |
|---|---|---|---|---|---|---|
| | #Items | Mean | Std dev | #Items | Mean | Std dev |
| Length: #Words | 15 | 37.29 | 8.92 | 30 | 29.28 | 9.68 |
| Vocabulary: Infrequent | 15 | 1.93 | 0.25 | 30 | 1.36 | 0.50 |
| Vocabulary: Specialized | 15 | 1.96 | 0.21 | 30 | 1.69 | 0.51 |
| Vocabulary: Ambiguous | 15 | 1.73 | 0.69 | 30 | 1.91 | 0.32 |
| Context: American | 15 | 1.02 | 0.72 | 30 | 1.78 | 0.44 |
| Context: British | 15 | 1.13 | 0.79 | 30 | 1.59 | 0.52 |
| Context: Other | 15 | 0.89 | 0.61 | 30 | 1.40 | 0.54 |
| Context: Academic | 15 | 0.91 | 0.63 | 30 | 1.69 | 0.49 |
| Context: Non-Academic | 15 | 0.91 | 0.63 | 30 | 1.47 | 0.62 |
| Relation to passage | 15 | 2.56 | 0.72 | 30 | 2.63 | 0.97 |
| Distribution of Info | 15 | 0.62 | 0.53 | 30 | 0.84 | 0.60 |
| Type Info: Abstract | 15 | 1.31 | 0.67 | 30 | 1.20 | 0.80 |
| Type Info: Negative | 15 | 1.62 | 0.49 | 30 | 1.93 | 0.29 |
| Type Info: Counterfactual | 15 | 1.91 | 0.29 | 30 | 1.79 | 0.53 |
| Topic: American | 15 | 0.22 | 0.64 | 30 | 0.96 | 0.87 |
| Topic: British | 15 | 0.33 | 0.67 | 30 | 0.29 | 0.60 |
| Topic: Academic | 15 | 0.00 | 0.00 | 30 | 0.47 | 0.64 |
| Topic: Technical | 15 | 0.16 | 0.37 | 30 | 0.33 | 0.52 |
| Genre/item type: Prep | 15 | 2.00 | 0.00 | 30 | 1.90 | 0.30 |
| Genre/item type: Unprep | 15 | 1.11 | 0.57 | 30 | 1.31 | 0.47 |
| Grammar: Rating | 15 | 0.73 | 0.58 | 30 | 1.00 | 0.70 |
| Grammar: Sentence type | 15 | 1.24 | 0.98 | 30 | 1.77 | 0.64 |
| Grammar: Embeddings | 15 | 0.49 | 0.51 | 30 | 0.24 | 0.48 |
| Grammar: Voice | 15 | 0.38 | 0.58 | 30 | 0.30 | 0.46 |
| Cohesion: Reference | 15 | 1.22 | 0.77 | 30 | 0.28 | 0.54 |
| Cohesion: Substitution | 15 | 0.00 | 0.00 | 30 | 0.01 | 0.11 |
| Cohesion: Adversatives | 15 | 0.01 | 0.00 | 30 | 0.00 | 0.00 |
| Cohesion: Causals | 15 | 0.02 | 0.15 | 30 | 0.01 | 0.11 |
| Cohesion: Temporals | 15 | 0.00 | 0.00 | 30 | 0.00 | 0.00 |
| Cohesion: Lexical | 15 | 0.07 | 0.25 | 30 | 0.04 | 0.21 |
| Illocution: Directness | 15 | 1.82 | 0.39 | 30 | 1.88 | 0.42 |
| Illocution: Number | 15 | 2.00 | 0.00 | 30 | 1.99 | 0.11 |
| Illocution: Variety | 15 | 2.00 | 0.00 | 30 | 2.00 | 0.00 |
| Sociolinguistic: Dialect | 15 | 2.00 | 0.00 | 30 | 2.00 | 0.00 |
| Sociolinguistic: Variety | 15 | 0.67 | 0.95 | 30 | 0.34 | 0.48 |
| Sociolinguistic: Register | 15 | 0.11 | 0.32 | 30 | 0.00 | 0.00 |

## Table 50

## Comparison of mean facet ratings for TMFs: Reading passages (FCE1 and TOEFL3)

| | | FCE1 | | | | | TOEFL3 | | | |
|---|---|---|---|---|---|---|---|---|---|---|
| | #Pass | Med | Mean | Q | Std dev | #Pass | Med | Mean | Q | Std dev |
| Length: #Words | 3 | 387.00 | 393.90 | 30.00 | 29.91 | 5 | 261.00 | 226.40 | 51.50 | 64.15 |
| Vocab: Infrequent | 3 | 2.00 | 1.67 | 0.50 | 0.50 | 5 | 1.00 | 1.00 | 0.00 | 0.38 |
| Vocab: Specialized | 3 | 2.00 | 1.67 | 0.50 | 0.50 | 5 | 1.00 | 1.47 | 0.50 | 0.52 |
| Vocab: Ambiguous | 3 | 2.00 | 2.00 | 0.00 | 0.00 | 5 | 2.00 | 1.93 | 0.00 | 0.26 |
| Context: American | 3 | 2.00 | 1.33 | 0.50 | 0.87 | 5 | 2.00 | 1.53 | 0.50 | 0.64 |
| Context: British | 3 | 2.00 | 1.44 | 0.50 | 0.73 | 5 | 1.00 | 1.20 | 1.00 | 0.86 |
| Context: Other | 3 | 1.00 | 1.11 | 0.50 | 0.93 | 5 | 1.00 | 1.00 | 1.00 | 0.85 |
| Context: Academic | 3 | 2.00 | 1.22 | 1.00 | 0.97 | 5 | 2.00 | 1.33 | 0.50 | 0.82 |
| Context: Non-Academic | 3 | 2.00 | 1.22 | 1.00 | 0.97 | 5 | 1.00 | 1.07 | 1.00 | 0.96 |
| Relation to passage | | | [Not relevant] | | | | | [Not relevant] | | |
| Distrib of Information | 3 | 1.00 | 0.67 | 0.50 | 0.71 | 5 | 1.00 | 0.67 | 0.50 | 0.62 |
| Type Info: Abstract | 3 | 1.00 | 1.44 | 0.50 | 0.53 | 5 | 1.00 | 1.33 | 0.50 | 0.62 |
| Type Info: Negative | 3 | 1.00 | 0.67 | 0.50 | 0.50 | 5 | 1.00 | 1.40 | 0.50 | 0.63 |
| Info: Counterfactual | 3 | 1.00 | 1.22 | 0.50 | 0.83 | 5 | 2.00 | 1.73 | 0.50 | 0.46 |
| Topic: American | 3 | 0.00 | 0.22 | 0.00 | 0.67 | 5 | 2.00 | 1.27 | 1.00 | 0.88 |
| Topic: British culture | 3 | 0.00 | 0.44 | 0.50 | 0.73 | 5 | 0.00 | 0.33 | 0.50 | 0.62 |
| Topic: Academic | 3 | 0.00 | 0.11 | 0.00 | 0.33 | 5 | 1.00 | 0.60 | 0.50 | 0.63 |
| Topic: Technical | 3 | 0.00 | 0.22 | 0.00 | 0.44 | 5 | 0.00 | 0.33 | 0.50 | 0.49 |
| Genre: Prepared | 3 | 2.00 | 1.89 | 0.00 | 0.33 | 5 | 2.00 | 1.80 | 0.00 | 0.41 |
| Genre: Unprepared | 3 | 2.00 | 1.44 | 0.50 | 0.73 | 5 | 1.00 | 1.13 | 0.00 | 0.52 |
| Grammar: Rating | | | [Not rated*] | | | | | [Not rated] | | |
| Grammar: Sentence type | | | [Not rated*] | | | | | [Not rated] | | |
| Grammar: Embeddings | | | [Not rated*] | | | | | [Not rated] | | |
| Grammar: Voice | | | [Not rated*] | | | | | [Not rated] | | |
| Cohesion: Reference | 3 | 2.00 | 2.00 | 0.00 | 0.00 | 5 | 2.00 | 1.87 | 0.00 | 0.35 |
| Cohesion: Substitution | 3 | 1.00 | 1.00 | 1.00 | 0.87 | 5 | 0.00 | 0.67 | 1.00 | 0.98 |
| Cohesion: Adversatives | 3 | 1.00 | 1.33 | 0.50 | 0.71 | 5 | 0.00 | 0.13 | 0.00 | 0.52 |
| Cohesion: Causals | 3 | 1.50 | 1.12 | 1.00 | 0.99 | 5 | 0.00 | 0.47 | 0.50 | 0.64 |
| Cohesion: Temporals | 3 | 1.00 | 1.00 | 1.00 | 0.87 | 5 | 0.00 | 0.40 | 0.00 | 0.83 |
| Cohesion: Lexical | 3 | 2.00 | 2.00 | 0.00 | 0.00 | 5 | 2.00 | 1.93 | 0.00 | 0.26 |
| Illocution: Directness | 3 | 2.00 | 1.44 | 0.50 | 0.73 | 5 | 2.00 | 1.93 | 0.00 | 0.26 |
| Illocution: Number | 3 | 2.00 | 1.67 | 0.50 | 0.50 | 5 | 2.00 | 1.93 | 0.00 | 0.26 |
| Illocution: Variety | 3 | 2.00 | 1.67 | 0.00 | 0.71 | 5 | 2.00 | 2.00 | 0.00 | 0.00 |
| Sociolinguistic: Dialect | 3 | 2.00 | 2.00 | 0.00 | 0.00 | 5 | 2.00 | 2.00 | 0.00 | 0.00 |
| Sociolinguistic: Variety | 3 | 0.00 | 0.67 | 1.00 | 1.00 | 5 | 0.00 | 0.47 | 0.50 | 0.52 |
| Sociolinguistic: Register | 3 | 0.00 | 0.67 | 0.50 | 0.87 | 5 | 0.00 | 0.07 | 0.00 | 0.26 |

* The facets for grammar, sentence type, embeddings and voice were not rated for passages, since they all would have had uniformly high values.

## Table 51

## Meaningful differences in CLA ratings

| Subtests | Facet | Difference magnitude* | Difference direction |
|---|---|---|---|
| Listening items | Syntax | 1.83 | TOEFL > FCE |
| Listening passages | Morphology | –/0.83 | TOEFL > FCE |
| | Syntax | 1.50/1.08 | TOEFL > FCE |
| | Register | 1.00/0.92 | FCE > TOEFL |
| Structure items | Strategic competence | 1.00 | FCE > TOEFL |
| Vocabulary items | Lexicon | 0.99 | TOEFL > FCE |
| Reading items | Lexicon | 0.63 | TOEFL > FCE |
| Reading passages | Lexicon | 1.00/0.53 | TOEFL > FCE |

* For passages, differences for both median and mean (median/mean) are given. The symbol – indicates that one of these differences (median or mean) was not meaningful.

## Table 52

## Meaningful differences in TMF ratings

| Subtests | Facet | Difference magnitude* | Difference direction |
|---|---|---|---|
| Listening items | Length: #Words | 28.20 | TOEFL > FCE |
| | Genre: Unprepared | 0.86 | FCE > TOEFL (+ familiar) |
| | Cohesion: Lexical | 0.97 | TOEFL > FCE |
| | Socioling: Register | 0.72 | TOEFL > FCE (+ casual) |
| Listening passages | Length: #Words | 293.50/228.80 | FCE > TOEFL |
| | Vocabulary: Specialized | 1.00/– | FCE > TOEFL (+ general) |
| | Context: British | 2.00/1.62 | FCE > TOEFL |
| | Context: Academic | 1.00/– | TOEFL > FCE (+ acad.) |
| | Distribution of Info | 1.00/0.62 | TOEFL > FCE (+ diffuse) |
| | Topic: American | 1.00/– | TOEFL > FCE |
| | Topic: British | 1.00/1.25 | FCE > TOEFL |
| | Topic: Academic | 1.00/1.00 | TOEFL > FCE |
| | Topic: Technical | 1.50/1.37 | TOEFL > FCE |
| | Genre: Unprepared | –/0.67 | FCE > TOEFL (+ familiar) |
| | Illocution: Number | 1.00/1.12 | TOEFL > FCE |
| | Variety of English | 1.50/1.50 | FCE > TOEFL (+ British) |
| Structure items | Vocabulary: Infrequent | 0.84 | FCE > TOEFL (+ frequent) |
| | Topic: British | 0.52 | FCE > TOEFL |
| Vocabulary items | Length: #Words | 5.35 | TOEFL > FCE |
| | Vocabulary: Infrequent | 1.12 | FCE > TOEFL (+ frequent) |
| | Vocabulary: Specialized | 0.73** | FCE > TOEFL (+ general) |
| | Type of information: Abstract | 0.76** | FCE > TOEFL (+ concrete) |
| | Topic: Academic | 0.71 | TOEFL > FCE |
| | Genre: Unprepared | 0.58** | TOEFL > FCE (+ familiar) |
| | Socioling: Register | 0.64 | FCE > TOEFL (+ casual) |
| Reading items | Vocabulary: Infrequent | 0.57 | FCE > TOEFL (+ frequent) |
| | Context: American | 0.76 | TOEFL > FCE |
| | Context: Academic | 0.78 | TOEFL > FCE |
| | Cohesion: Reference | 0.94 | FCE > TOEFL |
| Reading passages | Length: #Words | 126.00/167.50 | FCE > TOEFL |
| | Vocabulary: Infrequent | 1.00/0.67 | FCE > TOEFL (+ frequent) |
| | Vocabulary: Specialized | 1.00/– | FCE > TOEFL (+ general) |
| | Context: British | 1.00.00–** | FCE > TOEFL |
| | Type of Info: Negative | –/0.73 | TOEFL > FCE |
| | Type of Info: Counterfact | 1.00/– | TOEFL > FCE (+ factual) |
| | Topic: American | 2.00/1.05 | TOEFL > FCE |
| | Topic: Academic | 1.00/– | TOEFL > FCE |
| | Genre: Unprepared | 1.00/– | FCE > TOEFL (+ familiar) |
| | Cohesion: Adversatives | 1.00/1.20 | FCE > TOEFL |

* For passages, differences for both median and mean (median/mean) are given.
The symbol – indicates that one of these differences (median or mean) was not meaningful.
** Slightly below the criterion for meaningful difference.

## Listening tests

Applying the criterion for meaningful differences to the average CLA ratings for the listening tests revealed that there were relatively more similarities than perceived differences. Raters perceived several components of CLA (competence in morphology, cohesion, sensitivity to differences in dialect and register), as well as competence in manipulative, heuristic and imaginative functions, as generally not required for successful completion of the items in either of the two listening tests, while ideational functions and strategic competence were perceived as being somewhat involved. Raters perceived knowledge of lexicon as being critical at the basic to intermediate level for both tests. Since phonology/graphology ratings were fixed at "2" for these tests, no differences were observed on this facet.

Looking at the CLA ratings for the listening passages (Table 40), we can see that raters perceived that the level of lexical competence required for the passages was at a higher level (3.00 and 3.50) than that required for the items. As with the listening items, knowledge of morphology, dialect and the manipulative, heuristic and imaginative functions were judged not to be involved, while knowledge of cohesion and ideational functions were perceived as somewhat involved for the TOEFL and critical at a basic level for the FCE.

Examination of the CLA average ratings also reveals that there were sizeable differences in the judged importance of syntax for both items and passages, with syntax being perceived as more critical for the TOEFL listening subtest than for the FCE Paper 4 (Tables 39–40 and 51). The mean syntax rating for FCE4 items (.54) indicates that the raters perceived syntax as generally somewhat involved, but not critical to answering these items successfully, while the mean rating of 2.37 for TOEFL1 items indicates that syntax was perceived as critical, and at a level between "basic" and "intermediate". The median syntax rating for TOEFL1 passages (3.00) indicates that raters felt these required syntactic competence to a greater degree than did FCE listening passages (median = 1.50). Furthermore, raters perceived the FCE listening passages as requiring a higher level of syntactic competence than FCE items. This was also true, to a lesser degree, of the TOEFL listening passages. Two other meaningful differences for the listening passages were observed. The TOEFL listening passages were perceived as requiring a higher level of morphological competence (mean = 1.33) than the FCE listening passages (mean = .50), while the FCE passages were perceived as requiring a higher level of sensitivity to register than the TOEFL listening passages.

Examining the TMF ratings for the FCE and TOEFL listening tests (Tables 45–46 and 52) revealed that the listening items of the two tests were perceived as very similar, while a larger number of differences were perceived between the FCE and TOEFL listening passages. The two listening tests differed considerably in length. The average FCE listening passage is over twice as long as the average TOEFL passage; the TOEFL items, on the other hand, are about four times as long, on average, as the FCE items.

Both tests were perceived as including item types and passage genres that would be to some extent unfamiliar to "unprepared" test takers, but very familiar to "prepared" test takers. However, the TOEFL listening test was perceived as including item types and passage genres with which "unprepared" test takers would be less familiar than those included in the FCE listening test.

TOEFL listening test items were perceived as having a greater amount of lexical cohesion than those in the FCE listening test (ratings of .97 versus 0.00), while the FCE items were perceived as closer to "formal" register (rating of .24) and the TOEFL items as closer to "casual" register (.92).

In addition, the relationship of the items to the passage was judged to be different, with the TOEFL's higher mean rating (2.5) indicating that it has more items that relate to several specific parts of the passage, or to the entire passage, or that require the test taker to relate information in the passage to the real world, than does the FCE (rating of 2.0). Although this difference did not quite meet the criterion for meaningfulness, the standard deviation for the FCE (0.00) indicates that the items were perceived as consistently asking for specific information related to a single part of the passage.

A number of meaningful differences were found in the ratings of listening passages. Thus, FCE listening passages were judged to include more specific British cultural content, to use British English, and to be more highly contextualized for test takers familiar with British culture, while the TOEFL passages were perceived as including more specific American cultural content. In addition, TOEFL listening passages were perceived as including more specialized vocabulary, more academic and technical content and as being more highly contextualized for test takers who are academically oriented than did the FCE listening passages. These differences are not surprising in that they probably reflect differences in the design specifications for the two tests. That is, FCE listening passages are probably written or selected to reflect, to a large extent, British culture, and the TOEFL passages to reflect American culture. Furthermore, the TOEFL is specifically designed to provide information that will be useful to academic institutions in the US for making admissions decisions, while the FCE is intended to provide a certification of EFL proficiency of a more general nature.

Two differences in passage ratings that are less obviously explicable were in the distribution of information and number of illocutionary acts. TOEFL listening passages were perceived as being neither diffuse nor compact, while the FCE was perceived as being relatively compact. Bachman defines distribution of information as a continuum ranging from highly compact discourse, in which "new information is distributed over a relatively short space of time", to highly diffuse discourse, in which "new information is distributed over a relatively long space of time" (1990:134). He hypothesizes that information that is either highly compact or highly diffuse will be relatively more difficult to process than that which is neither compact nor diffuse. The relationship between distribution of information in test passages and the level of difficulty of items based on those passages is an area of research that is being pursued in CTCS follow-up studies (e.g., Bachman *et al*. 1991). Another meaningful difference was in the number of illocutionary acts, with the FCE listening passages being perceived as including a relatively large number of illocutionary acts and the TOEFL listening passages a very small number. This finding is consistent with that of Bachman, Kunnan, Vanniarajan and Lynch (1988), who found that CPE reading passages contained a greater variety of illocutionary acts than did the TOEFL reading section.

## Structure tests

As with the listening tests, there were generally more similarities than differences between the FCE and TOEFL structure tests. Looking at the CLA ratings (Table 41), we can see that lexicon and morphology were perceived as critically involved in successful completion of the structure items for both tests, with most other components of CLA being judged as somewhat or not involved. The only meaningful difference was in strategic competence, which was perceived as somewhat involved in the successful completion of the TOEFL items, and as critical at a basic level for the FCE structure items. This may suggest that "test-wiseness" is perceived as more important for these FCE items than it is for the TOEFL items.

The TMF ratings (Table 47) also indicate more similarity than difference between the two structure tests. The vocabulary of both was perceived as relatively general and unambiguous, while the content was judged to be relatively neutral with respect to cultural and academic contextualization (although the TOEFL items were perceived as somewhat more academically oriented), being neither highly compact nor highly diffuse, fairly concrete, positive and factual. Topics were not perceived as specifically American, British, academic or technical. The item types were perceived as very familiar for prepared test takers and somewhat unfamiliar for unprepared test takers. The grammar was perceived as relatively non-complex, with some complex and compound sentences and few embeddings or passives. There was a fair amount of reference and lexical cohesion, but very few instances of cohesive substitution, adversatives, causals and temporals. The raters perceived very few illocutionary acts and little variety in the acts performed in the structure items of both tests, while the illocutionary acts that were performed were expressed in a highly direct way.

There were only two meaningful differences in the TMF ratings of structure items, and these were minimal. The FCE structure items were judged to have slightly more frequent vocabulary and to include topics that were more specific to British culture than do the TOEFL items.

## Vocabulary subtests

Of the components of CLA (Table 42) only one – lexicon – was judged to be critical, and only one – syntax – was judged to be somewhat involved in the successful completion of vocabulary items for the two tests. All other components of CLA were judged to be generally not involved. Looking at Table 51, we can see that the only meaningful difference was in lexical competence, which was judged as being critical at an intermediate level for the TOEFL vocabulary items, while this component was judged as critical at the basic level for the FCE items.

Looking at the TMF ratings of the vocabulary items (Table 48) reveals a profile that is very similar to that for the structure items, with a few notable exceptions. The FCE vocabulary items were perceived as slightly more contextualized with respect to British, American and other cultures, as well as for both academics and non-academics, than either the FCE and TOEFL structure items or the TOEFL vocabulary items. In contrast, the FCE vocabulary items were perceived as less specific to British and American topics than were the FCE structure items. TOEFL vocabulary items, on the other hand, were perceived as slightly more American and academic than the TOEFL structure items. Another contrast between structure and vocabulary items was in sentence types; both the FCE and TOEFL structure items were perceived as including higher proportions of compound and complex sentences than their vocabulary items. Finally, FCE vocabulary items were perceived as less formal in register than the FCE structure items.

A number of meaningful differences between TMF ratings for the FCE and TOEFL vocabulary subtests emerged (Tables 48 and 52). TOEFL vocabulary items were about five words longer, on average, than FCE vocabulary items. The vocabulary used in the TOEFL items was judged to be considerably less frequent and slightly more specialized, while the information in the TOEFL items was judged to be slightly more abstract and the topics more academic than in the FCE vocabulary items. Another meaningful difference was in genre or item type, with the TOEFL item types judged to be more familiar to unprepared test takers than those from the FCE vocabulary subtest. A final meaningful difference was in register, with the FCE vocabulary items judged to be less formal than the TOEFL vocabulary items.

## Reading subtests

The CLA ratings for the items in the reading subtests reveal a now familiar pattern: knowledge of lexicon and syntax were considered critical at a basic to intermediate level, cohesion and ideational functions somewhat involved and all the other components perceived as not required (Table 43). For the reading passages this pattern was generally repeated, with knowledge of syntax and cohesion perceived as being critical but at slightly higher levels than was the case for the reading items (Table 44). Only two meaningful differences were observed in the CLA ratings (Table 51). TOEFL reading items and passages were judged to require a higher level of lexical knowledge than was required for the FCE.

The TMF ratings for the reading subtest items (Table 49) reveal profiles that are quite similar to those of the other subtests, with some noteworthy differences. The FCE reading items, for example, were perceived as more highly contextualized for test takers familiar with British culture than were items from any of the other FCE tests. Similarly, the TOEFL reading items were rated the most highly of all the TOEFL test items in terms of contextualization and topics related to American culture. These characteristics undoubtedly reflect similar ratings for the FCE and TOEFL reading passages, which are discussed below.

The TMF ratings for the reading subtest items also indicated several meaning-ful differences (Tables 49 and 52). As with the structure and vocabulary items, the TOEFL reading items were perceived as containing lower frequency vocabu-lary than the FCE reading items. The TOEFL reading items were also perceived as being more contextualized for those familiar with American culture and academic topics. The FCE reading items, on the other hand, were perceived as including more cohesive reference than do the TOEFL reading items.

Looking at the TMF ratings for the reading passages again reveals more similarities than differences, overall, between the FCE and TOEFL. At the same time, there were a number of meaningful differences. First, the FCE reading passages were considerably longer on average (median difference of 126 words) than the TOEFL passages. The vocabulary in the FCE reading passages was perceived as both more frequent and more general than that in the TOEFL passages. Interestingly, both the FCE and TOEFL reading passages were perceived as highly contextualized for test takers familiar with American culture and for academics, while the FCE passages were judged to be slightly more contextualized for those familiar with British culture. Meaningful differences were also perceived in the type of information in the passages, with the FCE passages judged to contain more negative and counterfactual information and more cohesive adversatives than the TOEFL passages. Differences were also perceived in topic, with the TOEFL passages judged to contain topics with more American cultural and academic content. With respect to genre, the FCE passages were judged to be more familiar for unprepared test takers than were the TOEFL passages.[1]

A number of differences in TMF ratings between the listening and reading passages of the two tests were observed (Tables 46 and 50). The TOEFL listening passages were considerably shorter than the FCE listening passages, which is the same as was observed for the reading passages. The ratings for degree of contextualization facets (Context: American, British, Other, Academic, Non-Academic) were generally higher for the reading passages than for the listening passages on both tests, suggesting that raters perceived the reading passages as generally more highly contextualized than the listening passages. The FCE listening passages were perceived as more highly compact than the FCE reading passages, while there was little difference between the TOEFL listening and reading passages on this facet. For both tests, the reading passages were perceived as more abstract than the listening passages. The TOEFL reading passages were judged to contain more negative information than the listening passages, while the FCE passages did not differ in this regard. The FCE passages were judged to contain more counterfactual information than the listening passages, while the TOEFL listening and reading passages did not differ on this facet. The FCE listening passages were judged to contain more British content than the FCE reading passages, while the TOEFL reading passages were judged to contain more technical content than the TOEFL listening passages. The TOEFL reading passages were perceived to contain more cohesive adversatives and temporals than its listening passages. The FCE listening passages were rated as using British English, while the reading passages were perceived as neutral with respect to variety of English, as were the TOEFL listening and reading passages. Finally, for both the FCE and the TOEFL, the register of the listening passages was perceived as less formal than that of their respective reading passages.

## Discussion

One finding of the content analysis is that it is possible to obtain subjective ratings of test content that are highly consistent across different raters. We would attribute this to two factors. One factor was the rating instrument itself, which forced raters to focus almost microscopically on very specific aspects of content, rather than on general categories, and provided a fixed range of judgments, as indicated in the rating scales for the various facets. While such constraints have contributed to the high degree of consistency in our ratings, we are fully aware of the potential problem that such a narrowing of focus may pose in terms of the validity of the ratings, or their sensitivity to the full range of content characteristics of a given test task. This is clearly an important question, and one that we intend to pursue in our continued research into content analysis.

The second factor in achieving high consistency of ratings has to do with the training of raters. As indicated above, the content analysis procedures evolved over a period of two years, and several of the raters were involved in this evolution from the very beginning. The analysis procedures and the rating instruments were developed through a cyclical process of trial, intense discussion of ratings among the raters, revision of the procedures and the instrument, and retrialling. This procedure might be criticized as either unrepresentative or unfeasible, but we would argue that it is exactly this sort of development and training that should go into the analysis of test content during the test development process itself, so that individuals responsible for the design, writing and moderation of the test are concurrently analyzing its content. At the same time, we believe it is essential that continued research be conducted to investigate ways of making the rating instruments more usable by other language testers.

The meaningful differences in facet ratings indicate that the TOEFL was generally perceived as having less frequent and more specialized vocabulary than the FCE, with a tendency toward more American cultural, academic and technical content. The FCE, on the other hand, was perceived as generally including more cohesive devices of the six types rated, with a tendency toward more British cultural topics and contextualization. There were also some interesting differences in perceived register. While the TOEFL structure, vocabulary and reading tests were perceived as more formal than their FCE counterparts, the reverse was the case with the listening test items, in which the TOEFL was perceived as more casual than the FCE. Looking at these ratings another way, we can see that the register ratings for the TOEFL structure, vocabulary and reading tests were all near zero, which is the rating for "formal" register, while the rating for the listening test items was .92, which is very close to the rating for "casual" register. Looking further at the listening tests, we can see that while the TOEFL listening items and passages were both perceived as essentially in a casual register, there was a difference between the FCE listening passages and items, with the former perceived as in a casual register and the latter nearer to a formal register. A similar but less marked difference can be seen in the FCE reading test as well, with the reading items perceived as more formal than the passages. The TOEFL reading passages and items, on the other hand, were perceived as nearly uniformly in a formal register.

Meaningful differences between the two tests were also found in the degree to which the item types or genres of passages were judged to be familiar to unprepared test takers. FCE listening items and passages and reading passages were rated as being more familiar for unprepared test takers than the corresponding TOEFL parts. The TOEFL vocabulary items, on the other hand, were judged to be more familiar for unprepared test takers than the FCE items.

In general, however, there were considerably higher proportions of similarities than differences between pairs of tests, particularly for the CLA ratings. Only 12% of the differences in CLA ratings across the six forms (eight out of 66 possible differences) were considered meaningful. For the TMF ratings, 19% (39 out of a possible 204 differences on the ten facets for each of the six forms) were considered meaningful. The only CLA component that was consistently rated as critical for successfully completing test tasks across all tests was lexicon. Knowledge of syntax was judged to be critically involved for all of the TOEFL subtests and for all of the FCE papers except listening. Knowledge of cohesion was perceived as critical only for the FCE listening and reading passages, while of the four areas of functional competence that were rated, only the ideational was judged to be critical, and that only for the FCE listening and reading passages. All the other components of CLA were judged to be not required, or occasionally somewhat involved, in the successful completion of test tasks.

These CLA ratings give the general impression that a fairly narrow range of language abilities, primarily lexical and syntactic, are measured by these two test batteries, with knowledge of cohesion and ideational functions measured to some extent by the FCE listening and reading tests. On the other hand, much greater variation in test method was observed across the two test batteries. Of the 36 TMFs that were rated, twenty, or 55%, yielded a meaningful difference for at least one pair of subtests.

The similarities and differences in perceptions of the abilities measured and the test methods used in these two test batteries that our ratings have revealed are intended to be descriptive, and should not be interpreted as in any way evaluative of the two test batteries. At the same time, we feel that it is useful to speculate about their causes. One possible explanation for the similarities is related to the sensitivity of the rating procedure itself to the different components of CLA and test method facets that were rated. There were a number of ratings that had zero variances, indicating that the ratings did not vary across either items or raters. For example, CLA ratings for illocutionary competence – manipulative, heuristic, imaginative – had zero variances for structure items (Table 41), while several TMF ratings for cohesion – substitution and lexical cohesion – had zero variances for listening items (Table 45). It is possible that raters simply did not have a clear idea of what was meant by some of the facets, while for some facets there was a clear ceiling effect.

A much more likely explanation, we believe, is to be found in the relatively restricted range of item types included in these tests, which may be a reflection of the test specifications of the two test batteries. Thus, the fact that both test batteries appear largely to measure knowledge associated with organizational competence – lexicon, syntax and cohesion – may reflect an essentially structure-based approach to EFL test design. The perceived differences in test method, on the other hand, probably reflect fundamental differences between Cambridge and ETS in both the specifications for their EFL tests, and in their test production strategies. It would thus appear, looking back to our introductory discussion of the Cambridge and ETS traditions in EFL testing, that the two test batteries incorporate very similar views of language ability, namely that this consists largely of lexical and syntactic knowledge. The major differences, on the other hand, appear to be in the characteristics of the test methods used. Thus, while we believe that this content analysis has revealed useful information about areas of similarity and difference between the FCE and the TOEFL, continued research into the instrument and rating procedure must include the analysis of a wider variety of tests and item types. A particularly fruitful area, we believe, would be to utilize these ratings in conjunction with an analysis of the written discourse in the FCE Paper 2 and TEW compositions and the oral discourse in the FCE Paper 5 interview and the SPEAK.

## Note

1 One major difference between the FCE and TOEFL reading passages that has been pointed out by Professor Gillian Brown (personal communications) is

that they use quite different genres. The FCE reading passages tend to be literary, and often contain bits of conversation, which are likely to express cultural values and to contain a variety of illocutionary acts. TOEFL reading passages, on the other hand, tend to be encyclopedia-like, where the primary illocutionary force is ideational, expressing factual information. Such passages may nevertheless include presuppositions and values that are more characteristic of North American than British culture. The fact that the raters perceived the TOEFL reading passages as more contextualized for test takers familiar with American culture and FCE passages as more contextualized for test takers familiar with British culture suggests that the facets included in the TMF instrument are sensitive to and able to capture such "global" differences as that in genre as perceived by applied linguists.

# 8 Implications and recommendations

The results of the study should be of interest to test users – individuals who take these tests and those who use the results of them in reaching decisions about admission to academic programs, employment, career advancement and so forth. The "study experience" is also relevant to the practical and theoretical interests of language test developers and language testing researchers in that it has addressed both the methodological problems involved in comparing different types of language test and the theoretical issues of investigating the constructs that such tests measure. In addition, the materials, data and instruments generated by the study constitute a valuable resource for future research in language testing and other areas of applied linguistics. Finally, the information gathered as part of the study provided the basis for specific recommendations regarding continuing research and development in the areas of test design, test administration and scoring procedures for Cambridge EFL examinations.

## Implications for test users

Prospective test takers currently have little information about the nature of the test tasks and test content in the FCE, TOEFL, TSE and TWE other than that published by Cambridge and ETS, to inform their decision whether to take one of these tests at all, or which one to take. This is not to imply that test takers decide which test to take solely on the basis of test content. The decision is made, in large part, on the basis of the test taker's educational or career goals. Nevertheless, we believe that it is in the best interests of test takers if their decisions are informed by as complete an understanding as possible of the differences and similarities in content, format and procedures of the two test batteries. While the published information that is available from the two test developers is reasonably complete with respect to their own tests, neither, as might be expected, provides any information about the other. Similarly, admissions officers, prospective employers and other individuals who rely on information from the two tests currently have an inadequate basis for making comparative evaluations of scores from the two tests. That is, even though each test has its own published norms, with associated interpretations, there is no basis for evaluating the extent to which the interpretations associated with these different norms are comparable.

This study makes available detailed comparisons of the two test batteries in terms of their content, item and question formats, and hence will hopefully provide a stimulus for bridging this information gap. Such information should be particularly useful to prospective test takers in reaching a decision about which test battery to take, in situations in which they have a choice. Comparative information about test content will also be useful to individuals who use scores from either test battery as part of the decision-making process, be it for college admission, employment or career advancement.

# Implications for the field of language testing

One of the most pressing issues in the field of foreign language testing at present is that of defining the construct "communicative competence" precisely enough to permit its assessment. This issue is of crucial importance for the development and use of language tests, since considerable effort is currently being expended in developing measures of "communicative competence" or "communicative language ability", which attempt to operationalize the broadened view of language and language use that has characterized recent thinking in linguistics and applied linguistics (e.g., Hymes 1972; Hymes 1982; Widdowson 1978; Munby 1978; Canale and Swain 1980a; Savignon 1983; Bachman 1990). An equally pressing issue is that of the effect of test method on test performance. This issue is of importance because much of the current research and development effort in language testing is informed by a concern that test tasks be "authentic", or related to non-test language use, and thus incorporate a wide variety of "performance" test tasks that are generally more complex and whose effects on test scores are less well understood than those of more traditional testing methods.

Current test development efforts in language testing include not only studies conducted by numerous individuals, but programs of research and development conducted by organizations and institutions. These latter include the Communicative Use of English as a Foreign Language (Royal Society of Arts Examination Board 1985; Morrow 1977), the Test of English for Educational Purposes (Associated Examining Board 1987; Weir 1988), the International English Language Testing System[1] (Seaton 1983; Criper and Davies 1988; Alderson 1988; Alderson 1993; Ingram and Wylie 1993; Clapham 1993) and the tests developed by the Assessment of Performance Unit at the National Foundation for Educational Research (Dickson *et al.* 1985; Dickson *et al.* 1986; Portal 1986; Gorman and Brooks 1986) in England, the Ontario Assessment Instrument Pool (Ontario Ministry of Education 1980; Canale and Swain 1980b), the Ontario Test of English as a Second Language (Wesche *et al.* 1986; Wesche 1987), and the tests developed for the Development of Bilingual Proficiency Project (Allen *et al.* 1983; Swain 1985; Harley *et al.* 1987) in Canada, to mention some of the largest of these institutional research and development programs.

These efforts have shared the same general goal of expanding both the range of foreign language abilities measured and the types of test tasks included, and have yielded useful measures for various needs and purposes. Nevertheless, while the result of this research and development has been an enriched pool of measures, the potential for genuine progress in the understanding of foreign language abilities has been limited by the diversity of approaches and theoretical frameworks that have been employed. Progress has also been limited by the disparity of data structure types utilized in different studies, which makes it difficult for data from different studies to be shared and analyzed.

Theoretical research into the assessment of communicative competence has been less extensive than the applied research and development mentioned above, but it has been no less influential in shaping and extending our conceptualization of communicative language abilities. This research includes the construct validation studies designed and carried out as a result of the first two international Language Testing Research Colloquia (Bachman and Palmer 1981; Bachman and Palmer 1982a), the validation research that was part of the Development of Bilingual Proficiency Project at the Ontario Institute for Studies in Education (Allen *et al.* 1982; Allen *et al.* 1983), and that conducted at the Max Planck Institute for Human Development and Education in Berlin (Sang *et al.* 1986). These studies have refined our framework of communicative competence and demonstrate the value of empirical research directed toward theory-building and explanation as a basis for language test development. At the same time, they demonstrate the inadequacy of the constructs they examined, and the need for a theory-based program of research and development in language testing.

In a recent position paper prepared as part of a national agenda for foreign language instruction in the United States, Bachman and Clark (1987) review the "state of the art" in language testing, identify areas of need, and outline a program of research and development for addressing these needs. This call for a unified agenda of research and development in language testing has been echoed by Clark and Lett (1988), and extended to include research in second language acquisition by Clark and O'Mara (1991). Bachman and Clark's research and development agenda includes

1  beginning with a single theoretical model of factors that affect performance on language tests – components of communicative language ability and aspects of test method – and refining that model;
2  developing operational definitions of components in that model, either from existing tests, or with new tests; and
3  embarking on a unified program of validation research that would include a variety of empirical methodologies, ranging from the qualitative analyses of test content and test taking processes, such as that employed by Cohen (1984) and Canale (1988), to the more commonly used quantitative approaches, such as experimental designs or the *ex post facto* analysis of covariance structures.

The research that has been conducted in the study represents an initial step in implementing Bachman and Clark's research and development agenda. The content analysis instruments developed as part of the study are based on a model of communicative language ability and test method facets, and provide a starting point for accurately describing the content of language tests and for investigating the relationship between test content and test performance. These instruments have already been used to characterize a variety of measures, ranging from "discrete-point" multiple-choice and completion items, to more "integrative" measures such as gap-filling passages. Research at Cambridge is extending to the use of these instruments in the content analysis of composition prompts and oral interviews.

Furthermore, while the focus of the study was not on construct validation, much of the information that was gathered about the measures examined is relevant to the validity of construct interpretations. In this regard, the finding that measures as diverse as those examined in the study tap virtually the same sets of language abilities may be surprising to the test developers. For language testing researchers, however, this provides yet another piece of evidence in support of both a multicomponential view of language proficiency and the influence of test method on test performance. The finding that a common higher-order factor underlies the primary ability factors is consistent with earlier work in that it reveals a picture of EFL proficiency that consists of multiple primary abilities that are related to each other. The finding that two of the primary factors are associated with specific test methods is also consistent with other research that has demonstrated the effects of testing method on test performance. With respect to the specific tests examined, it is encouraging to find that the theoretical constructs that "appear" to inform the measures (reading/writing, speaking, listening) are reflected in patterns of performance, and that the analytical procedures employed in the study were useful in making these patterns interpretable.

The study employed a variety of empirical approaches to research, both qualitatively for continued multi-modal research as proposed by Bachman and Clark, but also for future test comparison studies. Furthermore, the data preparation required by the study has increased our understanding of the complexities of multiple datasets and how these need to be structured so as to permit common analyses. As was discussed in Chapter 2, one of the challenges in conducting the study was in combining information contained in a number of datasets that differed widely not only in the variables contained, but more significantly, in how they were structured. Experience gained from the study has contributed to a formulation of a set of principles for designing "intelligent" databases so as to facilitate the sharing and common analysis of data from multiple studies (Davidson 1991; Parsaye *et al.* 1989). Thus, although a number of research design features had to be either changed or abandoned in the course of the study, we believe that in general the study design, procedures and analyses provide a useful model for the comparison of different batteries of language tests.

Finally, the materials, data and instruments from the study constitute a valuable resource for continued research. A number of research questions that could not be addressed in the study have been pursued in follow-up studies by members of the study staff since the study was completed. One such question, that is of interest to both language testers and researchers into second language acquisition, involves the investigation of the relationship between patterns of test performance on the one hand, and individual test taker characteristics, such as native language, time of first exposure to English, type (formal, informal), length and intensity of prior exposure to English, on the other. This question has been studied by Kunnan (1991), using structural equation modeling of the study data. Further research into this question will be facilitated by information on test taker characteristics that is now being collected routinely as part of operational administrations of the FCE by means of a short questionnaire, and that will be collected at regular intervals with samples of test takers who will complete a more extensive research questionnaire that is currently under development.

A second area of enquiry, that has been prompted by the results gained by using the Mantel-Haenszel procedure, is the study of possible sources of differential item function in items from both test batteries, which is explored in Ryan and Bachman (1992). A third question has to do with the relationships between item characteristics (difficulty, discrimination) and item content, which have been investigated for multiple forms of FCE Paper 1 (Bachman *et al.* 1991), using IRT and multiple linear regression analysis. The content analysis instruments that were developed for the study have been refined in follow-up studies, and constitute useful tools for use by other language testers. In this regard, one of the original objectives of the study was to provide an archive of materials, data and instruments for use by other researchers, in the hope that their availability would stimulate further research. To this end, these materials have now been archived and can be made available to other researchers upon request. [2]

## Recommendations for research and development

During the study it became apparent that we needed to place the comparison of the Cambridge and ETS measures of EFL within the broader context of the philosophical differences between the British and American educational measurement traditions.[3] These differences, as they inform the Cambridge and ETS tests of EFL, are discussed in Chapter 1. Our discussion of the differences between the American and British measurement traditions must be tempered to some degree by the understanding that EFL testing operates all over the world, and is thus less constrained by the measurement-curriculum link than either British examinations or American standardized achievement tests. Effectively, then, both Cambridge and ETS have a greater degree of philosophical and operational freedom in the design, construction and operation of their EFL tests than with the other test batteries they develop and administer in their own countries. Nevertheless, we feel it is fair to say that both the Cambridge and the

ETS tests of EFL are quite clearly products of different measurement traditions.

We have provided this brief overview of the cross-national context within which the study was conducted to place the recommendations for test development that we have made to Cambridge in an appropriate context. As mentioned above, one feature that distinguishes the FCE from the ETS tests of EFL is its relative complexity, in both design and procedures. This complexity is not fortuitous, but is a direct consequence of the positive value that is attached to a test design that includes a wide variety of test tasks and scoring procedures that include expert human judgment. That is, the British examinations system is particularly concerned with promoting positive effects of examinations on curricula and instruction, and thus is sensitive to including features in its examinations that are consistent with those found in instructional programs. At the same time, the extent to which this introduces variation in test performance that is unrelated to differences in levels of language ability has been made clear by this study and needs to be continuously evaluated.

The study has provided an opportunity to study the Cambridge EFL examinations in a way that has not generally been done in the past, and we believe our results suggest that the very features that are seen to be the strengths of the Cambridge exams are also potential sources of unreliability that need to be investigated in further studies. Specifically, we believe that the complexities of test design, test administration and marking procedures provide numerous sources of variation in test scores, whose effects need to be empirically examined to demonstrate that Cambridge examination scores are reliable indicators of the abilities they are intended to measure. In addition, we believe that many of these complexities could be either reduced or controlled with a few relatively minor changes in the system, without appreciably diminishing their value from the point of view of test content and procedures.

The FCE includes a number of variable features in both its design and in its procedures:

Paper 2: multiple topics
different topic types (literature/non-literature)
multiple markers

Paper 3: wide variety of question types
multiple markers

Paper 4: wide variety of question types
multiple forms

Paper 5: multiple information packages
different candidate grouping patterns
multiple examiners who administer the interview
multiple examiners who rate the interview

The variability and flexibility which these features afford are quite reasonably considered to be positive qualities in the British examinations tradition. Therefore, rather than eliminating these, it would be more prudent to assess the extent of their effects, and on the basis of this information, steps could be taken either to eliminate or to revise those features that are determined to be sources of measurement error. In this regard, a program of on-going research and development is being implemented by Cambridge to monitor the effects of these features on test scores regularly, in terms of both the reliability of test scores and whether the variety of features contributes to either the effectiveness of the examination as a measure of proficiency in EFL or the extent to which examinees perceive the test tasks as "authentic" instances of language use and perform accordingly.

## Equivalence of different forms

As indicated by our analyses, the effects of multiple forms on score equivalence are not uniformly serious. The two forms of FCE Paper 1 that were administered were determined to be equivalent, so that this did not constitute a source of error in the study. However, this finding was based on a single comparison of two forms and therefore cannot be regarded as complete assurance that different forms of FCE Paper 1 are always equivalent. One recommendation that was made in the study report was that procedures for routinely ensuring the statistical equivalence of scores from different examination papers from one operational administration to the next be instituted as part of the on-going program of test development. We are pleased to report that this recommendation has been followed and that an item-banking procedure has been developed that will be used for IRT equating of FCE Paper 1 forms, beginning with the coming year, and will be extended to include Papers 3 and 4 in the very near future. A PC-based item-banking system has been developed and is now an integral part of the test development and construction process. This system is also being used in research related to test content.

Since multiple forms of Paper 4 are routinely used operationally, their potential lack of equivalence is also of concern. Recognizing that it may not be feasible at many Cambridge centers to administer a single form of Paper 4, we recommended that first, Cambridge should limit considerably the number of forms that are used for any given operational administration of the exams; second, every effort be made to ensure that these forms are equivalent in the numbers and types of questions that are included; and third, scores from the different forms be regularly equated through appropriate statistical procedures. This recommendation has also been implemented. First, the number of Paper 4 forms in use has been reduced by 64% (from fourteen to five), and may be reduced even further as administrative constraints permit. Second, the scoring procedures have been changed, so that all forms will be machine-scanned. Third, as indicated above, the item-banking and IRT equating procedures developed for Paper 1 will be extended to include Paper 4.

Substantial additional research into the description of test content and its relationship to the equivalence of forms has also taken place (Bachman *et al.* 1991). This research has already been used in training programs for test writers and subject officers. It is anticipated that it will have an increasing impact on the test development process in the future. The equivalence of forms is perceived to be as much a function of content as statistics.

## Equivalence of Paper 2 topics

The variations in performance on the Paper 2 topics that do not require prior preparation appear to be minor. Nevertheless, we recommended that marks from the different Paper 2 topics be regularly analyzed to ensure that differences continue to be minor. The question of differences in performance on these topics and on the "literary" topics, for which candidates prepare, on the other hand, was largely unexplored in the study. Thus, although the study data suggest that individuals who select one of the "literary" topics perform, on the average, similarly to those who select other topics, there is no reason to expect that these two groups of individuals are at more or less the same level of writing ability or that the "literary" topics are at the same level of difficulty as the other topics. In response to this recommendation, Cambridge has already conducted preliminary studies, using generalizability theory, into differences across topics. These studies have indicated that differences in performance across topics are not significant. Further research into the routine double marking of all Paper 2 scripts has also taken place (Milanovic *et al.* 1991b).

## Equivalence of Paper 5 information packages and grouping patterns

Paper 5, the oral interview, is the most complex of the papers, in that it involves at least four dimensions of variation, the individual effects of which are potentially compounded by interactions among them. One set of possible interactions involves the examiner in the role of administrator and interlocutor. It is possible, for example, that some examiners choose some information packages more frequently than others, while avoiding other packages entirely. If a given information package is avoided at some centers because it is culturally offensive to members of some cultures, this would raise questions about the appropriateness of this package in general, and about its equivalence to other packages. Another interaction that may occur operationally is that between examiner and grouping pattern, with examiners at different centers favouring one pattern – single or group – over the other.

In the study we were able to assess the relative effects of but a single facet, information packages, which we found to be relatively minor. We were not able to investigate the effects of possible interactions between information packages and examiners, information packages and candidates, examiners and grouping patterns, and so forth. This is not to say that these interactions are necessarily problematic, and so our first recommendation was that these need to be investigated empirically. Our second recommendation was that those interactions that prove to be problematic then need to be eliminated where possible, and where this cannot be done, controlled. The procedures that have been used in the study – IRT modeling, generalizability theory and multiple linear regression analysis – provide some of the tools for the investigation and control of these effects in the Paper 5 oral interview. Again, this recommendation has been followed, and an initial investigation into the comparability of performance on different information packages has taken place. Findings so far do not indicate that the packages perform differentially. In an initial study (Milanovic *et al.* 1991c) 60 taped interviews were re-rated by a sample of twelve examiners. Inter-rater reliability was established at more than 0.7. In addition, work has been carried out by Young and Milanovic (1991) to investigate discourse variation in FCE oral interviews. This work has provided a useful model for the characterization of interview discourse. Two further research projects were carried out in the first half of 1992. Finally, the new Cambridge examination, the Certificate of Advanced English, was offered for the first time in December 1991. In this examination the format of the oral component has been fixed at two candidates and two examiners. This will allow for the routine monitoring and reporting of inter-rater reliability estimates in the oral interview. It is anticipated that the 2–2 format will become the default format for FCE in 1996. Furthermore, administrative procedures have been initiated to control the selection of information packages.

## Rater consistency

The last potential source of measurement error that we will address here is that of inconsistencies across raters, which is potentially a problem in Papers 2, 3 and 5. A preliminary analysis of the re-marking that is done routinely as part of the quality control procedure for Paper 2 suggested a high degree of consistency between first and second marks. However, as noted above in the section on reliability, this cannot be regarded as a demonstration of inter-rater reliability, since the second marker knows what the first marks are. We thus recommended that Cambridge routinely double mark all Paper 2 scripts and regularly monitor the consistency of marks. This recommendation has been implemented, and an initial study of Paper 2 rater consistency indicates that inter-rater reliability is in the region of 0.7–0.75. Double marking of the composition paper (Paper 2) in the Certificate of Advanced English is routine procedure. Research has indicated that inter-rater reliability in this examination is more than 0.8.

The conditions under which the Paper 5 oral interview are marked differ considerably from those of Papers 2 and 3, in which scripts are marked by a relatively small group of experienced examiners, with opportunity for re-marking as a means of maintaining consistency. Paper 5 oral interviews are conducted and rated at local centers all over the world, by a large number of individuals whose experience ranges from that of a short training period immediately prior to administering the interview to many years of administering interviews in a number of different countries. Furthermore, there is much greater variety in both format and content, due to differences in grouping patterns and information packages, than is the case with Paper 2 topics. As a result of these factors, there is much greater variation in the Paper 5 interview, and much less opportunity for quality control of marking than in Paper 2. Thus, in addition to the recommendations made above with regard to investigating the effects of variation in information packages and grouping patterns, we recommended that Cambridge initiate some means for routinely assuring that the marking of Paper 5 oral interviews is consistent across different centers, grouping patterns, information packages and examiners.

In addition to the complexities related to test design, administration and scoring, we pointed out the time-consuming and complex nature of producing an item-level test research database that characterized Cambridge's data processing procedures at the time of the study and recommended changes in these procedures that would lead to the routine compilation of item-level data for use in the research and development process. This recommendation has been implemented by the initiation and use of optical mark sheets for the capture of responses in Papers 3 and 4.

In summary, in our report to Cambridge we recommended that the sources of potential error of the Cambridge examinations be reduced as much as possible, consistent with the value placed on multiple tasks and human judgment, through adjustments in test design, administration and marking procedures. We also recommended that a program of research and development be initiated that would regularly monitor the characteristics of the various parts of the examinations and the scores that they yield. We believe that these steps will result in examinations that are both more efficient for both examiners and test takers and also provide scores that are demonstrably reliable indicators of language proficiency and that are equivalent from one test administration to the next. Needless to say, we are gratified that virtually all of our recommendations have already been implemented, or are planned for implementation.

The discussion of what we view to be potential concerns with the complexities of the Cambridge EFL examinations and the recommendations we have put forth are informed by the psychometric measurement tradition. This is a tradition that places value on minimizing potential sources of measurement error through an empirical, quantitative, statistically based process of test development and the standardization of test administration and scoring procedures. The net effect of these practices, in the case of the ETS tests of EFL, is a test battery that includes a fairly narrow range of task types, a set of administrative procedures that are uniformly followed in every operational administration, and a scoring system that is largely objective and, where subjective, includes specific criteria and procedures that do not vary from one test administration to the next. These operational procedures are closely integrated with an on-going program of research into the characteristics of the tests themselves, the test performance of various types and groups of test takers and the relationship of performance on the EFL tests to measures of other skills or abilities, and to future performance in both academic and professional settings.

The Cambridge EFL examination process reflects very thoroughly one English educational measurement tradition, discussed in Chapter 1. It is a system that provides opportunities for individuals to make alterations and adjustments at all stages – in the writing of examinations, in their administration, and in marking and setting grade boundaries. The alterations and adjustments are implemented largely by the expert senior staff, who use their collective experience and memory to guide the examinations year after year, often in the light of statistical information, but never directed wholly by statistics. In this educational measurement, therefore, any appeal to uniformity and standardization cannot rest solely upon psychometric grounds.

Given these fundamental differences, the issue in interpreting and utilizing the results of the study is not whether a reactive, mediational, experience-trusting, adjustment-laden system of assessment such as that of the Cambridge EFL examinations is appropriate on its own. That is an issue for the philosophers and researchers of British education. The relevant questions pertain to whether or not such a flexible and complex system can be equated to the rigid and relatively simple psychometric system on which the TOEFL is based, and also whether and to what extent the Cambridge system of EFL examinations needs to change to "fit" the mold of the ETS tests of EFL. In undertaking the study we perhaps naively assumed the answer to the first question to be "yes", and the comparisons we have made reflect this assumption. At the same time, we must recognize that our comparisons have only looked at products – papers/tests and item and test scores. That is, although we have commented upon and described the processes that produce papers/tests and test scores, we have not attempted to compare them systematically. Nor have we ventured into the area of test use.

With respect to the question of tailoring the Cambridge examinations of EFL to the ETS mold, we wish to make our position clear: the fact that our recommendations have been limited to the FCE should not be taken as an indication that we consider the ETS tests to be models for all tests of EFL. On the contrary, we believe the Cambridge examinations incorporate many important principles and values. These principles and values need not be abandoned, but could be enriched by incorporating some of the principles and values that underlie the ETS tests. By the same token, we believe that both the ETS and Cambridge tests could benefit by incorporating some of the features that typify other British EFL tests such as the IELTS. Furthermore, we believe that the presence of an examination like the Cambridge FCE would engender positive development in the US EFL proficiency testing marketplace.

While we believe that the study has provided some valuable information for test users, language testing researchers, and for Cambridge, a broader interest than the comparison of two specific EFL test batteries has motivated us in conducting the study. We believe that the study has demonstrated the usefulness of collaborative cross-national research among language testers in the United States and Britain. It has given us a better understanding of the differences between American and British EFL testing, and an appreciation of the complementarity of these traditions. It is our hope that such collaborative research will continue to be seen as valuable by language testers and other applied linguists. Some indication that this is happening can be seen in the reports by de Jong and Oscarson (1990) and Shohamy and Stansfield (1990) of cross-national collaborative research projects between researchers in the Netherlands and Sweden, and Israel and the US, respectively. It is also our hope that the mutual appreciation and respect for differing values and traditions of measurement that such research engenders will spur collaborative projects in which the subjective, qualitative judgments of "experts" are complemented by quantitative research and development methods.

## Notes

1  The International English Language Testing System (IELTS) superceded the earlier English Language Testing Service (ELTS)test.
2  Because of obvious concerns for test security, requests for access to materials and/or data will be considered on a case-by-case basis.
3  These differences, as well as issues related to cross-national comparison studies, are discussed in Davidson and Bachman (1990).

# Appendices

A Tests and administration times
B FCE papers used in the study
C Sample items from the TOEFL and SPEAK, and the TEW Prompt used in the study
D Background questionnaire
E Correlations among all tests, among FCE measures, among ETS measures, and among FCE and ETS tests
F Components of Communicative Language Ability
G Test rubric and test input facets
H CLA rating instrument and checklist
I TMF rating instrument and checklist

# Appendix A  Tests and administration times

## First Certificate in English (FCE)

| | Section | Administration | Time |
|---|---|---|---|
| I | Paper 1: Reading Comprehension (two forms: "old" and "new") | Group | 60 min (am) |
| | A  Section A  (25 mc/4) B  Section B, passage based (15 mc/4) | | |
| II | Paper 2: Composition | Group | 90 min (am) |
| | Two 120–180 word essays, Ratings: 6 bands, 0–20 | | |
| III | Paper 3: Use of English | Group | 120 min (pm) |
| | A  Section A1 (20 gap-filling, continuous prose) B  Section A2 (8 transformation, constructed response) C  Section A3 (5 gap-filling, separate sentences) D  Section A4 (5 gap-filling, separate sentences) E  Section A5 (8 rewording, constructed response, forming continuous prose) F  Section B (table/graphic-based, two paragraphs) | | |
| IV | Paper 4: Listening Comprehension | Group | approximately 30 min |
| | Number of items, score-per-item, and item type vary per test form; 10 forms sent by Cambridge to CTCS sites. | | within 5-week period centred on the date Papers 1, 2, and 3 are administered |
| V | Paper 5: Interview | Individual or Group | 15 min |
| | The interview uses themes based on information packages. 15 FCE packages available to interviewers in the CTCS. | | within 5-week period centred on the date Papers 1, 2, and 3 are administered |
| | A  Stage 1: general conversation (brief) B  Stage 2: picture(s): describe, discuss C  Stage 3: theme-related passage(s): read and discuss D  Stage 4: discussion task, problem-solving task, role play, etc. | | |
| | Ratings: Fluency, Accuracy, Pronunciation (segmentals), Pronunciation (suprasegmentals), Communicative Ability, Vocabulary; all on scales of 0–5 | | |

Total FCE time as used in the CTCS, assuming 30 min for Paper 4: 315 minutes (5 hours, 15 minutes)

## Test of English as a Foreign Language (TOEFL)

| | Section | Administration | Time |
|---|---|---|---|
| I | Section 1: Listening Comprehension | Group | 29 min |
| | A  Choose best paraphrase (15 mc/4) | | |
| | B  Answer question on dialogue (15 mc/4) | | |
| | C  Short talks, questions (15 mc/4) | | |
| II | Section 2: Structure and Written Expression | Group | 25 min |
| | A  Incomplete sentences (15 mc/4) | | |
| | B  Error detection (25 mc/4) | | |
| III | Section 3: Vocabulary and Reading Comprehension | Group | 45 min |
| | A  Synonym recognition (30 mc/4) | | |
| | B  Reading passages (30 mc/4) | | |

## Speaking Proficiency in English Assessment Kit (SPEAK)

| | Section | Administration | Time |
|---|---|---|---|
| A | Section One: Warm-up (not scored) | Group | 22 min |
| B | Section Two: Read passage aloud | | |
| C | Section Three: Complete sentences | | |
| D | Section Four: Tell story describing a series of pictures | | |
| E | Section Five: Answer spoken questions about a single picture | | |
| F | Section Six: Answer questions (longer responses) | | |
| G | Section Seven: Describe printed summary | | |

Ratings: pronunciation, grammar, fluency;
all on scales of 0-3

## Test of English Writing (TEW)

| Section | Administration | Time |
|---|---|---|
| 200–300 word pro-con essay<br>Ratings: Holistic scale, 0–6 | Group | 30 min |

Total TOEFL-SPEAK-TEW time: 151 minutes (2 hours, 31 minutes)
Total Combined Test Times, as used in the study: TOEFL-SPEAK-TEW + FCE
time: 466 minutes (7 hours, 46 minutes)

# Appendix B  FCE Papers used in the study

**0100/1**

UNIVERSITY OF CAMBRIDGE
LOCAL EXAMINATIONS SYNDICATE

## First Certificate in English

Tuesday   13 December 1988   Morning   1 hour

---

## PAPER 1   READING COMPREHENSION

*Answer all questions. Indicate your choice of answer in every case* **on the separate answer sheet** *already given out, which should show your name and examination index number. Follow carefully the instructions on how to record your answers. Give* **one answer only** *to each question. Marks will not be deducted for wrong answers: your total score on this test will be the number of correct answers you give.*

**[Turn over**

---

# Appendices

## Section A

*In this section you must choose the word or phrase which best completes each sentence.*
**On your answer sheet** *indicate the letter A, B, C or D against the number of each item* **1** *to* **25** *for the word or phrase you choose.*

1   It's a terribly expensive restaurant - they .............. you twenty pounds for even a simple meal.
   A  price          B  cost          C  take          D  charge

2   He's sold one million ................. of the book since it was published.
   A  examples     B  issues       C  copies       D  samples

3   I don't feel well: I wish I .................. so much at dinner.
   A  didn't eat    B  couldn't eat    C  hadn't eaten    D  mightn't eat

4   ................... up a child on your own is a big responsibility.
   A  Training     B  Growing     C  Bringing     D  Taking

5   He turned the wheel sharply to ................. a tractor and his car went into a ditch.
   A  prevent     B  avoid      C  preserve     D  lose

6   I can't open this jar – the lid is too .................... .
   A  firm         B  strong      C  tight       D  close

7   Their neighbours made them ................... down some of their trees.
   A  to chop     B  chop       C  chopping     D  chopped

8   He ...................... to us that it wouldn't be long before he returned.
   A  told         B  hoped      C  explained     D  promised

9   They spent a long time looking for curtains which ................. the wallpaper.
   A  agreed with    B  fitted      C  matched     D  suited

10   It will be difficult for the mountaineers to carry on with their climb now that winter has set ................. .
   A  on          B  off         C  up         D  in

11   My friend offered to take me out to dinner ................... buying me a birthday present.
   A  in place of    B  instead of    C  on account of    D  in case of

12   I'm very much looking forward ................... your brother.
   A  to meet     B  to have met    C  to meeting    D  meeting

144

**13** In my opinion, schools should spend more time teaching the .................. which are useful in life.
  A abilities     B skills     C capabilities     D information

**14** Some students did not know .................. fill in the exam paper.
  A how     B how they     C how to     D to

**15** Tell her to take a map in case she .................. lost.
  A gets     B got     C will get     D would get

**16** Eating too many potatoes is .................. to make you fat.
  A involved     B considered     C supposed     D regarded

**17** He had changed so much that .................. anyone recognised him.
  A almost     B hardly     C not     D nearly

**18** Fortunately, .................. from a sprained wrist, she suffered no serious injuries from her fall.
  A other     B except     C besides     D apart

**19** When I left the theatre last night I discovered that my bicycle had been .................. .
  A burgled     B robbed     C stolen     D gone

**20** Would you .................. asking her to come in and see me?
  A like     B mind     C please     D possibly

**21** You are advised to .................. your eyes checked every eighteen months.
  A have     B let     C make     D organise

**22** If you see anything suspicious you should .................. it to the police immediately.
  A report     B say     C confirm     D notice

**23** There was a .................. accident last night in which two people were killed.
  A deadly     B murderous     C cruel     D fatal

**24** People are .................. to want to travel by train when it's cheaper and easier by car.
  A impossible     B improbable     C incapable     D unlikely

**25** There have been many .................. of measles in the school this year.
  A occasions     B cases     C circumstances     D opportunities

*Appendices*

Section B

*In this section you will find after each of the passages a number of questions or unfinished statements about the passage, each with four suggested answers or ways of finishing. You must choose the one which you think fits best.* **On your answer sheet**, *indicate the letter A, B, C or D against the number of each item* **26–40** *for the answer you choose. Give* **one answer only** *to each question. Read each passage right through before choosing your answers.*

## FIRST PASSAGE

When I was a boy growing up in India, my father, who was a Christian missionary, was my hero. He never turned away from anyone in need who came to him. Only once did I see him hesitate to help – when I was seven, and three strange men walked up the rough track to our mountain home.

At first glance these three seemed like hundreds of other strangers who came to our home for medical treatment. But as they approached, I noticed differences: their skin was covered with sores and their foreheads and ears were swollen. Looking more closely, I realized they also lacked fingers and toes.

My mother did not react in her normal welcoming manner. Her face took on a pale, tense appearance. 'Run and get your father' she whispered to me. 'Take your sister, and both of you stay in the house!'

My sister obeyed perfectly, but I came back to see what was happening. When I saw the same look of uncertainty, almost fear, pass across my father's face I was very puzzled. He stood by the three nervously, awkwardly, as if he didn't know what to do. I had never seen my father like that.

The three men bowed very low, a common action that my father disliked. 'I'm not God,' he would usually say, and lift the people to their feet. But not this time. He stood still. Finally, in a weak voice he said, 'There's not much we can do. I'm sorry. I'll do what I can'.

He washed the strangers' feet, treated them with disinfectant and bandaged them.

That incident was my first experience of leprosy, a terrible skin disease. For the past thirty years I have been among people with this disease. During that time, my mistaken fears and prejudices about leprosy have disappeared, at least in the medical profession. Partly because of effective drugs, leprosy is now thought of as a controllable disease and it is one which fewer people now catch.

However, in most parts of the world less than a quarter of leprosy patients are actually under any form of treatment. Thus, to many it is still a disease that can have terrible physical effects.

26  Why did the boy particularly remember this incident?
   A   He didn't know the three men.
   B   The three men frightened him.
   C   The three men were dressed in a strange way.
   D   His father seemed unwilling to help the three men.

27  The boy's mother told the children to stay inside the house because she did not want
   A   the children to be frightened of the men.
   B   the children to hear what she said to the men.
   C   the children's behaviour to embarrass the men.
   D   the children to get close to the men.

28  What did the boy's father do when he met the three men?
   A   He helped them to their feet.
   B   He gave them what treatment he could.
   C   He said there was nothing he could do.
   D   He nervously asked them to leave.

29  What is the writer's attitude to leprosy now?
   A   He is afraid of it.
   B   He is sad it cannot be cured.
   C   He believes it to be more widespread.
   D   He thinks it is still a serious problem.

30  Among people who catch leprosy
   A   many are not offered treatment.
   B   some refuse treatment.
   C   many recover without treatment.
   D   a few are permanently affected.

## SECOND PASSAGE

The training given to police dogs today is very much better than it was only twenty years ago.

Previously, once a dog had been released to chase an escaping criminal, it was usually so excited that few trainers — or handlers, as they are called — would have claimed to have any control over its actions until the man had been stopped. In addition, the earlier training in searching for people was very inefficient compared with modern methods.

For some reason, police dogs were usually trained by being ordered to find a man who had been told to climb a tree. In the rather small training areas which were available, the dogs soon learned all the likely hiding-places. Therefore, instead of using their sense of smell, and searching systematically, the dogs would simply run aimlessly from tree to tree, looking for the man.

When the man was found, he would put on a show for the benefit of onlookers, calling to the dog from the safety of the tree until it was wild with excitement and rage. This kind of training was dangerous, and the dogs also became confused when asked to carry out a search on unfamiliar ground. Moreover, the encouragement given to the dogs to bite made it risky to employ them in searching for lost or injured people.

In contrast to this, the new training emphasises the importance of handlers being in complete control of the dog at all times. The dogs are taught not to bite when they catch up with the person they are chasing, but to bark only, and to continue to do this until the handler arrives on the scene.

These revised ideas on training have made it necessary for some thought to be given to the selection of dogs and handlers. It is essential that handlers should not be men who place all their faith in powerful and aggressive animals. For the training to be successful, and a good all-purpose dog produced, the nervous excitable dog has had to go, and it has been replaced by one of a calmer nature. Each handler has to learn thoroughly the particular character of his dog and be capable of developing a close relationship of trust and affection with it so that man and dog can work confidently together as a team.

**31**  Under the old system of training, once a chase had begun, the dogs
    A    would not usually obey their handlers.
    B    never stopped until the man was caught.
    C    seemed to enjoy their work more than they do today.
    D    ran too fast for the handlers to keep up with them.

**32**  Why was the earlier training in searching inefficient?
    A    The dogs took too long to learn the necessary skills.
    B    Too many dogs were trained together in the space available.
    C    The dogs were allowed to run around too much and get tired.
    D    The dogs were not encouraged to exercise their special abilities.

**33**  What unsatisfactory result did the earlier training methods produce?
    A    The dogs would not work because they were excited.
    B    The dogs failed to cope with real situations.
    C    The dogs became confused about who to chase.
    D    The dogs tended to attack anyone who approached them.

**34**  A good handler is a person who
    A    forces his dog to obey.
    B    trains his dog to be aggressive.
    C    has confidence in his dog.
    D    gives all his affection to his dog.

**35**  What kind of dogs make good police dogs?
    A    large and aggressive
    B    gentle and affectionate
    C    calm and trustworthy
    D    excitable and intelligent

## THIRD PASSAGE

The major supposition of this book is that you want to give up smoking. It is not going to encourage you to take half measures. It won't suggest that you can be satisfied with cutting down, changing to cigars or starting to smoke a pipe. It is tough. It asks you to give up tobacco of all kinds for the rest of your life.

What it asks is much easier for some than they ever expected. However, the majority of people think that it is going to be difficult and this is an obstacle. You may have tried to give up smoking before and, having failed, may feel disheartened. You may not want to try again. A few of you really will find it difficult.

What this book will make you realise is this: if you want to give up smoking, there is nothing that can stop you. Even if you think you don't have enough will-power, you will find it. This book can't help you to want to give up smoking but, if you want to, it can help to stop and to stay stopped.

You will still have to make quite an effort regardless of what you have been told or read. There is no substitute for will-power, and it is only by using your will-power that you will become a non-smoker. Don't doubt for one minute that you have the will-power. You certainly have. I hope that you will find that you have more will-power than you ever thought, and be proud of it.

This book will give you clear and practical step-by-step guidelines, a programme to help you to stop smoking. It sets out to answer most of the questions you have ever had about giving up smoking. It aims to give you support—when your will-power may weaken, when the desire gets great, when you feel like giving in, and having a cigarette. It will cheer you up and keep you going. It is a friend. There is something in it somewhere that will help you through the difficult times.

Keep it with you. Put it in your pocket or your handbag. Turn to it if you need to refresh your memory about some of the things you should be doing. Dip into it when the going gets tough. Re-read its messages, so that you believe them and you think positively. It is the kind of friend you can refer to at any time and be sure you will get suggestions on how to cope with difficult situations. Don't go anywhere without it.

**36** The book is intended to show people

  A    how they can cut down their smoking.

  B    that giving up smoking can be done gradually.

  C    that pipes are less harmful than cigarettes.

  D    how to give up smoking altogether.

**37** What do most people think about giving up smoking?

  A    If they fail at first they may never succeed.

  B    It is easier to give up cigarettes if you smoke cigars instead.

  C    Friends can make it hard for you to stop.

  D    They expect it to be harder than it is.

**38** What does success in giving up smoking depend on?

  A    how long you have been a smoker

  B    how clear and practical the instructions are

  C    how strongly you want to stop smoking

  D    how much pride you have

**39** What does the writer expect her programme to do?

  A    to take away the desire to smoke

  B    to make people want to give up smoking

  C    to make people feel ashamed they smoke

  D    to provide encouragement at all times

**40** How should readers use this book?

  A    read it carefully from cover to cover

  B    memorise the answers to the questions

  C    read some parts of it more than once

  D    use it only when they have problems

*Appendices*

**0100/2**

UNIVERSITY OF CAMBRIDGE
LOCAL EXAMINATIONS SYNDICATE

**First Certificate in English**

Tuesday   13 December 1988   Morning   1 hour 30 minutes

## PAPER 2   COMPOSITION

**[turn over**

*Write two only of the following composition exercises. Your answers must follow exactly the instructions given and must be of between 120 and 180 words each.*

I    You have heard from a friend that your brother, who will be seventeen next month, is behaving foolishly and upsetting your parents. Write a letter to him for his birthday but at the same time try to persuade him to mend his ways.

2    Your neighbours are exchanging houses for a month with a family from another country, and have asked you to welcome the family and give them some useful information. Write what you say.

3    A little girl was lost and asked for your help. Describe what you did and how you found her family.

4    Describe some of the things people should do to stay fit and healthy.

5    Based on your reading of *one* of these books, write on one of the following.

Zero Hour (Cambridge University Press)

Describe **one or more** of these stories which give a particularly bitter picture of marriage.

DONN BYRNE: Mahatma Gandhi - The man and his message

'My life is my message'. What was Gandhi's message and how did his life illustrate it?

L. P. HARTLEY: The Go-Between

How far do you consider Marian's affection for Leo was genuine? Support your opinion with examples from the text.

*Appendices*

**0100/3**

UNIVERSITY OF CAMBRIDGE
LOCAL EXAMINATIONS SYNDICATE

## First Certificate in English

Tuesday   13 December 1988   Afternoon   2 hours

## PAPER 3   USE OF ENGLISH

Candidate's name ................................................................................................................

Candidate's index number ...........................................................

*Your answers must be written in ink in this booklet, using the spaces provided.*

**[Turn over**

1   *Fill each of the numbered blanks in the following passage.  Use only* **one** *word in each space.*

He was born in a very poor part of London.  His father ........................ (1) a

comedian and his mother worked ........................ (2) a dancer and singer.

........................ (3) of them was very successful, however, and the family had very

........................ (4) money; at one time they were ........................ (5) poor that he

and his brothers had only one pair of shoes ........................ (6) them and they had to

take turns wearing them. The first time he himself earned any money,

........................ (7) dancing and singing, he was only five years old. He did many

kinds of jobs, but what he loved ........................ (8) was working in the theatre.


........................ (9) he was about 15 he joined a travelling theatre company and went

on trips to America. On ........................ (10) such tour he was offered a part in a

film, so he went to Hollywood, ........................ (11) he eventually became both an

actor and a film director. He was known to be a perfectionist, and sometimes

........................ (12) the other actors repeat a scene many times ........................ (13)

he was finally satisfied with it.


Many people found ........................ (14) difficult and some accused him of

........................ (15) mean, but it was really his early experiences of poverty

........................ (16) made him careful with his ........................ (17).


He died in Switzerland in 1977, ........................ (18) the age of 88. ........................ (19)

is now a statue of him in Leicester Square, London, the city of his ........................ (20)

and early upbringing.  His name was Charlie Chaplin.

**2**   *Finish each of the following sentences in such a way that it means exactly the same as the sentence printed before it.*

EXAMPLE: I haven't enjoyed myself so much for years.

ANSWER: It's years ...*since I enjoyed myself so much*..................................

(a)   "Will I ever find a job?" Tim said to himself.

Tim wondered ...........................................................................................................

(b)   You should take a map because you might get lost in those mountains.

In case ...................................................................................................................

(c)   Temperature is measured by a thermometer.

A thermometer is ...................................................................................................

(d)   You remembered to post the letter, didn't you?

You didn't ..........................................................................................................?

(e)   Mr Dryden mended the washing machine for me.

I had ......................................................................................................................

(f)   Pat is the tallest girl in her class.

No one ...................................................................................................................

(g)   To get the 40% discount, you must buy all twelve books at the same time.

You can only ........................................................................................................

(h)   "I'm sorry I gave you the wrong number," said Paul to Susan.

Paul apologised ....................................................................................................

(i)   Samuel started keeping a diary five years ago.

Samuel has ............................................................................................................

(j)   Please don't smoke in the kitchen.

I'd rather ...............................................................................................................

**3** *Complete the following sentences with a phrase formed with* **out of** ...................

EXAMPLE:   After running twenty kilometres he was ........ ..... .................
ANSWER:   After running twenty kilometres he was ..*out of breath*...

(a)   Keep this plant in the house. It won't survive ........ ..... ...................

(b)   Steve has been ........ ..... ....................for two years and doesn't think he will ever find a job.

(c)   They watched the ship until it was ........ ..... .................... .

(d)   They had to use the stairs because the lift was ........ ..... .................... .

(e)   This information is ........ ..... .................... . Haven't you got the latest figures?

**4** *Complete the following sentences with* **one** *word related to the world of work.*

EXAMPLE:   Edward found a good ................... in an office close to his home.
ANSWER:   Edward found a good ....*job*........ in an office close to his home.

(a)   A ................... has arisen for a new Director of Studies at the language school.

(b)   He got the ................... because he was always late for work.

(c)   Applications are invited for the ................... of secretary to the Director.

(d)   The new car factory is expanding and expects to ................... a thousand more local people.

(e)   Mary wanted to work for that particular organisation because there were good chances of ................... to a senior level.

*Appendices*

5   *Make all the changes and additions necessary to produce, from the following sets of words and phrases, sentences which together make a complete letter. Note carefully from the example what kind of alterations need to be made. Write each sentence in the space provided.*

> EXAMPLE:    I be very surprised / receive / letter / you this morning.
>
> ANSWER:    *I was very surprised to receive a letter from you this morning.*

1 Poachers Walk
Cambridge
5 May 1988

The Manager
Royal Hotel
Kings Road
TORQUAY
TO5 7KM

Dear Sir/Madam

I stay/your hotel/24 April/30 April/room 415.

(a)   .........................................................................................................................................

On arrive/home, I realise/I leave/book/room.

(b)   .........................................................................................................................................

I wonder/it be find/hand in.

(c)   .........................................................................................................................................

It be/small, hardback book/blue cover call "Gallions Reach"/H.M. Tomlinson.

(d)   .........................................................................................................................................

I be very anxious/get/book back because it be now out/print/it be difficult/find/ bookshops.

(e)   .........................................................................................................................................

Also,/book be give/me/author,/signature be/front cover.

(f)   .........................................................................................................................................

I enclose/cheque/£1.50/cover/cost/post it back/me.

(g)   .........................................................................................................................................

If, unfortunately, you not find/book, please return/cheque.

(h)   .........................................................................................................................................

I look forward to hearing from you soon.
Yours faithfully


Peter Hackett

6    *In the town of Mudleigh, the Council has to make a decision about what to do with a large empty field. At a recent meeting, five suggestions were made. Look at each of these, together with the other information given below, and then write two paragraphs. In your first paragraph, say which plan **you** think would be best and why. In the second paragraph, say which plan you think should definitely **not** be chosen, giving your reasons for your decision.*

|         |                                              | **Cost**      |
|---------|----------------------------------------------|---------------|
| Plan A  | Build 150 houses                             | £7,500,000    |
| Plan B  | Create a new park                            | £50,000       |
| Plan C  | Build a Sports Centre                        | £600,000      |
| Plan D  | Build a factory for making<br>wooden furniture | £10,000,000 |
| Plan E  | Take no action                               | £0            |

**MAP OF CENTRE OF MUDLEIGH**

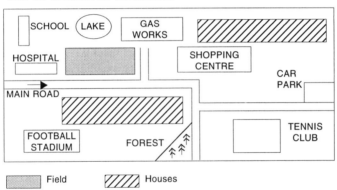

Field       Houses

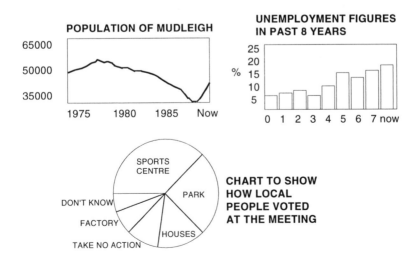

**POPULATION OF MUDLEIGH**

**UNEMPLOYMENT FIGURES IN PAST 8 YEARS**

**CHART TO SHOW HOW LOCAL PEOPLE VOTED AT THE MEETING**

# Appendices

*First paragraph*

_____

_____

_____

_____

_____

_____

_____

_____

_____

_____

*Second paragraph*

_____

_____

_____

_____

_____

_____

_____

_____

_____

_____

UNIVERSITY OF CAMBRIDGE                    **0100/4**
LOCAL EXAMINATIONS SYNDICATE               **0101/4**

**First Certificate in English**

PAPER 4   LISTENING COMPREHENSION          **Test 20**
(Approx. 30 minutes)

Candidate's name.........................................................................................................................................

Candidate's index number ...........................................................................

*Further instructions will be given on the recording. Your answers must be written in ink in this booklet,*
*using the spaces provided.*

⨠→

S237R

## Appendices

### FIRST PART

*You will hear a court case about a road accident. For each of the questions 1–10 tick (√) one box to show whether each statement is true or false.*

|  |  | True | False |
|---|---|:---:|:---:|
| 1 | Martha Dobbs lives at 42 South Mansions. | | |
| 2 | The accident happened just after Christmas. | | |
| 3 | The pedestrian crossing is near a junction. | | |
| 4 | It was already very dark. | | |
| 5 | The roads were wet. | | |
| 6 | The man started to cross without looking. | | |
| 7 | She said the car was going too fast. | | |
| 8 | The motor-cycle hit the car. | | |
| 9 | The pedestrian was injured in the accident. | | |
| 10 | She wasn't sure about the number of the motor cycle. | | |

*Appendices*

SECOND PART

*You will hear a conversation about birthday presents. Choose from the following list the items that best apply to the opinions expressed and write them down in the spaces provided (numbered 11–15).*

record

camera

watch

books

handbag

perfume

food

jewellery

picture

glasses

11  ..................................  possibly, but probably not a present she will enjoy that much

12  ..................................  likely to have them already

13  ..................................  used this idea at Christmas

14  ..................................  in the circumstances, not very suitable

15  ..................................  good idea, even if they may be quite expensive

S237                              [4]

# Appendices

## THIRD PART

*Listen to the description of the De Luxe Gas Cooker and then for question 16 tick (√) one or more boxes to show which of the following features have been mentioned.*

| 16 | | | |
|---|---|---|---|
| a glass oven door | A | |
| a fold-away grill | B | |
| a fold-away drawer | C | |
| a self-cleaning oven | D | |
| an automatic oven | E | |
| a plate rack | F | |
| four high-speed burners | G | |
| an oven light | H | |
| a double oven | I | |
| electronic controls | J | |

**FOURTH PART**

*You will hear a recorded telephone announcement giving a recipe for stuffed pancakes.*

17    Tick (✓) one of the boxes, A, B, C or D to show which quantities of cheese, butter and milk are needed for the filling of the pancakes according to the recipe.

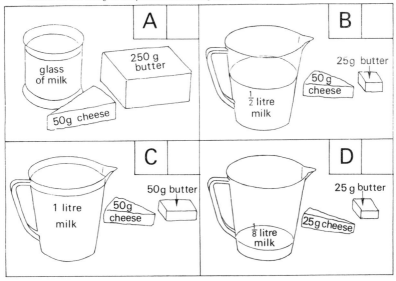

18    Tick (✓) one of the boxes A, B, C or D to show which other items are needed for the recipe.

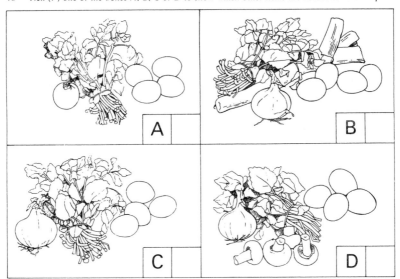

## Appendices

*For question 19 fill in the missing information in the spaces provided.*

Now to make: cook eight .................................. and keep warm.

Fry onions in butter, stir in .................................. and cook for a further 2 minutes.

Remove from heat, add .................................. and bring it to the boil.

Cook for two minutes.

Add the cheese and watercress to the sauce with ..................................

Season and divide between the pancakes.

Roll them up and reheat.

Tasks

Candidates are invited to participate in one or more communicative activities

1.  Candidates are asked to look at the "Boys and Girls" leaflet. They are
    then invited to comment on this and say what relevant advice they would
    give to the people in the photographs. They may also be asked about the
    extent to which they themselves follow the advice given in the leaflet.

Discussion

Candidates are asked to look at the
"Boys and Girls" leaflet and then
invited to talk about

-   children working in their own
    country
-   their own childhood work experiences
-   whether children should be paid to
    help in the home

## BOYS & GIRLS

Are you 13 or over?
Do you need extra pocket money?
Can you spare a couple of hours on Thursdays?

**WE HAVE A 'WEEKLY NEWS'
DELIVERY ROUND VACANCY
IN YOUR VICINITY.**

Phone now **Cambridge 358877** Ext 452

2.  Decisions

    Leaflet "Saturday Activities"

    Ask candidate(s) to look at the "Saturday Activities" below and

    -   explain what they think the activities are
    -   choose two out of three to make up an interesting Saturday for a
        12-15 year old
    -   talk about the best kind of activity for making friends

JEB/PMS11/EFL4

*Appendices*

FCE/5 SAMPLE PACKAGE D

**Family Life**

Photographs

Candidates are asked to look at one or more photographs and a short time is
allowed for study. Conversation is initiated by the examiner on the lines
suggested. (Group variation) Individual candidates are encouraged to initiate
discussion on one topic, and other candidates are invited to comment.

1.

2.

3.

    (a)   Describe/compare the people
                        the activity
                        the setting

    (b)   Discuss caring for children
                        learning and play
                        how adults help/guide children

Passages

Candidates are shown one or more short passages and are invited to try and
match the texts with the appropriate photographs, giving reasons for their
choice and commenting on the content. (It is not necessary for a whole text to
be read aloud)

1.    We decided to take the children to visit a farm while we were on holiday,
      so that they could see milk, eggs and vegetables being produced. Living
      in a city, they thought these things only came from the supermarket

2.    There's no need to spend money on buying lots of toys. Many ordinary
      household objects make good playthings. When you do buy toys, make sure
      they are strong, safe and easy to keep clean

3.    Every night there has to be at least one story - usually the longest in
      the book! And, of course, Sam knows the story off by heart and corrects
      me if I get anything wrong or leave anything out

# Paper 5 [UCLES 1988:2–3]

## General

1 The oral test carries a substantial mark weighting in the examination, equal to each of the written papers 1, 2, and 3 (40 marks after final adjustment) and giving the examination an oral/aural weighting of one third in combination with the Listening Comprehension's 20 marks. The oral examiner's role, as the most personally encountered part of the examination process, is a sensitive and important one. Examiners represent the Syndicate to the public, and are responsible for the satisfactory conduct of the tests in exact accordance with these instructions.

2 It is important that examiners are completely familiar with the procedure and marking criteria:
   i   as described in this booklet;
   ii  as exemplified by the range and character of the material and tasks;
   iii as further described at the preliminary examiners' meetings held before the examining period begins, and in the course of the joint assessment of candidates during the examination sessions.

3 The test consists of a theme-directed conversation on a variety of stimuli, with assessment on six marking scales [fluency, grammatical accuracy, pronunciation – sentences, pronunciation – individual sounds, interactive communication, and vocabulary resource] applied simultaneously through the interview. The examiner's folders of material for each level consist of a number of separate "packages" with photographs and other discussion and activity material broadly related in theme. A further package with material for basing the interview on a background text is also provided. Each package contains detailed guidelines for descriptive, discursive, role play or problem-solving activities.

4 The material attempts to incorporate a careful balance between realism and international viability, and is designed to encourage candidate initiative yet provide a firm structuring of themes and activities. The full range of packages should be consistently used; examiners are encouraged to submit comments on examining material and tasks after the examining period.

## Conduct of the interview

5 The examiner's main considerations must be to:
   i   create a positive atmosphere in which candidates, whether examined singly or in a pair or group, can demonstrate their ability. Minor changes to the position of chairs, tables, clocks, etc. may help improve a potentially intimidating situation;
   ii  conduct the interview in full accordance with instructions and expectations, bearing in mind that preparation of candidates is very often specific and intensive;

iii give a fair and objective mark for each separate aspect of performance under test, as indicated in the marking scales;

iv make it clear to candidates at all times that the assessment is not being made on background knowledge or particular viewpoints, or personality factors of any kind.

6 Begin the interview with a greeting, linked with a check on the correctness of names and index numbers on the mark sheets ... . To create a friendly and encouraging atmosphere there may be some general warming-up conversation, but with an eye to making a choice of theme in line with the candidate's interests and experience. This should not last more than a minute. The basic format and material must be kept to, and general conversation must not be allowed to predominate.

7 Develop conversation on the lines indicated in the package selected. The sets of photographs, with their indications for developing discussion, will usually provide a reassuring introduction to the interview situation and establish the theme. The passages are not to be read aloud, although candidates may quote from them. The relative time spent on the photographs, passages and other material cannot be precisely regulated, although the passages usually require less time. Remember that most candidates, through practice and preparation, expect to participate in three distinct stages of the interview, and this format must be respected by the examiner.

8 A careful and positive approach to the assimilation of all material presented is necessary. Candidates must not be hurried, but not given the impression that close and complete reading of all material is needed. The items are chosen for authenticity and, where unedited, may have culture-loaded aspects or more detail than is relevant to the test activity. Candidates should be steered round apparent difficulties in an encouraging and natural manner, and the activity developed along expected lines. In the case of activities (angled discussion, role play, etc.) prompted verbally or with minimal visual input, similar attention should be given to seeing that candidates are given appropriate presentation time and have understood the task. Rough paper and pencil for making notes should be at hand for activities and discussions which may require them.

9 Candidates should at all times be given reasonable openings for extended remarks, and encouraged to take the initiative and speak a number of connected sentences without interruption. The conversation should tend always to open towards broader concepts (why, how, etc.) rather than the narrowly specific (yes/no, which, who, etc.). Particularly in the case of candidates examined in pairs or groups, it is possible for the interview to move productively beyond the basic examiner/teacher, candidate/pupil relationship which is felt to be an inadequate model for the kind of realistic interchange aimed at. For example, in a group, one of the candidates can be given an active role in introducing and developing a particular task. Conversely the examiner

may participate freely in debate, role play, etc., a practice which also widens the range of material which can be used for single-candidate interviews.

10  With pairs and groups, take care to establish a good balance of contributions, with no over-dominance by yourself or any one group member, and with deliberate bringing out of reticent candidates. Be conscious also of the need to offset any negative effects of too little (or too great) similarity of background or level within the group. The arrangement of chairs needs to be considered; the interlocutor-examiner will need to be part of the group, whereas a separate assessor requires a discreet, unobtrusive position.

# Appendix C  Sample items from the TOEFL and SPEAK, and the TEW prompt used in the study

These sample TOEFL and SPEAK items were extracted from the following ETS publications, and are reproduced here with permission:
Educational Testing Service. 1987. *TOEFL Test and Score Manual.* Princeton.
Educational Testing Service. 1985. *A Guide to SPEAK.* Princeton.

## TOEFL

### Section 1 (Listening comprehension)

**Part A, 20 items (choose option closest in meaning):**

Example item: (spoken, not written)

"Mary swam out to the island with her friends."

(written)    (A) Mary outswam the others.
             (B) Mary ought to swim with them.
             (C) Mary and her friends swam to the island.
             (D) Mary's friends owned the island.

(correct response C)

**Part B, 15 items (interpret a short dialogue):**

Example item: (spoken, not written)

(Man:)       "Professor Smith is going to retire soon, what kind of gift shall we give her?"
(Woman:)     "I think she'd like to have a photograph of our class."
(3rd voice:) "What does the woman think the class should do?"

(written)    (A) Present Professor Smith with a picture.
             (B) Photograph Professor Smith.
             (C) Put glass over the photograph.
             (D) Replace the broken headlight.

(correct response A)

Appendices

**Part C, 15 items (interpret a monologue):**

Example item: (spoken, not written)

"Balloons have been used for about a hundred years. There are two different kinds of sport balloons, gas and hot air. Hot air balloons are safer than gas balloons which may catch fire. Hot air balloons are preferred by most balloonists in the United States because of their safety. They are also cheaper and easier to manage than gas balloons. Despite the ease of operating a balloon, pilots must watch the weather carefully. Sport balloon flights are best early in the morning or late in the afternoon when the wind is light."
(Other voice:)"Why are gas balloons considered dangerous?"

(written)   (A) They are impossible to guide.
              (B) They may go up in flames.
              (C) They tend to leak gas.
              (D) They are cheaply made.

(correct response B)

# Section 2 (Structure and written expression)

**Part 1, 15 items (recognize appropriate language):**

Example item:
Vegetables are an excellent source _____ vitamins.

        (A) of
        (B) has
        (C) where
        (D) that

(correct response A)

**Part 2, 25 items (error detection):**

Example item:

A ray of light passing through the center of a thin lens keep its original direction.
              A           B               C        D
(correct response C)

# Section 3 (Vocabulary and reading comprehension)

**Part 1, 30 items (vocabulary – choose closest meaning):**

Example item:

Passenger ships and aircraft are often equipped with ship-to-shore or air-to-land radio telephones.

173

(A) highways
(B) railroads
(C) planes
(D) sailboats

(correct response C)

**Part 2, 30 items (reading comprehension):**

(*Note*: Section 3 has four passages with at least four items per passage.)

Example item:

(passage)
The rattles with which a rattlesnake warns of its presence are formed by loosely interlocking hollow rings of hard skin, which make a buzzing sound when its tail is shaken. As a baby, the snake begins to form its rattles from the button at the very tip of its tail. Thereafter, each time it sheds its skin, a new ring is formed. Popular belief holds that a snake's age can be told by counting the rings, but this idea is fallacious. In fact, a snake may lose its old skin as often as four times a year. Also, rattles tend to wear or break off with time.
(sample item for this passage)

A rattlesnake's rattles are made of

(A) skin
(B) bone
(C) wood
(D) muscle

(correct response A)

# SPEAK

## Section 1:

In this section, the source tape asks the candidate several general questions about him/herself, e.g. "What is your name", "How many brothers and sisters do you have?".

## Section 2:

In this section the candidate reads a paragraph aloud. The paragraph in the CTCS version of the SPEAK concerned the issue of increasing use of parks and natural wilderness areas in the USA.

## Section 3:

Here, the candidate completes partial sentences. For example, one item, spoken on the source tape and printed in the booklet, reads: "When the library opens ...".

The candidate repeats those words and finishes the sentence.

## Section 4:

In Section 4, a series of photographs is given in the booklet. The candidate is asked to examine these and narrate a story suggested by the photos. In the SPEAK used in the CTCS, the photographs show a narrative concerning the use of a library.

## Section 5:

Here, the candidate is given one photograph. The source tape then asks some questions about it, questions which are also printed in the booklet. In the CTCS SPEAK, the photograph shows some fishermen sorting through a day's catch.

## Section 6:

This section asks the candidate to speak on several very general questions of current interest and/or to describe some common objects.

## Section 7:

Here, the candidate is given a class schedule for an imaginary organizational meeting, such as a club or university class. The candidate then has to imagine him/herself as a leader/teacher of that group, meeting the people for the first time, and explaining the schedule to the group's members. It should be noted that this item directly reflects the original market of the SPEAK: on-site testing at US universities of international students who wish to become teaching assistants.

# TEW Prompt

(time limit: 30 minutes)

Some people believe that it is important for old people to continue living with members of their own families. Others believe that old people are happier living with people of their own age and interests. What are the advantages of each situation? Which do you personally think is better for the old person?

# Appendix D  Background questionnaire

(Original English version)

This questionnaire is designed to provide us with information of interest for research purposes. Your answers to these questions will be kept strictly confidential. Please answer each question as accurately as you can. Thank you for your cooperation.

## DIRECTIONS:

Please provide the information on the top portion of the answer sheet as instructed. For each question below, darken the appropriate circle on the answer sheet using the pencil provided. All answers should be given on the answer sheet provided. Do not mark anything on this questionnaire.

1  What is your current educational status?
   (A) enrolled in a secondary school
   (B) enrolled part-time in a college, university or other institution of higher education
   (C) enrolled full-time in a college, university or other institution of higher education
   (D) enrolled in a language institute or English course given where I work
   (E) not currently enrolled as a student

2  Have you ever or are you currently taking a course to prepare for the TOEFL?
   (A) yes
   (B) no

3  Have you ever or are you currently taking a course to prepare for the FCE?
   (A) yes
   (B) no

4  Have you ever or are you currently taking a course to prepare for the CPE?
   (A) yes
   (B) no

5  At what age did you begin to learn or use English?
(A)  1–5 years          (D)  14–17 years
(B)  6–9 years          (E)  18 or more years
(C)  10–13 years

6  Have you ever studied English in school or in a language institute in the country you consider to be your home country?
(A)  yes
(B)  no

IF YES, ANSWER QUESTIONS 7–13. IF NO, GO TO QUESTION 13 ON PAGE 3.

7  How many years have you studied English in school or in a language institute?
(A)  less than 1 year   (D)  7–9 years
(B)  1–3 years          (E)  10 or more years
(C)  4–6 years

8  How old were you when you first began to study English in school or in a language institute?
(A)  1–5 years          (D)  14–17 years
(B)  6–9 years          (E)  18 or more years
(C)  10–13 years

How many hours per week did you spend in English class ...

9  ... in elementary school?
(A)  none               (D)  7–9 hours
(B)  1–3 hours          (E)  10 or more hours
(C)  4–6 hours

10  ... in secondary school?
(A)  none               (D)  7–9 hours
(B)  1–3 hours          (E)  10 or more hours
(C)  4–6 hours

11  ... in college and/or language institute?
(A)  none               (D)  7–9 hours
(B)  1–3 hours          (E)  10 or more hours
(C)  4–6 hours

12  How many hours are you currently spending in English class?
(A)  none               (D)  7–9 hours
(B)  1–3 hours          (E)  10 or more hours
(C)  4–6 hours

13  Have you used English at home with your family or friends in the country you consider to be your home country?
    (A) yes
    (B) no

IF YES, ANSWER QUESTIONS 14–18. IF NO, GO TO QUESTION 18 ON PAGE 4.

14  How many years have you used English at home?
    (A) none            (D) 4–6 years
    (B) less than 1 year (E) 7 or more years
    (C) 1–3 years

15  How old were you when you first started to use English at home?
    (A) 1–5 years        (D) 14–17 years
    (B) 6–9 years        (E) 18 or more years
    (C) 10–13 years

16  How much did you use English at home?
    (A) not at all
    (B) a little
    (C) about half the time
    (D) most of the time
    (E) all the time

17  How much do you currently use English at home?
    (A) not at all
    (B) a little
    (C) about half the time
    (D) most of the time
    (E) all the time

18  Have you ever learned or used English while visiting or living in an English-speaking country?
    (A) yes
    (B) no

IF YES, ANSWER QUESTIONS 19–21. IF NO, GO TO QUESTION 30 ON PAGE 6.

19  How old were you when you first went to an English-speaking country?
    (A) 1–5 years        (D) 14–17 years
    (B) 6–9 years        (E) 18 or more years
    (C) 10–13 years

20  How many years in total did you spend there?
    (A)  1 year or less    (D)  8–10 years
    (B)  2–4 years         (E)  11 or more years
    (C)  5–7 years

21  Did you study English in school or in a language institute in the English-speaking country?
    (A)  yes
    (B)  no

IF YES, ANSWER QUESTIONS 22–27. IF NO, GO TO QUESTION 27 ON PAGE 5.

22  How many years did you study English in school or in a  language institute in an English-speaking country?
    (A)  less than 1 year    (D)  7–9 years
    (B)  1–3 years           (E)  10 or more years
    (C)  4–6 years

23  How old were you when you first began to study English in  school or in a language institute in an English-speaking country?
    (A)  1–5 years     (D)  14–17 years
    (B)  6–9 years     (E)  18 or more years
    (C)  10–13 years

How many hours per week did you spend in English class ...

24  ... in elementary school?
    (A)  none         (D)  7–9 hours
    (B)  1–3 hours    (E)  10 or more hours
    (C)  4–6 hours

25  ... in secondary school?
    (A)  none         (D)  7–9 hours
    (B)  1–3 hours    (E)  10 or more hours
    (C)  4–6 hours

26  ... in college and/or language institute?
    (A)  none         (D)  7–9 hours
    (B)  1–3 hours    (E)  10 or more hours
    (C)  4–6 hours

27  Did you use English at home with family or friends in the English-speaking country?
    (A)  yes
    (B)  no

IF YES, ANSWER QUESTIONS 28–66. IF NO, GO TO QUESTION 30 ON
PAGE 6.

28 How many years did you use English at home with family or friends in the
English-speaking country?
(A) none                    (D) 4–6 years
(B) less than 1 year        (E) 18 or more years
(C) 1–3 years

29 How old were you when you first started to use English at home in the
English-speaking country?
(A) 1–5 years               (D) 14–17 years
(B) 6–9 years               (E) 18 or more years
(C) 10–13 years

The following statements describe some possible reasons why people learn
English. For each statement, darken the circle on your answer sheet by the
response which is most appropriate for you – i.e., the response which best
describes why you want to learn English.

A = strongly agree        (SA)
B = agree                 (A)
C = disagree              (D)
D = strongly disagree     (SD)

|  |  | SA | A | D | SD |
|---|---|---|---|---|---|
| 30 | I want to be able to read English books, reports, articles, etc. in my field of specialization | A | B | C | D |
| 31 | I want to think and behave as people from America or Great Britain do | A | B | C | D |
| 32 | I want to be able to write professional reports in English | A | B | C | D |
| 33 | I want to fit into an English-speaking community | A | B | C | D |
| 34 | I enjoy learning English as a second or foreign language | A | B | C | D |
| 35 | As an international language, English is useful for communicating with other people whose native language I do not know | A | B | C | D |
| 36 | I want to understand American or British people and culture | A | B | C | D |
| 37 | English is important for career purposes | A | B | C | D |

38 When you hear (or listen to) a mistake in English, do you know it is a mistake because it "sounds" wrong to you, or do you understand why it is wrong?
   (A) Only because it "sounds" wrong.
   (B) Usually because it "sounds" wrong, but sometimes I understand why it is wrong.
   (C) I usually understand why it is wrong.
   (D) I almost always understand why it is wrong.

39 When you see (or read) a mistake in English, do you know it is a mistake because it "looks" wrong to you, or do you understand why it is wrong?
   (A) Only because it "looks" wrong.
   (B) Usually because it "looks" wrong, but sometimes I understand why it is wrong.
   (C) I usually understand why it is wrong.
   (D) I almost always understand why it is wrong.

40 When you speak, do you just say what "sounds" correct, or do you think about the English rules you know?
   (A) I say what "sounds" correct.
   (B) I usually say what "sounds" correct, but sometimes I think about rules.
   (C) I usually think about rules, but I also say what "sounds" correct.
   (D) I always think about rules.

41 When you write, do you just write what "looks" correct or do you think about the English rules you know?
   (A) I write what "looks" correct.
   (B) I usually write what "looks" correct, but sometimes I think about rules.
   (C) I usually think about rules, but I also write what "looks" correct.
   (D) I always think about rules.

How often do you forget to use the English rules you know ...

42 ... in speaking?
   (A) almost always     (C) not very often
   (B) often             (D) almost never

43 ... in writing?
   (A) almost always     (C) not very often
   (B) often             (D) almost never

44 How often can you tell (while listening) when a speaker breaks a rule of English you know?
   (A) almost always     (C) not very often
   (B) often             (D) almost never

45  How  often can you tell (while reading) when a writer  breaks  a rule of English you know?
(A) almost always      (C) not very often
(B) often              (D) almost never

How often do you think you don't know ...

46  ... how to speak English?
(A) almost always      (C) not very often
(B) often              (D) almost never

47  ... correct English pronunciation?
(A) almost always      (C) not very often
(B) often              (D) almost never

48  ... correct English grammar?
(A) almost always      (C) not very often
(B) often              (D) almost never

49  ... correct English vocabulary?
(A) almost always      (C) not very often
(B) often              (D) almost never

50  ... how to put several English sentences together in a row?
(A) almost always      (C) not very often
(B) often              (D) almost never

51  ... how to use the right kind of English with different kinds of people (professors, friends, children, etc.)?
(A) almost always      (C) not very often
(B) often              (D) almost never

52  ... how to write English?
(A) almost always      (C) not very often
(B) often              (D) almost never

How often do you think you make mistakes in ...

53  ... speaking English?
(A) almost always      (C) not very often
(B) often              (D) almost never

54  ... English pronunciation?
(A) almost always      (C) not very often
(B) often              (D) almost never

55 ... English grammar?
   (A) almost always     (C) not very often
   (B) often            (D) almost never

56 ... English vocabulary?
   (A) almost always     (C) not very often
   (B) often            (D) almost never

57 ... putting several English sentences together correctly?
   (A) almost always     (C) not very often
   (B) often            (D) almost never

58 ... using the right kind of English with different kinds of people?
   (A) almost always     (C) not very often
   (B) often            (D) almost never

59 ... writing English?
   (A) almost always     (C) not very often
   (B) often            (D) almost never

In general, can you tell when someone makes a mistake in ...

60 ... speaking English?
   (A) almost always     (C) not very often
   (B) often            (D) almost never

61 ... English pronunciation?.
   (A) almost always     (C) not very often
   (B) often            (D) almost never

62 ... English grammar?
   (A) almost always     (C) not very often
   (B) often            (D) almost never

63 ... English vocabulary?
   (A) almost always     (C) not very often
   (B) often            (D) almost never

64 ... putting several English sentences together correctly?
   (A) almost always     (C) not very often
   (B) often            (D) almost never

65 ... using the right kind of English with different kinds of people?
   (A) almost always     (C) not very often
   (B) often            (D) almost never

66 ... writing English?
   (A) almost always     (C) not very often
   (B) often            (D) almost never

# Appendix E  Correlations among all tests, among FCE measures, among ETS measures, and among FCE and ETS tests

**Intercorrelations among all tests** (pair-wise deletion of cases; total scores included. This correlation matrix was not used for the factor analyses.)

| | TLC STD | TSW STD | TVR STD | TST DTOT | TEW | SP COMP | ETS TTOT | F1 SCALD | F2 SCALD | F3 SCALD | F4 SCALD | F5 SCALD | SUM SCALD | TEST GRAD |
|---|---|---|---|---|---|---|---|---|---|---|---|---|---|---|
| TLCSTD | 1.00000 | | | | | | | | | | | | | |
| TSWSTD | .58117 | 1.00000 | | | | | | | | | | | | |
| TVRSTD | .60804 | .72837 | 1.00000 | | | | | | | | | | | |
| TSTDTOT | .83494 | .88612 | .89327 | 1.00000 | | | | | | | | | | |
| TEW | .44430 | .53706 | .52455 | .58163 | 1.00000 | | | | | | | | | |
| SPCOMP | .63971 | .47260 | .44086 | .60066 | .43701 | 1.00000 | | | | | | | | |
| ETSTTOT | .79243 | .80380 | .78551 | .92257 | .77165 | .78785 | 1.00000 | | | | | | | |
| F1SCALD | .61380 | .56381 | .61853 | .69422 | .42672 | .53349 | .68976 | 1.00000 | | | | | | |
| F2SCALD | .54035 | .50427 | .49121 | .59408 | .44588 | .53812 | .65353 | .57981 | 1.00000 | | | | | |
| F3SCALD | .59096 | .62753 | .63723 | .71745 | .52616 | .54467 | .73600 | .70763 | .66806 | 1.00000 | | | | |
| F4SCALD | .60906 | .43645 | .49843 | .59538 | .41612 | .53156 | .62664 | .53678 | .49466 | .56553 | 1.00000 | | | |
| F5SCALD | .55869 | .41133 | .42187 | .53713 | .38318 | .57347 | .59731 | .46881 | .44726 | .47772 | .49294 | 1.00000 | | |
| SUMSCALD | .72249 | .64548 | .66695 | .78544 | .54578 | .68473 | .82644 | .82103 | .82116 | .86539 | .72569 | .73582 | 1.00000 | |
| TESTGRAD | .66704 | .59016 | .59091 | .71409 | .49956 | .62126 | .75307 | .75149 | .75435 | .77162 | .66244 | .65090 | .90250 | 1.00000 |

**Intercorrelations among FCE Papers** (list-wise deletion of cases; N = 1,332)

| | F1 SCALD | F2 SCALD | F3 SCALD | F4 SCALD | F5 SCALD |
|---|---|---|---|---|---|
| F1SCALD | 1.00000 | | | | |
| F2SCALD | .58054 | 1.00000 | | | |
| F3SCALD | .70730 | .66754 | 1.00000 | | |
| F4SCALD | .53710 | .49427 | .56614 | 1.00000 | |
| F5SCALD | .46457 | .44448 | .47369 | .49554 | 1.00000 |

## Intercorrelations among ETS tests (list-wise deletion of cases; N = 1,282)

| | TLC STD | TSW STD | TVR STD | TEW | SP GRAM | SP PRON | SP FLCY | SP COMP |
|---|---|---|---|---|---|---|---|---|
| TLCSTD | 1.00000 | | | | | | | |
| TSWSTD | .55197 | 1.00000 | | | | | | |
| TVRSTD | .56483 | .71597 | 1.00000 | | | | | |
| TEW | .44761 | .54038 | .51739 | 1.00000 | | | | |
| SPGRAM | .58395 | .43680 | .38214 | .38866 | 1.00000 | | | |
| SPPRON | .58779 | .46374 | .47350 | .45019 | .64165 | 1.00000 | | |
| SPFCLY | .61484 | .41868 | .41163 | .43372 | .78437 | .67494 | 1.00000 | |
| SPCOMP | .64026 | .47326 | .44279 | .43503 | .89268 | .75249 | .87286 | 1.00000 |

## Intercorrelations among FCE Papers AND ETS tests (list-wise deletion of cases; N = 1,226)

| | TLC STD | TSW STD | TVR STD | TEW | SP GRAM | SP PRON | SP FLCY | SP COMP | F1 SCALD | F2 SCALD | F3 SCALD | F4 SCALD | F5 SCALD |
|---|---|---|---|---|---|---|---|---|---|---|---|---|---|
| TLCSTD | 1.00000 | | | | | | | | | | | | |
| TSWSTD | .55354 | 1.00000 | | | | | | | | | | | |
| TVRSTD | .56500 | .71801 | 1.00000 | | | | | | | | | | |
| TEW | .43919 | .54284 | .51782 | 1.00000 | | | | | | | | | |
| SPGRAM | .58721 | .43657 | .38292 | .38729 | 1.00000 | | | | | | | | |
| SPPRON | .58578 | .47240 | .47637 | .44754 | .64102 | 1.00000 | | | | | | | |
| SPFLCY | .61731 | .42348 | .40753 | .42906 | .78855 | .66837 | 1.00000 | | | | | | |
| SPCOMP | .64193 | .47819 | .44714 | .43305 | .89324 | .74693 | .87416 | 1.00000 | | | | | |
| F1SCALD | .60579 | .57021 | .62738 | .44062 | .47310 | .52405 | .50064 | .53396 | 1.00000 | | | | |
| F2SCALD | .53629 | .51820 | .50162 | .47045 | .50129 | .56657 | .48799 | .53821 | .57632 | 1.00000 | | | |
| F3SCALD | .58680 | .62876 | .63841 | .52807 | .49123 | .59153 | .52199 | .54648 | .69970 | .66234 | 1.00000 | | |
| F4SCALD | .61123 | .44312 | .49670 | .42396 | .49685 | .52697 | .52437 | .53489 | .52980 | .49364 | .56273 | 1.00000 | |
| F5SCALD | .55493 | .40958 | .40419 | .36558 | .54278 | .53077 | .56055 | .57177 | .45530 | .45189 | .47376 | .49156 | 1.00000 |

# Appendix F  Components of Communicative Language Ability

(Bachman 1990)

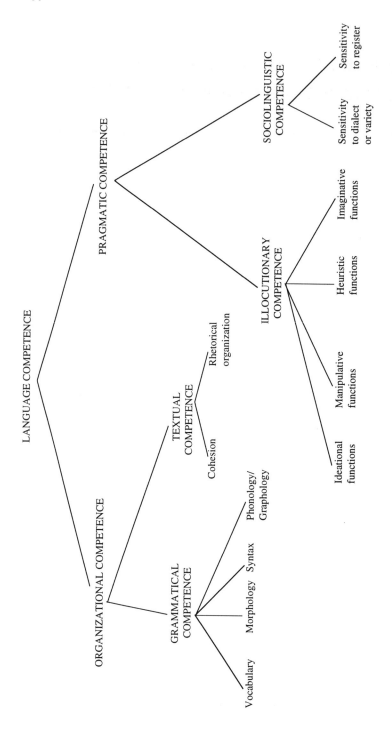

(Bachman 1990)

# Appendix G  Test rubric and test input facets

(Bachman 1990)

## Facets of the test rubric

### Test organization

Salience of parts
Sequence of parts
Relative importance of parts

### Time allocation

### Instructions

Language (native, target)
Channel (aural, visual)
Specification of procedures and tasks
Explicitness of criteria for correctness

## Facets of the input

### Format

Channel of presentation (aural, visual)
Mode of presentation (receptive)
Form of presentation (language, non-language, both)
Vehicle of presentation ("live", "recorded", both)
Language of presentation (native, target, both)
Identification of problem (specific, general)
Degree of speededness

# Nature of language

## Length

## Propositional content

Vocabulary (frequency, specialization)
Degree of contextualization (embedded/reduced)
Distribution of new information (compact/diffuse)
Type of information (concrete/abstract, positive/negative, factual/counterfactual)
Topic
Genre

## Organizational characteristics

Grammar
Cohesion
Rhetorical organization

## Pragmatic characteristics

Illocutionary force
Sociolinguistic characteristics

# Appendix H CLA rating instrument and checklist

---

(Revised March 13 1989)

If the ability is not required for successful completion of the task, write "0"; if the ability may be involved, but is not critical to the successful completion of the task, write "1"; if the ability is critical to successful completion of the task, and at a basic level, write "2"; if critical, but intermediate level, write "3"; and if critical and advanced level, write "4".

In the following example, no ability other than lexical competence is critical to correctly answering the item:

"Sylvia Plath's The Bell Jar was written <u>a decade</u> after the occurrence of the events it describes."

    a  a short time
    b  several months
    c  ten years
    d  a century

This is because the test taker can simply match the underlined phrase "a decade" with its meaning, "ten years", without even reading the rest of the stem.

| Not required | Somewhat involved | Critical basic | Critical intermediate | Critical advanced |
|---|---|---|---|---|
| 0 | 1 | 2 | 3 | 4 |

**Grammatical competence**

LEX:  Lexis
MOR: Morphology
STX:  Syntax
PG:    Phonology/Graphology

*Note*: PG will always be "2" for these tests.

**Textual competence**

COH: Cohesion

Cohesion refers to explicitly marked relationships across clauses and sentences.

This explicit marking may be in the form of lexical connectors or of specific grammatical patterns that provide appropriate topicalization.

ORG: Rhetorical organization

*Note*: ORG will always be "0" for single-sentence items.

**Illocutionary competence**

IDE: Ideational functions

This refers to the expression of information – ideas or feelings. The level of ability required can be considered to be a function of the amount and complexity of the information and the directness or indirectness with which it is expressed.

MAN: Manipulative functions
HEU: Heuristic functions
IMG: Imaginative functions

*Note*: IMG does not refer to how imaginative the text is, but to whether the test taker must perceive an imaginative function in order to answer the item correctly. For example, the following item does not require the test taker to perceive imaginative function in order to answer the item correctly, even though it includes a figure of speech, a simile:

"Rough diamonds look like <u>pebbles</u> made of glass."

    a. gems
    b. bubbles
    c. stones
    d. beads

**Sociolinguistic competence**

DIA: Dialect
REG: Register

**Strategic competence (STC)**

|  | Very much |  | Not at all |
|---|---|---|---|
| Degree to which engaged | 2 | 1 | 0 |

If engaged, describe:

*Note*: Include in STC the skills associated with "test wiseness".

# Example Communicative Language Abilities checklist

Test: _____     Part: _____

Rater: _____     Date: _____

0 = not involved, 1 = involved, 2 = critical basic, 3 = critical intermediate
4 = critical advanced

Item #  LEX MOR STX  PG  COH ORG  IDE MAN HEU IMG DIA  REG STC

Passage
1
2
3
4
5
6
7
8
9
10

Passage
11
12
13
14
15
16
17
18
19
20

# Appendix I  TMF rating instrument and checklist

(Revised March 13 1989)

## Test takers' characteristics

Differences in test takers' characteristics will undoubtedly be a factor in test performance. The problem is how the possible interaction between these characteristics and test method facets (TMFs) can be captured in ratings. One possible approach, which will be taken in our ratings, is to give different ratings on the TMFs for different types of test takers. There are three differences that we will attempt to capture in differential ratings:
1  test preparation;
2  cultural background/orientation; and
3  academic background/orientation.

### Differences in test preparation

For the facets of rubric, and some of the input facets, two ratings should be given: one for "prepared" test takers and one for "unprepared" test takers (ignoring, for the purpose of the analysis, the question of how they prepare). For purposes of analysis, we should consider "prepared" test takers to be those who have either undergone an extensive preparation course (as is normally the case with Cambridge candidates), or in the case of the TOEFL, to have undergone some sort of coaching course or to have taken the TOEFL at least once before. "Unprepared" test takers are those who have not taken any sort of preparation course and have not taken the test before.

The rating for prepared test takers should be given first, followed by the rating for unprepared test takers. Thus a rating of "1/0" on relative importance of parts, for example, would mean that the facet is "sufficiently clear" for prepared test takers, but "not at all clear" for unprepared test takers. A "2" on these facets means that the specification is explicit, and "very clear", even for unprepared test takers.

Double ratings – for prepared and unprepared test takers – should be given for the following facets:

RUBRIC:
Salience of parts

Relative importance of parts
Specification of procedures
Specification of tasks
Specification of ability measured
Criteria for correctness

INPUT:
Identification of problem
Genre

## Differences in cultural background/orientation

For some of the input facets, separate ratings should be given for test takers of different cultural backgrounds. For purposes of analyses, cultural background/ orientation will include three categories: "Americans", "British", and "Others". As well as Americans, the catagory "Americans" includes individuals who may be oriented primarily toward America, and hence may have learned about aspects of American culture. As well as the British, the category "British" includes individuals who may be oriented primarily toward Britain. "Others" includes those individuals who cannot be assumed to know much about either American or British culture.

## Differences in academic background/orientation

For some of the input facets, separate ratings should be given for test takers of different academic background or orientation. For purposes of analyses, academic background/orientation will include two categories: "academic" and "non-academic". "Academic" includes individuals who either have a tertiary level academic background or who plan to attend a tertiary level academic program in the US or Britain. "Non-academic" includes all others, such as individuals in the government or the private sector who may want to take the tests for employment or advancement. Separate ratings for different cultural and academic backgrounds or orientations should be given for degree of contextualization, under input.

# Ratings

In general, all scales are intended to be directional, so that a larger value would be expected to make the item easier. This is merely a matter of convenience, since it means that whatever relationships we observe among these ratings and other variables in the study should be positive. At the same time, remember that these are not direct ratings of difficulty, but rather represent ratings of value on the specific facets. That is, the ratings on these facets will enable us to look at how these characteristics of test tasks and content relate to difficulty, but they are not in themselves ratings of difficulty.

In the list of facets that follows, the type of information to be recorded is indicated for each facet. That is, for most of the facets subjective ratings will be given, but for some specific features will be counted, and for others both ratings and counts will be used. For all facets, verbal descriptions or comments should be given to supplement the ratings where necessary.

The abbreviations in parentheses correspond to the scales on the "checklist".

# Facets of the testing environment

These facets should be rated on the basis of administrative conditions at the time of the tests. There should be a verbal description where indicated, along with ratings on the features indicated.

**Familiarity**

|  | Unfamiliar |  | Very familiar |
|---|---|---|---|
| Familiarity of place | 0 | 1 | 2 |
| Familiarity of equipment | 0 | 1 | 2 |
| Familiarity of personnel | 0 | 1 | 2 |

Verbal description/comments: _____

_____

**Time of testing (time of the day)**

|  | Not conducive to good test performance |  | Very conducive to good test performance |
|---|---|---|---|
| Time of testing | 0 | 1 | 2 |

Verbal description/comments: _____

_____

**Physical conditions**

|  | Bad | OK | Good |
|---|---|---|---|
| Weather | 0 | 1 | 2 |
| Physical conditions of room | 0 | 1 | 2 |
| Temperature in room | 0 | 1 | 2 |
| Seating | 0 | 1 | 2 |
| Lighting | 0 | 1 | 2 |

Verbal description/comments: _____

# Facets of the test rubric

## Test organization

| | |
|---|---|
| Salience of parts: | *TO BE RATED ON THE* |
| Relative importance of parts: | *SCALES BELOW* |

The facet "salience of parts" has to do with how clearly distinguished the parts are from each other. Whether or not "what is being tested" is clear is a function of the facets of instructions as given below.

Separate ratings for "prepared" and "unprepared" test takers should be given for these two facets. The following ratings are possible:

0/0 = not at all clear for both prepared and unprepared
1/0 = sufficiently clear for prepared, not clear for unprepared
1/1 = sufficiently clear for both prepared and unprepared
2/2 = very clear for both prepared and unprepared

| | Not at all clear | Sufficiently clear, making some assumptions about test takers | Very clear; explicit, making no assumptions about test takers |
|---|---|---|---|
| Salience of parts | 0 | 1 | 2 |
| Relative importance of parts | 0 | 1 | 2 |

Verbal description/comments: _____

## Time allocation

This facet should be quantified, so that the actual amount of time (minutes/seconds) per part, passage, and item is reported. Be as precise as possible. For reading, for example, the number of minutes per passage can be found by dividing the total amount of time allocated for this part by the number of passages. The fact that some passages are longer than others will be reflected below, under "length". For listening comprehension, this facet will include the number of seconds between items, or the number of seconds allowed per item, along with the amount of time each listening passage takes. For the writing tests, this will be the amount of time divided by the number of compositions required. For the SPEAK, we can count the amount of time allowed per item and section. It is not at all clear whether this facet for the oral interviews can be quantified.

## Instructions

| Language: | native = 0 | both = 1 | target = 2 |
|-----------|-----------|----------|------------|
| Channel:  | visual = 0 | both = 1 | aural  = 2 |

Specification of procedures:
Specification of tasks:                 *ALL TO BE RATED ACCORDING*
Specification of ability measured:     *TO THE SCALES BELOW*
Criteria for correctness:

"Specification of procedures" includes instructions about how the responses are to be recorded on the test booklet or answer sheet, the order in which the parts are to be taken, etc.

"Specification of tasks" includes instructions that indicate to the test taker how he or she is to arrive at the answer to be recorded.

Separate ratings for "prepared" and "unprepared" test takers should be given for these four facets. The following ratings are possible:

0/0 = not at all clear for both prepared and unprepared
1/0 = sufficiently clear for prepared, not clear for unprepared
1/1 = sufficiently clear for both prepared and unprepared
2/2 = very clear for both prepared and unprepared

|  | Not at all clear | Sufficiently clear, making some assumptions about test takers | Very clear; explicit, making no assumptions about test takers |
|---|---|---|---|
| Specification of procedures | 0 | 1 | 2 |
| Specification of tasks | 0 | 1 | 2 |
| Specification of ability measured | 0 | 1 | 2 |
| Criteria for correctness | 0 | 1 | 2 |

Verbal description/comments: _____

_____

# Facets of input

## Format

| Channel: | visual = 0 | both = 1 | aural = 2 |
| Form of presentation: | language = 0 | both = 1 | non-language = 2 |
| Vehicle of presentation: | taped = 0 | both = 1 | live = 2 |
| Language of presentation: | native = 0 | both = 1 | target = 2 |

Verbal description/comments: _____

---

### Identification of problem

For "identification of problem", separate ratings for "prepared" and "unprepared" test takers should be given, following the procedure described above, for
the facets of rubric.

| | Vague; not at all specifc | Sufficiently specific, making some assumptions about test takers | Explicit; very specific, making no assumptions about test takers |
|---|---|---|---|
| Identification of problem | 0 | 1 | 2 |

Verbal description/comments: _____

---

## Nature of language

### Length

number of words (#WDS)

For individual items, count number of words in both stems and choices.

Verbal description/comments: _____

---

## Propositional content

Vocabulary
This includes not only single words, but also fixed phrases that may function as single units of meaning.

| Infrequent (INF) | 0 | 1 | 2 | Frequent |
|---|---|---|---|---|
| Specialized (SPC)<br>(e.g., technical,<br>jargon, slang) | 0 | 1 | 2 | General |
| Ambiguous (AMB)<br>(e.g., polysemy,<br>unclear reference) | 0 | 1 | 2 | Clear |

Verbal description/comments: _____

---

Degree of contextualization

| In rating this facet, only the content culture (BR) | 0 | 1 | 2 |
|---|---|---|---|
| For those familiar with neither American nor<br>  British culture (OT) | 0 | 1 | 2 |
| For academics (AC) | 0 | 1 | 2 |
| For non-academics (NAC) | 0 | 1 | 2 |

*Note*: For single-sentence items, the highest possible rating for this facet will be "1".

Verbal description/comments: _____

---

Relationship of item to passage (RTP)
5 = Requires test taker to relate information in passage to the real world
4 = Item relates to the entire passage, and requires an understanding of the entire passage
3 = Relates to several specific parts of the passage, or requires test taker to relate one part of the passage to several others
2 = Relates to a specific part of the passage, and requires only localized understanding of that part
1 = No relationship to the passage; items can be answered without reference to the passage, *or* relationship of item to passage is not clear

Verbal description/comments: _____

---

Distribution of new information

|  | Highly compact |  | Highly diffuse |
|---|---|---|---|
| Distribution of new information (C/D) | 0 | 1 | 2 |

Verbal description/comments: —————————————————

---

Type of information
This can be rated in terms of how many occurrences of the feature there are (none, one, several). What is of concern here is the information contained in the text, and not how the test taker is expected to process that information.

| Abstract (ABS) | 0 | 1 | 2 | Concrete |
|---|---|---|---|---|
| Negative (NEG) | 0 | 1 | 2 | Positive |
| Counterfactual (CTF) | 0 | 1 | 2 | Factual |

Verbal description/comments: ———————————————

---

Topic
This facet has to do with the topic, or "subject" of the text (passage, item), and not whether the test taker is American, British or academic. Thus, for example, a text that has a great deal of specific British cultural content is highly specific to this category, and would be rated "2", irrespective of whether a given test taker is of British background or orientation.

|  | Not at all specific |  | Highly specific |
|---|---|---|---|
| American culture (TAM) | 0 | 1 | 2 |
| British culture (TBR) | 0 | 1 | 2 |
| Academic (TAC) | 0 | 1 | 2 |
| Technical/esoteric (TTEC) | 0 | 1 | 2 |

Verbal description/comments: —————————————————

*Appendices*

Genre
For "genre" separate ratings for "prepared" and "unprepared" test takers should
be given, following the procedure described above.

For individual items, "genre" should be considered to mean "item type". For
example, the following two items are different item types, and therefore different
genres:

Amish settlers who <u>arrived</u> in Iowa <u>on</u> 1825 <u>constructed</u> the first sod <u>houses</u> in
America.        A            B              C                    D

As you see / address above, / we move house.

|  | Very unfamiliar |  | Very familiar |
|---|---|---|---|
| Genre (GEN) | 0 | 1 | 2 |

Verbal description/comments: _____

_____

**Organizational characteristics**
Grammar

|  | Very simple |  | Very complex |
|---|---|---|---|
| Rating (GRTG) | 0 | 1 | 2 |

Sentence type (STY):  0 = complex
                      1 = compound
                      2 = simple

Embeddings (EMB):  0 = none
                   1 = one
                   2 = more than one

Embeddings include relative clauses and noun phrase complement structures:

    factive:    The fact that Harry was dirty angered his boss.
    gerundive:  Harry's being dirty angered his boss.
    infinitival: For Harry to be dirty angered his boss.

Voice (VC):  0 = no passives
             1 = at least one passive (main or subordinate clause)
             2 = more than one passive

*Note*: For purposes of these analyses, an arbitrary categorization will be made.
Count something as passive only if it is a clause, that is, if it contains at least the
auxiliary verb form and participle as remnants. Thus, the participial phrase,
*known . . .* in the sentence, *John Henry, known for his prodigious strength,*

*expired at the short ends of two twenty-pound sledge hammers*, will not be counted as a passive. If the unreduced relative clause, *who was known for his prodigious strength*, were included, this would count as a passive, and would also count as an embedding (relative clause).

Plus counts of the following for each *passage*:
number of simple sentences (SMP)
number of compound sentences (CPD)
number of complex sentences (CPX)
number of passive sentences (PAS)
number of active sentences (ACT)
total number of sentences (TOT)
number of relative clauses (REL)
number of infinitival complements (INF)
number of gerundive complements (GER)
number of factive complements (FAC)

Verbal description/comments: _____

_____

Cohesion

|  | Does not occur | One occurrence | More than one occurrence |
|---|---|---|---|
| Reference (REF) | 0 | 1 | 2 |
| Substitution (SUB) | 0 | 1 | 2 |
| Adversatives (ADV) | 0 | 1 | 2 |
| Causals (CAU) | 0 | 1 | 2 |
| Temporals (TMP) | 0 | 1 | 2 |
| Lexical cohesion (LEX) | 0 | 1 | 2 |

*Note*: While the distance between elements in a cohesive relationship may be an aspect of this facet, this will be difficult to include at this time. It may also prove useful to distinguish between anaphora and cataphora, but this will be a refinement to be considered at a later time.

Verbal description/comments: _____

_____

Rhetorical organization
Rating should be made relevant to the particular text (written passage, conversational exchange), but not at the item level. This facet should be rated in terms of how complex the rhetorical organization is, not on how familiar test takers are with it. This complexity will be a function not only of the order of the specific pattern of rhetorical organization (in the classical rhetorical sense, e.g., narrative < description < comparison and contrast < argumentation) but also of the number of specific patterns in a particular text.

| | Very simple | | Very complex |
|---|---|---|---|
| Rhetorical organization (RHET) | 0 | 1 | 2 |

| | One | Two | Three or more |
|---|---|---|---|
| Number of specific types of rhetorical organization (NUMR) | 0 | 1 | 2 |

Verbal Description/comments: _____

_____

**Pragmatic characteristics**
Illocutionary acts

| | Highly indirect | | Highly direct |
|---|---|---|---|
| Directness (IDIR) | 0 | 1 | 2 |

| | Very large | | Very small |
|---|---|---|---|
| Number of speech acts (INUM) | 0 | 1 | 2 |
| Variety of different speech acts (IVAR) | 0 | 1 | 2 |

Verbal description/comments: _____

_____

Sociolinguistic characteristics
Dialect (SDIA):  "Standard" = 2    "non-standard" = 0
Variety (SVAR):  "British" = 2     "American" = 1     "neutral" = 0
Register (SREG):  intimate = 2      casual = 1         formal = 0

# Example test method facets checklist

Test                                    Part
Rater                                   Date

## I Rubric

Salience of parts              _____
Relative importance of parts   _____


Verbal description/comments:  —————————————————————————————

_____


Time allocation
Total time for this part      _____
Time per passage              _____
Time per item                 _____
Time between items            _____

Verbal description/comments:  —————————————————————————————

_____


Instructions
Language                      _____
Channel                       _____
Specification of procedures   _____
Specification of tasks        _____
Specification of ability
  measured                    _____
Criteria for correctness      _____

Verbal description/comments:  —————————————————————————————

_____  ——————————————————————————————————

## II Input

Channel      _____
Form of presentation      _____
Vehicle of presentation      _____
Language of presentation      _____
Identification of problem      _____

Verbal description/comments: _____

_____

### Nature of Language

**Passage/**
**Item #**

| | Len | | Vocab | | | Deg of Context | | | | Type of Info | | | |
|---|---|---|---|---|---|---|---|---|---|---|---|---|---|
| | #WDS | INF | SPC | AMB | BR | OT | AC | NAC | RTP | C/D | ABS | NEG | CTF |
| **Pass** | | | | | | | | | | | | | |
| 1 | ___ | ___ | ___ | ___ | ___ | ___ | *** | ___ | ___ | ___ | ___ | ___ | ___ |
| **Item** | | | | | | | | | | | | | |
| 1 | ___ | ___ | ___ | ___ | ___ | ___ | ___ | ___ | ___ | ___ | ___ | ___ | ___ |
| 2 | ___ | ___ | ___ | ___ | ___ | ___ | ___ | ___ | ___ | ___ | ___ | ___ | ___ |
| 3 | ___ | ___ | ___ | ___ | ___ | ___ | ___ | ___ | ___ | ___ | ___ | ___ | ___ |
| 4 | ___ | ___ | ___ | ___ | ___ | ___ | ___ | ___ | ___ | ___ | ___ | ___ | ___ |
| 5 | ___ | ___ | ___ | ___ | ___ | ___ | ___ | ___ | ___ | ___ | ___ | ___ | ___ |
| 6 | ___ | ___ | ___ | ___ | ___ | ___ | ___ | ___ | ___ | ___ | ___ | ___ | ___ |
| 7 | ___ | ___ | ___ | ___ | ___ | ___ | ___ | ___ | ___ | ___ | ___ | ___ | ___ |
| 8 | ___ | ___ | ___ | ___ | ___ | ___ | ___ | ___ | ___ | ___ | ___ | ___ | ___ |
| 9 | ___ | ___ | ___ | ___ | ___ | ___ | ___ | ___ | ___ | ___ | ___ | ___ | ___ |
| 10 | ___ | ___ | ___ | ___ | ___ | ___ | ___ | ___ | ___ | ___ | ___ | ___ | ___ |

Verbal description/comments: _____

_____

Passage/
Item #

| | Len | Vocab | | | Deg of Context | | | | | Type of Info | | | |
|---|---|---|---|---|---|---|---|---|---|---|---|---|---|
| | #WDS | INF | SPC | AMB | BR | OT | AC | NAC | RTP | C/D | ABS | NEG | CTF |
| **Pass** | | | | | | | | | | | | | |
| 1 | — | — | — | — | — | — | *** | — | — | — | — | — | — |
| **Item** | | | | | | | | | | | | | |
| 11 | — | — | — | — | — | — | — | — | — | — | — | — | — |
| 12 | — | — | — | — | — | — | — | — | — | — | — | — | — |
| 13 | — | — | — | — | — | — | — | — | — | — | — | — | — |
| 14 | — | — | — | — | — | — | — | — | — | — | — | — | — |
| 15 | — | — | — | — | — | — | — | — | — | — | — | — | — |
| 16 | — | — | — | — | — | — | — | — | — | — | — | — | — |
| 17 | — | — | — | — | — | — | — | — | — | — | — | — | — |
| 18 | — | — | — | — | — | — | — | — | — | — | — | — | — |
| 19 | — | — | — | — | — | — | — | — | — | — | — | — | — |
| 20 | — | — | — | — | — | — | — | — | — | — | — | — | — |

Passage
Item #

| | Topic | | | | | Grammar | | | |
|---|---|---|---|---|---|---|---|---|---|
| | TAM | TBR | TAC | TTEC | GEN | GRTG | STY | EMB | VC |
| **Pass** | | | | | | | | | |
| 1 | — | — | — | — | — | *** | *** | *** | *** |
| **Item** | | | | | | | | | |
| 1 | — | — | — | — | — | — | — | — | — |
| 2 | — | — | — | — | — | — | — | — | — |
| 3 | — | — | — | — | — | — | — | — | — |
| 4 | — | — | — | — | — | — | — | — | — |
| 5 | — | — | — | — | — | — | — | — | — |
| 6 | — | — | — | — | — | — | — | — | — |
| 7 | — | — | — | — | — | — | — | — | — |
| 8 | — | — | — | — | — | — | — | — | — |
| 9 | — | — | — | — | — | — | — | — | — |
| 10 | — | — | — | — | — | — | — | — | — |

*Appendices*

**Passage**
**Item #**

| | | | Topic | | | | Grammar | | |
|---|---|---|---|---|---|---|---|---|---|
| | TAM | TBR | TAC | TTEC | GEN | GRTG | STY | EMB | VC |

Pass
2 — — — — — *** *** *** ***

Item

| 11 | — | — | — | — | — | — | — | — | — |
| 12 | — | — | — | — | — | — | — | — | — |
| 13 | — | — | — | — | — | — | — | — | — |
| 14 | — | — | — | — | — | — | — | — | — |
| 15 | — | — | — | — | — | — | — | — | — |
| 16 | — | — | — | — | — | — | — | — | — |
| 17 | — | — | — | — | — | — | — | — | — |
| 18 | — | — | — | — | — | — | — | — | — |
| 19 | — | — | — | — | — | — | — | — | — |
| 20 | — | — | — | — | — | — | — | — | — |

Verbal description/comments: ⎯⎯⎯⎯⎯⎯⎯⎯⎯⎯⎯

| Passage | SMP | CPD | CPX | PAS | ACT | TOT | REL | INF | GER | FAC |
|---|---|---|---|---|---|---|---|---|---|---|
| Pass 1 | — | — | — | — | — | — | — | — | — | — |
| Pass 2 | — | — | — | — | — | — | — | — | — | — |

Verbal description/comments: ⎯⎯⎯⎯⎯⎯⎯⎯⎯⎯⎯

**Item #**

| | REF | SUB | ADV | CAU | TMP | LEX | RHET | NUMR | IDIR | INUM | IVAR | SDIA | SVAR | SREG |
|---|---|---|---|---|---|---|---|---|---|---|---|---|---|---|
| Pass | | | | | | | | | | | | | | |
| 1 | — | — | — | — | — | — | — | — | — | — | — | — | — | — |

Item

| | REF | SUB | ADV | CAU | TMP | LEX | RHET | NUMR | IDIR | INUM | IVAR | SDIA | SVAR | SREG |
|---|---|---|---|---|---|---|---|---|---|---|---|---|---|---|
| 1 | — | — | — | — | — | — | | | — | — | — | — | — | — |
| 2 | — | — | — | — | — | — | | | — | — | — | — | — | — |
| 3 | — | — | — | — | — | — | | | — | — | — | — | — | — |
| 4 | — | — | — | — | — | — | | | — | — | — | — | — | — |
| 5 | — | — | — | — | — | — | | | — | — | — | — | — | — |
| 6 | — | — | — | — | — | — | | | — | — | — | — | — | — |
| 7 | — | — | — | — | — | — | | | — | — | — | — | — | — |
| 8 | — | — | — | — | — | — | | | — | — | — | — | — | — |
| 9 | — | — | — | — | — | — | | | — | — | — | — | — | — |
| 10 | — | — | — | — | — | — | | | — | — | — | — | — | — |

**Item #**

| | REF | SUB | ADV | CAU | TMP | LEX | RHET | NUMR | IDIR | INUM | IVAR | SDIA | SVAR | SREG |
|---|---|---|---|---|---|---|---|---|---|---|---|---|---|---|
| Pass | | | | | | | | | | | | | | |
| 2 | — | — | — | — | — | — | — | — | — | — | — | — | — | — |

Item

| | REF | SUB | ADV | CAU | TMP | LEX | RHET | NUMR | IDIR | INUM | IVAR | SDIA | SVAR | SREG |
|---|---|---|---|---|---|---|---|---|---|---|---|---|---|---|
| 11 | — | — | — | — | — | — | | | — | — | — | — | — | — |
| 12 | — | — | — | — | — | — | | | — | — | — | — | — | — |
| 13 | — | — | — | — | — | — | | | — | — | — | — | — | — |
| 14 | — | — | — | — | — | — | | | — | — | — | — | — | — |
| 15 | — | — | — | — | — | — | | | — | — | — | — | — | — |
| 16 | — | — | — | — | — | — | | | — | — | — | — | — | — |
| 17 | — | — | — | — | — | — | | | — | — | — | — | — | — |
| 18 | — | — | — | — | — | — | | | — | — | — | — | — | — |
| 19 | — | — | — | — | — | — | | | — | — | — | — | — | — |
| 20 | — | — | — | — | — | — | | | — | — | — | — | — | — |

Verbal description/comments: _____

_____

# References

Alderman, D. L. and P. W. Holland. 1981. Item performance across native language groups on the Test of English as a Foreign Language. *TOEFL Research Report* 9. Princeton: Educational Testing Service.

Alderson, J. C. 1987. An overview of ESL/EFL testing in Britain. In J. C. Alderson, K. J. Krahnke and C. W. Stansfield (Eds.) *Reviews of English Language Proficiency Tests.* Washington, D.C.: TESOL, pp. 3–4.

Alderson, J. C. 1988. New procedures for validating proficiency tests of ESP? Theory and practice. *Language Testing* 5 (2): 220-32.

Alderson, J.C. 1989. Reaction paper to Bachman *et al.*: An investigation into the comparability of two tests of EFL. In *Cambridge TOEFL Comparability Study: Responses to the Final Report.* Cambridge: University of Cambridge Local Examination Syndicate.

Alderson, J. C. 1990a. Testing reading comprehension skills: Part one. *Journal of Reading in a Foreign Language* 6 (2): 425–38.

Alderson, J. C. 1990b. Testing reading comprehension skills: Part two. *Journal of Reading in a Foreign Language* 7 (1): 465–503.

Alderson, J. C. 1993. The relationship between grammar and reading in an English for academic purposes test battery. In D. Douglas and C. Chapelle (Eds.) *A New Decade of Language Testing Research.* Alexandria, VA:TESOL, pp. 203–19.

Alderson, J.C. and Y. Lukmani. 1989. Cognition and reading: Cognitive levels as embodied in test questions. *Journal of Reading in a Foreign Language* 5 (2): 253–70.

Allen, P., E. Bialystok, J. Cummins, R. Mougeon and M. Swain. 1982. *Development of Bilingual Proficiency: Interim Report on the First Year of Research.* Toronto: Ontario Institute for Studies in Education.

Allen, P., J. Cummins, R. Mougeon and M. Swain. 1983. *Development of Bilingual Proficiency: Second Year Report.* Toronto: The Ontario Institute for Studies in Education.

Angoff, W. H. 1971. Scales, norms, and equivalent scores. In R. L. Thorndike (Ed.) *Educational Measurement*, 2nd edn. Washington, D.C.: American Council on Education, pp. 508–600.

Angoff, W. H. 1982. Summary and derivation of equating methods used at ETS. In P.W. Holland and D. B. Rubin (Eds.) *Test Equating.* New York: Academic Press, pp. 55–69.

Angoff, W. H. and A. T. Sharon. 1972. Patterns of test and item difficulty for foreign language groups on the Test of English as a Foreign Language. *Research Bulletin RB–72–2*. Princeton: Educational Testing Service.

Ashton-Tate, Inc. 1985. *Learning and Using dBase III Plus*. Los Angeles: Ashton-Tate, Inc.

Associated Examining Board. 1987. *Test in English for Educational Purposes (TEEP)*. Aldershot, Hampshire: Associated Examining Board.

Bachman, L. F. 1990. *Fundamental Considerations in Language Testing*. Oxford: Oxford University Press.

Bachman, L. F. and J. L. D. Clark. 1987. The measurement of foreign/second language proficiency. *Annals of the American Academy of Political and Social Science* 490: 20–33.

Bachman, L. F., F. Davidson and B. Lynch. 1988. Test method: the context for performance on language tests. Paper presented at the 1988 Annual Meeting of the American Association for Applied Linguistics, New Orleans, Louisiana, December 1988.

Bachman, L. F., F. Davidson, B. Lynch and K.E. Ryan. 1989. Content analysis and statistical modeling of EFL proficiency tests. Paper presented at the 11th Annual Language Testing Research Colloquium, San Antonio, Texas, March 1989.

Bachman, L.F., F. Davidson and M. Milanovic. 1991. The use of test method characteristics in the content analysis and design of EFL proficiency tests. Paper presented at the 13th Annual Language Testing Research Colloquium, March 21–23, Princeton, Educational Testing Services.

Bachman, L. F., A.J. Kunnan, S. Vanniarajan and B. Lynch. 1988. Task and ability analysis as a basis for examining content and construct comparability in two EFL proficiency test batteries. *Language Testing* 5 (2): 128–59.

Bachman, L. F. and A. S. Palmer. 1981. The construct validation of the FSI oral interview. *Language Learning* 31 (1): 67–86.

Bachman, L. F. and A. S. Palmer. 1982a. The construct validation of some components of communicative proficiency. *TESOL Quarterly* 16 (4): 449–65.

Bachman, L. F. and A. S. Palmer. 1982b. A scoring format for rating components of communicative proficiency in speaking. Paper presented at the Pre-conference on Oral Proficiency Assessment, Georgetown University.

Bachman, L.F. and A.S. Palmer (forthcoming). *Language testing in practice: Designing and developing useful language tests*. Oxford University Press.

Bejar, I. I. 1980. A procedure for investigating the unidimensionality of achievement tests based on item parameter estimates. *Journal of Educational Measurement* 17: 283–96.

Birnbaum, A. 1968. Some latent trait models and their use in inferring an examinee's ability. In F. M. Lord and M. R. Novick. *Statistical Theories of Mental Test Scores*. Reading, MA: Addison-Wesley.

Brown, G. 1989. Comments. In *Cambridge-TOEFL Comparability Study:*

*Responses to the Final Report.* Cambridge: University of Cambridge Local Examinations Syndicate.

Buros, O.K. 1959. *The Fifth Mental Measurements Yearbook.* Highland Park, NJ: The Gryphon Press.

Burt, C.L. 1921. *Mental and Scholastic Tests.* London: London County Council.

Butler, N.M. 1926. How the College Entrance Examination Board came to be. In College Entrance Examination Boards (Eds.) *The Work of the College Entrance Examination Board: 1901–1925.* Boston: Ginn and Company, pp. 1–6.

Canale, M. 1988. The content validity of some oral interview procedures: an analysis of communication problems and strategies. Paper presented at the 10th Annual Language Testing Research Colloquium, March 1988, Urbana, Illinois.

Canale, M. and M. Swain. 1980a. Theoretical bases of communicative approaches to second language teaching and testing. *Applied Linguistics* 1 (1): 1–47.

Canale, M. and M. Swain. 1980b. A domain description for core FSL: Communication skills. In *The Ontario Assessment Instrument Pool: French as a Second Language, Junior and Intermediate Divisions.* Toronto: Ontario Ministry of Education.

Carroll, J.B. 1961. Fundamental considerations in testing for English language proficiency of foreign students. In *Testing the English Proficiency of Foreign Students.* Washington D.C.: Center for Applied Linguistics, pp. 30–40.

Carroll, J. B. 1983. Psychometric theory and language testing. In J. W. Oller Jr. (Ed.) *Issues in Language Testing Research.* Rowley, MA: Newbury House.

Carroll, J. B. 1989. *Exploratory Factor Analysis Programs for the IBM PC (and Compatibles).* Chapel Hill: J. B. Carroll.

Choi, I-C. 1992. An application of item response theory to language testing. *Theoretical Studies in Second Language Acquisition.* Vol. 2. New York: Peter Lang.

Choi, I-C. and L. F. Bachman. 1992. An investigation into the adequacy of three IRT models for data from two EFL reading tests. *Language Testing* 9 (1): 51–78.

Clapham, C. 1993. Is ESP testing justified? In D. Douglas and C. Chapelle (Eds.) *A New Decade of Language Testing Research.* Alexandria, VA: TESOL, pp. 257–71.

Clark, J.L.D. 1989. Comments on draft of CTCS Final Report. In *Cambridge-TOEFL Comparability Study: Responses to the Final Report.* Cambridge: University of Cambridge Local Examinations Syndicate.

Clark, J. L. D. and J. Lett. 1988. A research agenda. In P. Lowe Jr. and C. W. Stansfield (Eds.) *Second Language Proficiency Assessment: Current Issues.* Englewood Cliffs, N J: Prentice-Hall, pp. 53–82.

Clark, J. L. D. and F. E. O'Mara. 1991. Measurement and research implications of Spolsky's Conditions for Second Language Learning. *Applied Language Learning* 2 (1): pp. 71–113.

Clark, J. L.D. and S. S. Swinton. 1980. The Test of English as a Spoken Language as a measure of communicative ability in English-medium instructional settings. *TOEFL Research Report* 7. Princeton: Educational Testing Service.

Code, L. 1991. *What Can She Know? Feminist Theory and the Construction of Knowledge.* Ithaca: Cornell University Press.

Cohen, A. D. 1984. On taking tests: what the students report. *Language Testing* 1 (1): 70–81.

College Entrance Examination Board. 1929. *Twenty-ninth Annual Report of the Secretary.* New York: College Entrance Examination Board.

College Entrance Examination Board. 1932. *Thirty-second Annual Report of the Secretary.* New York: College Entrance Examination Board.

College Entrance Examination Board. 1934. *Thirty-fourth Annual Report of the Secretary.* New York: College Entrance Examination Board.

College Entrance Examination Board. 1935. *Thirty-fifth Annual Report of the Secretary.* New York: College Entrance Examination Board.

College Entrance Examination Board. 1946. *Forty-sixth Annual Report of the Secretary.* New York: College Entrance Examination Board.

Cowell, W. R. 1982. Item-response theory pre-equating in the TOEFL testing program. In P.W. Holland and D. B. Rubin (Eds.)*Test Equating.* New York: Academic Press, pp. 149–61

Crick, J. E. and R. L. Brennan. 1983. *Manual for GENOVA: A Generalized Analysis of Variance System.* (ACT Technical Bulletin No. 43). Iowa City: American College Testing Program.

Criper, C. and A. Davies. 1987. *Edinburgh ELTS Validation Project: Project Report.* London: The British Council.

Criper, C. and A. Davies. 1988. *ELTS Validation Project Report.* The British Council and the Unversity of Cambridge Local Examinations Syndicate.

Davidson, F. 1988. An exploratory modeling survey of the trait structures of some existing language test datasets. (Doctoral dissertation, University of California at Los Angeles). Dissertation Abstracts International, 49, 1441. UMI Order Number DA8815771.

Davidson, F. 1991. Designing an "intelligent" SLA research computer database. Paper presented at the conference on "Theory Construction and Methodology in Second Language Research", East Lansing, Michigan, October 1991.

Davidson, F. and L.F. Bachman, 1990. *The Cambridge-TOEFL comparability study: An example of the cross-national comparison of language tests.* In J. H. A. L. de Jong (Ed.) Standardization in language testing. *AILA Review* 7: 24–45.

de Jong, J. H.A. L. and M. Oscarson. 1990. Cross-national standards: A Dutch-Swedish collaborative effort in national standardized testing. In J. H. A. L. de Jong (Ed.) Standardization in language testing. *AILA Review* 7: 62–78.

Dickson, P., C. Boyce, B. Lee, M. Portal and M. Smith. 1985. *Foreign Language Performance in Schools: Report on 1983 Survey of French, German and Spanish.* London: HMSO.

Dickson, P., C. Boyce, B. Lee, M. Portal and M. Smith. 1986. *Foreign Language Performance in Schools: Report on 1984 Survey of French.* London: HMSO.

Edgeworth, F.Y. 1888. The statistics of examinations. *Journal of the Royal Statistical Society* 51: 599–635.

Educational Testing Service (ETS).1982. *Test of Spoken English: Manual for Score Users.* Princeton: Educational Testing Service.

Educational Testing Service (ETS). 1985. *A Guide to SPEAK.* Princeton: Educational Testing Service.

Educational Testing Service (ETS). 1987. *TOEFL Test and Score Manual.* Princeton: Educational Testing Service.

Educational Testing Service (ETS). 1989. *Test of Written English Guide.* Princeton: Educational Testing Service.

Evangelauf, J. 1990. Reliance on multiple-choice tests said to harm minorities and hinder reform: Panel seeks a new regulatory agency. *The Chronicle of Higher Education* 26: 37A1 + A31.

Fair Test Examiner 4, 2 (Spring 1990). Cambridge, MA: National Center for Fair and Open Testing.

Fair Test Examiner 4, 3 (Summer 1990). Cambridge, MA: National Center for Fair and Open Testing.

Federal Trade Commission, Bureau of Consumer Protection (FTC). 1979. Effects of standardized admission examinations: Revised statistical analyses of data gathered by Boston regional office of the Federal Trade Commission. Washington, D.C.: FTC.

Gorman, T. and G. Brooks. 1986. Assessing oracy. In M. Portal (Ed.) *Innovations in Language Testing.* Windsor: NFER-Nelson, pp. 68–92.

Hale, G.A., C.W. Stansfield, and R.P. Duran. 1984. Summaries of studies involving the test of English as a Foreign Language, 1963–1982. *TOEFL Research Report* 16, Princeton: Educational Testing Service.

Hambleton, R. K. and H. Swaminathan. 1985. *Item Response Theory: Principles and Applications.* Boston: Kluwer-Nijhoff.

Harley, B., P. Allen, J. Cummins and M. Swain. 1987. *The Development of Bilingual Proficiency: Final Report.* Toronto: Modern Language Centre, Ontario Institute for Studies in Education.

Hartog, P., P.B. Ballard, P. Gurrey, H.R. Hamley and C. E. Smith. 1941. *The Marking of English Essays.* London: Macmillan and Company Ltd.

Hartog, P. and E.C. Rhodes. 1935. *An Examination of Examinations, being a summary of investigations on comparison of marks allotted to examination scripts by independent examiners and boards of examiners, together with a section on viva voce examinations.* London: Macmillan and Company Ltd.

Hartog, P. and E.C. Rhodes. 1936. *The Marks of Examiners, being a comparison of marks allotted to examination scripts by independent examiners and boards of examiners, together with a section on viva voce examinations.* London: Macmillan and Company Ltd.

Hattie, J. A. 1985. Methodology review: assessing dimensionality of test and items. *Applied Psychological Measurement* 9: 139–64.

Henning, G. 1988. The influence of test and sample dimensionality. *Language Testing* 5 (1): 83–99.

Henning, G., T. Hudson and J. Turner. 1985. Item response theory and the assumption of unidimensionality. *Language Testing* 2 (2): 141–54.

Hicks, M. M. 1984. A comparative study of methods of equating TOEFL test scores. *Research Report RR–84–20*. Princeton: Educational Testing Service.

Holland, P. W. 1985. On the study of differential item difficulty without IRT. *Proceedings of the Military Testing Association.*

Holland, P. W. and D. T. Thayer. 1986. Differential item performance and the Mantel-Haenszel procedure. *Research Report 86–31*. Princeton: Educational Testing Service.

Hymes, D.H. 1972. On communicative competence. In J. B. Pride and J. Holmes, (Eds.) *Sociolinguistics*. Harmondsworth: Penguin.

Hymes, D. H. 1982. *Toward Linguistic Competence*. Philadelphia: Graduate School of Education, University of Pennsylvania. (Mimeo).

Ingram, D. E. and E. Wylie. 1993. Assessing speaking proficiency in the International English Language Testing System. In D. Douglas and C. Chapelle, (Eds.) *A New Decade of Language Testing Research*. Alexandria, VA: TESOL, pp. 220–34.

Junker, B. 1988. *User's Guide to Computer Programs for Stout's Unidimensionality Statistic*. Urbana: University of Illinois. Photocopy.

Kaplan, R.B. 1989. Comments on the Final Report. In *Cambridge-TOEFL Comparability Study: Responses to the Final Report*. Cambridge: University of Cambridge Local Examinations Syndicate.

Kunnan, A. J. 1991. *Modeling relationships among some test taker characteristics and performance on tests of English as a foreign language*. Unpublished dissertation. University of California at Los Angeles, CA.

Levine, R. S. 1955. Equating the score scales of alternate forms administered to samples of different ability. *Research Bulletin 55–23*. Princeton: Educational Testing Service.

Linn, R. L., M. V. Levin, C. N. Hastings and J. L. Wardrop. 1981. Item bias in a test of reading comprehension. *Applied Psychological Measurement* 5: 159–73.

Lord, F. M. 1980. *Applications of Item Response Theory to Practical Testing Problems*. Hillsdale, NJ: Lawrence Erlbaum.

Lord, F. M. and M. R. Novick. 1968. *Statistical Theories of Mental Test Scores*. Reading, MA: Addison-Wesley.

Maley, A. 1989. Comments on the Final Report. In *Cambridge-TOEFL Comparability Study: Responses to the Final Report*. Cambridge: University of Cambridge Local Examinations Syndicate.

Mantel, N. and W. Haenszel. 1959. Statistical aspects of the analysis of data from retrospective studies of disease. *Journal of the National Cancer Institute* 22: 719–48.

Mcpeek, W. M. and C. L. Wild. 1986. Performance of the Mantel-Haenszel statistic in a variety of situations. Paper presented at the annual meeting of the American Educational Research Association, San Francisco.

Messick, S. M. 1980. *The Effectiveness of Coaching for the SAT: Review and Reanalysis from the Fifties to the FTC.* Princeton: Educational Testing Service.

Milanovic, M., N. Saville and S. Shen. 1991a. *The Marking of FCE and CPE Paper IV: A Report and Guidelines.* Cambridge: University of Cambridge Local Examinations Syndicate.

Milanovic, M., N. Saville and S. Shen. 1991b. *Research Report: an Investigation of the Viability of Double-Marking FCE Compositions.* Cambridge: University of Cambridge Local Examinations Syndicate.

Milanovic, M., N. Saville and S. Shen. 1991c. *Research Report: an Investigation of the Inter-rater and Intra-rater Reliability of FCE Oral Interviews.* Cambridge: University of Cambridge Local Examinations Syndicate.

Mislevy, R. J. and R. D. Bock. 1986. *PC-BILOG: Item Analysis and Test Scoring with Binary Logistic Models.* Mooresville, IN: Scientific Software Inc.

Montanelli, R. G. and L. G. Humphreys. 1976. Latent roots of random data correlation matrices with squared multiple correlations on the diagonal. *Psychometrika* 41: 341–8.

Morrow, K. 1977. *Techniques of Evaluation for a National Syllabus.* London: Royal Society of Arts.

Munby, J. 1978. *Communicative Syllabus Design.* Cambridge: Cambridge University Press.

National Council on TOEFL. 1964. Minutes of the 25 March 1964 meeting of the Executive Committee. In College Board Archives.

Oller, J. W. JR. 1979. *Language Tests at School.* London: Longman.

Ontario Ministry of Education. 1980. *The Ontario Assessment Instrument Pool: French as a Second Language, Junior and Intermediate Divisions.* Toronto: Ontario Ministry of Education.

Parsaye, K., M. Chignall, S. Khoshafian and H. Wong. 1989. *Intelligent Databases: Object-oriented, Deductive, Hypermedia Technologies.* New York: John Wiley & Sons.

Peterson, N. S., M. J. Kolen and H. D. Hoover. 1989. Scaling, norming and equating. In R. L. Linn (Ed.) *Educational Measurement.* 3rd Edn. New York: American Council on Education/Macmillan, pp. 221–62.

Phillips, A. and P. W. Holland. 1987. Estimators of the variance of the Mantel-Haenszel loggs-odds-ratio estimate. *Biometrics* 43: 425–31.

Portal, M. 1986. Methods of testing speaking in the Assessment of Performance Unit (APU) French surveys. In M. Portal (Ed.) *Innovations in Language Testing.* Windsor: NFER-Nelson. pp. 41–54.

Powers, D. E. 1985. Effects of coaching on the GRE aptitude test scores. *Journal of Educational Measurement* 22: 121–36.

Powers, D. E. 1986. Relations of test item characteristics to test preparation/test practice effects: A quantitative summary. *Psychological Bulletin* 100: 67–77.

Reckase, M. D. 1979. Unifactor latent trait models applied to multifactor tests: results and implications. *Journal of Educational Measurement* 4: 207–30.

Roach, J.O. 1936. The reliability of school certificate results. *Overseas Education: a Journal of Educational Experiment and Research in Tropical and Sub-tropical Areas* 7 (3): 113–8.

Roach, J.O. 1945. *Some problems of oral examinations in modern languages: an experimental approach based on the Cambridge Examinations in English for foreign students, being a report circulated to oral examiners and local examiners for those examinations.* Cambridge: Local Examinations Syndicate.

Roach, J.O. 1983. My work with the Local Examinations Syndicate 1925–45. Unpublished manuscript.

Royal Society of Arts Examination Board. 1985. *The Communicative Use of English as a Foreign Language.* Orpington, Kent: Royal Society of Arts Examination Board.

Ryan, K.E. 1988. Mantel-Haenszel program: A computer program for detecting DIF with the Mantel-Haenszel procedure. Department of Educational Psychology. University of Illinois, Urbana-Champaign, IL.

Ryan, K. E. and L. F. Bachman. 1992. Differential item functioning on two tests of EFL proficiency. *Language Testing* 9 (1): 12–29.

Sang, F., B. Schmitz, H. J. Vollmer, J. Baumert and P. M. Roeder. 1986. Models of second language competence: a structural equation approach. *Language Testing* 3 (1): 54–79.

Saretsky, G.D. 1984. History of the EEFS. Unpublished manuscript, EEFS Papers, Educational Testing Service Archives.

SAS Institute Inc. 1985. *SAS Language Guide.* Cary, NC: SAS Institute Inc.

Savignon, S. J. 1983. *Communicative Competence: Theory and Classroom Practice.* Reading, MA: Addison-Wesley.

Schmid, J. and J. M. Leiman. 1957. The development of hierarchical factor solutions. *Psychometrika* 22: 53–61.

Seaton, I. 1983. The English Language Testing Service (ELTS): Two issues in the design of the new "non-academic module". In A. Hughes and D. Porter (Eds.) *Current Developments in Language Testing.* London: Academic Press.

Shepard, L. A., G. Camilli and D. M. Williams. 1985. Validity of approximation techniques for detecting item bias. *Journal of Educational Measurement* 22: 77–105.

Shephard, W. 1989. Conversation with Bernard Spolsky.

Shohamy, E. and C. W. Stansfield. 1990. The Hebrew Speaking Test: An example of international cooperation in test development and validation. In J. H. A. L. de Jong (Ed.) Standardization in language testing. *AILA* 7: 79–90.

Spolsky, B. 1978. Introduction: Linguists and language testers. In B. Spolsky (Ed.) *Approaches to Language Testing*. Arlington, VA: Center for Applied Linguistics, pp. v–x.

Spolsky, B. 1990a. Oral Examinations: An historical note. *Language Testing* 7 (2): 158–73.

Spolsky, B. 1990b. The prehistory of TOEFL. *Language Testing* 7 (1): 98–118.

SPSS Incorporated. 1988. *SPSS-X User's Guide*. 3rd Edn. Chicago: SPSS, Inc.

Stout, W. 1987. A nonparametric approach for assessing latent trait unidimensionality. *Psychometrika* 52 (4): 589–617.

Strevens, P. 1989. Comments. In *Cambridge-TOEFL Comparability Study: Responses to the Final Report*. Cambridge: University of Cambridge Local Examinations Syndicate.

Swain, M. 1985. Large-scale communicative language testing: A case study. In Y. P. Lee, A. C. Y. Y. Fok, R. Lord and G. Low (Eds.) *New Directions in Language Testing*. Oxford: Pergamon Press.

Swinton, S. S. and D. E. Powers. 1980. Factor analysis of the Test of English as a Foreign Language for several language groups. *TOEFL Research Report* 6. Princeton: Educational Testing Service.

Tucker, L. R. and C. T. Finkbeiner. 1981. Transformation of factors by artificial personal probability functions. *Research Report 81–58*. Princeton: Educational Testing Service.

University of Cambridge Local Examinations Syndicate (UCLES). 1988. *Instructions to Oral Examiners: First Certificate and Certificate of Proficiency in English*. Internal Brochure. Cambridge: University of Cambridge Local Examinations Syndicate.

University of Cambridge Local Examinations Syndicate (UCLES). 1989. *Cambridge Examinations in English: Survey for 1988*. Cambridge: University of Cambridge Local Examinations Syndicate.

Van Ek, J.A. and J. L. M. Trim. 1991a. *Threshold Level 1990*. Council of Europe Press.

Van Ek, J.A. and J.L. M. Trim. 1991b. *Waystage Level 1990*. Council of Europe Press.

Wainer, H. 1989. The future of item analysis. *Journal of Educational Measurement* 26: 191–207.

Weir, C. 1988. The specification, realization and validation of an English language proficiency test. In A. Hughes (Ed.) *Testing English for University Study*. ELT Documents 127. Oxford: Modern English Press, pp. 46–110.

Wesche, M. 1987. Second language performance testing: the Ontario Test of ESL as an example. *Language Testing* 4 (1): 28–47.

Wesche, M., M. Canale, E. Cray, S. Jones, D. Mendelsohn, M. Tumpane and M. Tyacke. 1986. *Ontario Test of ESL: Final Report*. Ottawa: Ontario Ministry of Colleges and Universities.

Widdowson, H. G. 1978. *Teaching Language as Communication*. Oxford: Oxford University Press.

Wilson, K.M. 1982. A comparative analysis of TOEFL examinee characteristics, 1977–1979. *TOEFL Research Report* 11. Princeton: Educational Testing Service.

Wilson, K.M. 1987. Patterns of test-taking and score change for examinees who repeat the Test of English as a Foreign Language. *TOEFL Research Report* 22. Princeton: Educational Testing Service.

Wright, B. D. and R. J. Mead. 1976. BICAL calibrating of rating scales with the Rasch Model. *Research Memorandum 23*. Chicago: Statistical Laboratory, University of Chicago.

Young, R. and M. Milanovic. 1991. Discourse variation in oral proficiency interviews. Cambridge: University of Cambridge Local Examinations Syndicate.

# Subject Index

**A**
Advisory Committee   11, 22
American Association of Collegiate Registrars   4
Analysis of residuals   87

**B**
Background questionnaire   48
Bejar's method   89
BILOG   86
British Council   7

**C**
Cambridge-dominant sites   34, 35
Canonical discriminant analysis   46
Certificate of Proficiency   1, 3
Chief Examiner   29
CITO   10
College Board   4, 6
College Board English Examination for Foreign Students   6
College Entrance Examination Board   3
Communicative language ability   101
  Components   100
  Instrument   102
Content analysis   20, 101, 122

**D**
DAPPFR   64, 65, 68
Data preparation   31
Differential item functioning   75, 76

**E**
Educational Testing Service   8, 9, 15, 26
Effect of test preparation   73
English Competence Examination   3

# Author Index